Ann Morrow was born and author of three previous bo *Highness: The Maharajahs o* of the *Daily Telegraph*, she now works and magazines, and lives in Pimlico, London.

By the same author

The Queen
Highness: The Maharajahs of India
The Queen Mother

ANN MORROW

Picnic in a Foreign Land

The Eccentric Lives of the Anglo-Irish

GRAFTON BOOKS

A Division of the Collins Publishing Group

LONDON GLASGOW
TORONTO SYDNEY AUCKLAND

Grafton Books
A Division of the Collins Publishing Group
8 Grafton Street, London W1X 3LA

Published in paperback by Grafton Books 1990
9 8 7 6 5 4 3 2 1

First published in Great Britain by
Grafton Books 1989

Copyright © Ann Morrow 1989

A CIP catalogue record for this book is available
from the British Library

ISBN 0–586–20999–9

Printed and bound in Great Britain by
Collins, Glasgow

Set in Bembo

CONTENTS

ACKNOWLEDGEMENTS

To Molly Keane, my thanks for all her encouragement and introductions to a firmament of friends; to Robin Montgomery, Mike Reid, Sir Robin and Lady Kinahan, delightful hosts who opened my eyes to life – and a special people – in Northern Ireland; and to Jim Fahy, RTE's western correspondent, who has a way with words even by Irish standards.

For their kindness and help, I am grateful to Patrick and Jane Annesley; Dean Baker, Rachel Bendon Paul and Arabella Burton; Captain M.B. Chavasse, Harold and George Clarke, Sir Richard Colthurst, Alfred Corcoran, Lady Mollie Cusack Smith; Lady Katharine Dawnay, Garech de Brun, the Duke of Devonshire, Lord and Lady Dunsany; Chris Everton, Brigadier Denis Fitzgerald, DSO, OBE, Joe Fleming, the Knight of Glin, Lord Gowrie; Hurd Hatfield, Bob Heapes, Lord and Lady Hemphill, Joyce and Louis Hill, Major Walter Joyce, Lord Kilbracken, Lord Kingsale, Tessa and Jeffry Lefroy, Malcolm Lysaght, John and Lucy Madden, Brigadier Edmond Mahony, Hugh Montgomery-Massingberd, Lady Diana Mosley, Lord Moyola, Dame Iris Murdoch, Tiffany Nicholson, Professor David Norris, Mrs Mafra O'Reilly, Sandy and Debonnaire Perceval, Mark Rowlette, Peter Smethwick, KM, Lord Strathloch, Robert Towers, the late Honor Tracy, the Marquis of Waterford, Bridie Whoriskey.

I appreciate the trust of Lord Altamount, Lady Jennifer Bernard, Mrs Bowes Daly, Gordon and Sylvia Brickenden, Kitty Fleming, Lord Gormanston, Mrs Leila McGarel-Groves, Joyce Walpole and Richard Wood in lending family photographs and albums.

For the insight and background provided in *Twilight of the Ascendancy* I am indebted to Mark Bence-Jones, to Gifford Lewis for *Somerville and Ross*, to J.C. Beckett for *The Anglo-Irish Tradition*, to Michael McConville for *Ascendancy to Oblivion*, and Patricia Cockburn for *Figure of Eight*.

I owe thanks to Conor Brady, editor of the *Irish Times* and his librarians, William Garner, *The Architectural Archives*; the team at *Burke's Peerage*; Geraldine Murtagh of Elegant Ireland; the inimitable monocled John Colclough of Hidden Ireland; Jeri Ward of The Western People; Philomena Byrne of The Royal Hospital, Kilmainham; Frank Hamilton and Gerry McKeown of Shannon Development, Edda Tasiemka's Archives, the London Library; Arthur Prager, Irish-Georgian Society, New York.

For a base in one of Dublin's remaining elegant Georgian houses, my gratitude to Mrs Josie Harrison and to Frances Hishon at Cork University for her hospitality and charmed view of that city. For help on some of many visits across the Irish Sea, thanks to Bill Maxwell, Chief Press Officer at Aer Lingus; all their planes are blessed. To the Irish Tourist Board who gave me shelter at Ballymaloe, Kinsale and Bunratty and to Matt McNulty, now its Director General, for sharing his affectionately indulgent view of Ascendancy Ireland.

Most special thanks go to Richard Johnson, editorial director at Grafton, for his support and enthusiasm for the Irish; to my agent Mike Shaw at Curtis Brown, for sustaining encouragement; to editors Janice Robertson, to whom I owe so much, and Anne Charvet for calm direction; and to Katherine Everett for her felicitous way with pictures.

To my personal assistant, Angie Montfort Bebb, my thanks for her sparky contributions, and to Valerie Castle, for assured and vital help at the keyboard in time of need.

Finally, two precious links with Ireland: Derry, a last and favourite Morrow uncle, and Stella Treanor, a cousin, for all her generosity; this book is for them, and as always, for G.

Introduction

IN ASPIC

Ruled by fairies, ruined by curses, riding like Genghis Khan, the Anglo-Irish were a wild splendid people; loyal to the Crown, loyal to the half crown; leading lives of such strenuous leisure that the Irish RM's wife thought it all a gigantic 'picnic in a foreign land'; their godparents were Queen Victoria's children; their wives, mistresses of kings; devoted to the monarchy, they served the Empire, produced sons like Wellington, writers like Beckett and Shaw; their friends were Russian aristocrats, Prince Yusupov who killed Rasputin; they would bring to Ireland cricket, glorious neo-classical visionary architecture and an aura of prosperity.

Their histories reach back into Ireland's past; they tell you they came over with Strongbow in the eleventh century, but many were soldiers and courtiers rewarded with shamrocked acres by Crown or Commonwealth. Everyone loves the Anglo-Irish, mention them and a slow smile spreads across people's faces. Jane Austen thought the very name suggested distinction.

Dublin was their 'high jinks' capital; Ireland was a colonial oligarchy. Their heyday was the eighteenth century, their golden time. They had their own Parliament until a broken-hearted Henry Grattan struggled to the Irish House of Commons to lament an Ireland 'not dead but in a swoon'. When power transferred to England on 1 January 1801, they were flattered into taking their seats at Westminster. But nothing would be the same again for them. It marked the start of their decline and they have remained sublimely isolated, galloping each day across the greenest fields, leading lives of careless stylishness, though 'doomed', as the Church of Ireland rector and novelist George Birmingham predicted eighty years ago.

Confident, extraordinarily brave, when the IRA were burning their houses down, one old Admiral complained that all he was worried about was his wife's soufflé. Even the terrorists were won over, telling off old ladies for leaving their handbags open on the hall table as they got a petrol can ready to throw the place sky high.

They produced women who stopped civil wars, matriarchs, semi-dowagers who kept diaries about sons who were generals, others wore frocks; they had daughters who shot tigers or hunted while carrying a 'quelque chose', the unborn baby could not have too early an experience of the saddle. They went to London for the Season; on their marriage certificates under Rank they wrote Gentleman; they built Hindu Gothic archways to celebrate a darling daughter's return from honeymoon.

The Ascendancy created Dublin's elegance, their gift to the green land was Georgian mansions in the country, Restoration houses at places called Carrick-on-Suir; and for their vicars, parsonages at places called Knockgrafton, where pale heroines drove to eighteenth-century Galway in a glass coach to treat the beggars to 'Hot Toast, Tea and Chocolate'.

You could tell the importance of their houses by the length of the avenue, once through the tall gates with griffins, stone lions or pineapples, the symbol of hospitality, quite unassailable for generations. They owned vast estates with forests spreading to the next county, and lakes, drowsy in summer with dragon and butterflies, flecked with foam in spring or the water reflecting the autumn gold of turning beech trees. Today they may live in the gate lodge.

High grey-stoned Palladian crescents remain elegant as Bath today with mouth watering interiors, decorative icing cake stucco, medallions of nymphs and wheatsheafs on dining-room walls once lit by Waterford crystal and reflecting burnished silver soup tureens; garlanded cornices, triumphant engraved ceilings with harps and trumpets, and in music rooms violins and songbooks; entrance halls of Aubussons and mosaic tiles from Pompeii; tiny love birds billing above flying staircases, to walk up was to go to heaven. Doors of rich mahogany led to libraries of uncut first editions, Swift and Goldsmith in green leather gold embossed binding; Crusader shell symbols, cherubs trailing petals and grapes above architraves; swans supporting baskets of flowers in florid hunting women's boudoirs; Bacchus and Ariadne in ballrooms; this riot of rococo, extravagant and indulgent was not unlike the owners. They made Ireland bloom. Some had gardens like miniature Versailles with elegant allées, temples and statues of Bacchus and Diana; others were simpler with Gloire de Dijon roses, wisteria and lavender still blooming.

For their children with English nannies there were seaside cottages, any hint of a brogue, saying 'cooat', was frowned on, simply 'bad form', repugnant to the Anglo-Irish. A girl's education might be informal reading of Gibbon's *Decline and Fall*; school in England merely wiped out any traces of an Irish accent.

They had daughters of such beauty, people would stand on walls to catch a glimpse. Girls were presented – 'Daddy kept buttery sandwiches soaking in his bearskin'; land if possible married land, a self-perpetuating Ascendancy. In the best tradition, some went feral, others ran and married god-like feckless young men; Ireland was the inspiration for Evelyn Waugh's sad hedonistic Sebastian in *Brideshead Revisited*.

Their thin women watched their waistlines though never eating less than seven courses: pâté de foie gras, plovers' eggs; fish or sweetbreads; a roast; champagne with the pudding; a savoury; and game was usually served as another entrée in between. 'Footmen kept filling your glass and as young girls we had four brimming at one time.' Wine was the footman's prerogative; occasionally they became 'legless'. 'Jones – stay where you are and don't touch any of the ladies' ankles.'

Parties went on for weeks; aunts and cousins in wide-brimmed hats, inside bee nets, fluttered round these warm old-fashioned houses vicariously enjoying the tennis parties at which the butler served homemade lemonade on a silver tray; extravagant fancy dress parties, girls dressing as flowers and boys as vegetables at the Flower Ball; the foreignness of it all, keeping up Edwardian standards in a remote corner of Ireland, *fêtes champêtres*, syllabub parties, gambling, race-going; and playing cricket for Na Shuler, The Wanderers, the Irish equivalent of I Zingari, inviting the great W. G. Grace to play at Blarney in the hope of a few tips for the local batsmen.

They had the best of all possible worlds, English in Ireland, in England the indulged lovable Anglo-Irish.

They valued and understood their grooms, their ghillies, their Flurrys and their Bridies, and appreciated the Irish charm, the innate courtesy, the silver-tongued compliment: 'Welcome, tis fine and gross you are.' It was the O'Pooters they could never stand; Ascendancy Ireland never allowed an aspiring middle class.

No people talked more about 'beautiful manners'. They mattered very much to them, forgiving anything if it was correctly done. When Oscar Wilde's mother was asked to receive a young woman who was respectable, Lady Wilde replied, 'You must never employ that description in this house. It is only trades people who are respectable. We are above respectability.' When a girl was expelled from Ireland's principal Ascendancy public school St Columba's, the parents were outraged by the suggestion that any daughter of theirs could not hold her drink.

Not easily frightened, they lived with family legends, the darker side, how foxes gather whenever Lord Castletown died, deer for the Donerailes: spells, smells and bells. They believe in fairies and love being surrounded by ghosts, ghoulies and goblins; they enjoy the occult; Charlotte Bingham Carter experienced manifestations as a cat three times in one evening. A beautiful woman washed up on the shores of Dublin Bay and married to a Baron would disappear and from time to time return as a small rat. The Gaisford St Lawrences, in every other way a sensible family, still set a spare place every night in the dining room in case a huffy ghost who was turned away in her lifetime should return.

All the things you expect in Ireland happen in an Ascendancy house; jars in the larder full of coffee are labelled salt; husbands are very uncertain about the whereabouts of the kitchen. You are asked to refrain from pulling the curtains in a half-acre pink guest room in Sligo because they were put up in 1845.

Some let their houses; one Knight lets his castle to rich Americans for £2,000 a week and disappears into a turret for the duration of their stay. But most of the landed eccentrics prefer to open the house to themselves twice a year.

They have always had an aristocratic lack of earnestness, not a hint of endeavour or self-reliance. Ascendancy women were never a bit interested in good works. If they are important enough they still appear in *Who's Who*; there is no authoritative equivalent in Ireland. They are cheerful and resilient, to whinge and complain is something for the lower orders. They despise weather chat and anything smacking of Ruth Draper.

The north, by comparison, is all rather Scottish, partition once almost a joke is now their figleaf. Their houses are very much better kept and better run and the Protestant work ethic triumphs. The best education is to be found in the north but there isn't the same fun, except for the elderly aristocrat who always wore unusual homemade brooches – the skull of a snipe or a brooch made out of the small bones of a rabbit. Sir Richard Keane, a Waterford baronet, cuts the shape of the lavatory seat from *The Times* when he is abroad.

Far from being resented, the Anglo-Irish remain at their most splendid, appreciated for their resilient spirit and for their gentle dottiness which the Irish have always loved. They had wives called Bunny, but many came to the end of the possibility of being generous and had to set up tents in their own drawing rooms.

Elizabeth Bowen, an Anglo-Irish writer, once told Derek Hill, a landscape artist who is Ireland's answer to Constable and Corot, that for all of her kind there was probably 'just one moment' of knowing who they really were or where they truly belonged, a second's enlightenment, perhaps on the boat or train as they made that old-fashioned journey between Dublin and London.

Today many of their houses are exceptionally bleak, though it seems not to deter one or two of their retainers from coming to the table in the nude – nobody takes the slightest notice. Butlers' ear-trumpets are found in shattered, roofless windswept mansions where an ageing manservant totters in with the drinks trolley ten minutes before dinner; the savoury tends to be a runny scrambled egg. The host may offer a nip of poteen.

Even in decline, there is a distinction, though the branches of the silver epergne may hold a few Fisherman's Friend lozenges rather than little baskets of French sugared violet petals. Even the names are perfect: Mooney of the Doon, houses called Drumnabreeze and Miss Blennerhassett of Ballyseedy, a niece of the Knight of Glin.

The Irishness of the south has diluted the Ascendancy, a once phlegmatic race now quirky and unconventional, captivated by a land of squelchy grass and fey enchantment. Today the leprechaun and his pot of gold is even more elusive in this country of rainbows and runny blue skies, mockingly tangible and yet impossible to reach like a rainbow spanning across fields, then skipping behind white cottages showing a smiling front of pink hydrangeas, ever tantalizing, a celestial crescent.

The Anglo-Irish are outdoor people rather than reflective; equestrian rather than creative; whatever their circumstances nothing can change the magic of the daytime in Ireland, that softness, the moistness in the air; the day is the thing and there could be no better country for them; here they can fish in romping rivers of unpolluted gold and land a glistening mother-of-pearl salmon leaping as high as the bank of fresh lemony green moss or, in the cool clear water of a private lake, a speckled brown trout for lunch. Winter is for the joy of flying over high stone-faced banks, on over hawthorn hedges riding across country, across everybody's land for the best hunting in the world. A horse is a god; Brendan Behan defined the Anglo-Irishman as 'A Protestant on a horse'.

John Betjeman, long before he was Poet Laureate, lived in Ireland and thought it the most perfect place on earth, something the Anglo-Irish have always known. They survive, as if in aspic, in this country of dreamers, stargazers and rainbow enthusiasts.

1

GOING AWAY FOREVER

It had been a bit of a fairy story. Now it was all over; it was true and not a child's dream.

It is the year 1981. Mrs Olive Pakenham Mahon, daughter of one of the great Ascendancy houses in Ireland, is, in her eighties, preparing to leave Ireland and a declining ancestral home forever. Called Strokestown, it had been in her family for 300 years.

'Pack my ballgown and a tiara . . . I shall need it for Buckingham Palace,' she instructs her housekeeper, the far from infirm eighty-seven-year-old Miss Bessie.

Often a little absentminded, the old housekeeper reeled slightly, but the woman she and Massie the butler always called 'Madam', once so striking, erect and tall, now ailing, gave one of her looks which could still unnerve. Miss Bessie nodded. Shuffling back from the library with its faded early nineteenth-century gold paper, the poignancy of this last request was not lost. On and off for the last sixty-six years Mrs Pakenham Mahon had been leaving for each London season.

These shrivelled relics of what had been one of the most distinguished houses in Ireland found little else to put into Mrs Pakenham Mahon's brown leather trunk. Already she had packed a bundle of old love letters from her first husband Captain Edward Stafford-King-Harman whom she always called 'my darling

Edward' and who had been killed in the First World War. She never stopped loving him.

Hers had been a gilded childhood; when she was born celebration bonfires were lit all over the county, also when she married, just like the royal family, and barrels of beer were placed outside the great Georgian-Gothic arch for the villagers.

The Pakenham Mahons had been a typical Anglo-Irish family, arriving first in Ireland in the seventeenth century to pick up a gift of 27,000 acres and a royal deer park from Charles II, a token of appreciation for Nicholas Mahon's continuing loyalty to the Royalists long after Charles I's execution.

In the flat lands of Roscommon, the Mahons built their ornate neo-Palladian country house and called it Strokestown. In the best and continuing tradition of housebuilding, work begun in 1660 was still not quite finished for another thirty-six years. Later with the help of Richard Cassels, a German architect who had created some of Ireland's finest houses including Carton, Leinster House and Russborough, it would become more opulent: a ballroom with bow and coved ceiling, a library of French first editions gracing a Chinese Chippendale bookcase; a Bossi inlaid marble table where the men could stretch their legs and companionably drink claret till the small hours, throwing the empty bottles into a specially attached net.

Every imaginable whim was anticipated. There was a gallery in the kitchen so that the chatelaine never had to set foot on the stone-flagged floor but could watch the servants from a dress circle view and at a savoury distance.

On Mondays a selection of menus for the week fluttered down, dropped from jewelled hands. In the eighteenth century, when tea was a luxury, the housekeeper was given her supply in a little brown mahogany teapot lowered in a basket; enough for the week.

Even the stables with their vaulted ceilings were handsome and described as an 'equine cathedral'. The Irish always like a religious analogy. Tenants would queue up by the stable pavilion on Fridays, the women in black shawls not fully appreciating the beauty of the Doric columns as they filed up the steep stone staircase rummaging deep in the pockets of their long flannel skirts for the rent.

The Mahons loved Ireland but were fervent believers that Union with Britain was best. In 1800, Maurice Mahon became Baron Hartland of Strokestown; the family was now truly established if only for a brief but 'glorious' time.

During the early part of the nineteenth century, Lord Hartland having added to the house, now wanted it to have the widest street in Europe. So in this tiny midland village just ninety miles from Dublin, a street was grandly created to rival the Ringstrasse in Vienna or the Champs Élysée in Paris.

Ireland was not always irresponsibly served by its aristocracy. This ambitiously broad 147-foot-wide street, lined with trees, had a hundred pleasant tall stone houses where tenants were kept warm and dry with good slate roofs imported from Wales. Strokestown was quite unlike many other Irish villages. Here the 'Big House' did not stand in isolation behind high walls, blinkered from squat ugly granite artisan houses in a horseshoe of drab streets outside the demesne.

The early Hartlands were set to enjoy a life of charm, beauty, wealth and style. There seemed no reason to suppose that the good order and stability at Strokestown would ever change.

But the peerage ended abruptly in 1845 with the insanity of Lord Hartland and later the death of a childless third Baron Hartland, who was a vicar. The estate, horribly mismanaged and run down, passed on to Major Denis Mahon who also inherited £30,000 arrears of rent.

A benevolent but autocratic rule was restored over a happy enough tenantry until the time of Famine, when landlords and tenants began to be terrified of each other: tenants dreading eviction if they could not pay their rent and landowners frightened of assassination.

In country villages it is word of mouth which does the damage and the rumour spread quickly that ships chartered by Major Mahon to take his tenants to a new life in America were the dreaded 'coffin ships' which sank in mid-Atlantic.

On his way home from Roscommon in November 1847, Denis Mahon was murdered, near Carntryla, the Hill of the Corncrakes, by a man called Hasty and another known as Kill-Commings. The

gun, an unwanted souvenir, would be handed over to the family
years later and Hasty and Commings were hanged publicly in
Roscommon.

For her definitive book on the Famine, Cecil Woodham-Smith
studied family papers kept at Strokestown, and with consummate
fairness points out that the Major had been to a Board of Guardians
Meeting. There he had been pleading that they should not shut
down the workhouse so there could be some shelter for his
emaciated tenants, 'many in dire distress'.

Denis Mahon's daughter Grace, on honeymoon after her marriage
to Henry Sandford-Pakenham of Castlerea at the time of her father's
assassination, vowed she would never go back to Strokestown. But
her son Henry Pakenham Mahon loved the house, though he never
persuaded his mother to return; she died in 1913. He married Colonel
Sidney Burrard's only daughter, such a great beauty that people
would stand on walls and each other's shoulders to catch a glimpse of
her. Their daughter Olive inherited her mother's looks, large
expressive eyes and a soft mouth. She grew up at Strokestown but the
family spent half the year in London in their house in Bond Street,
ideal for the launching of their daughter in society.

'Miss Olive's Coming Out' and being presented at Court was all
rather puzzling to the villagers in Strokestown, where the Court
Circular was not often seen. They could hardly understand the
subtleties of a Pakenham Mahon background which epitomized the
Anglo-Irish flirtation with Ireland, these impeccable credentials
enabling them to enjoy the best of both countries.

'I took it for granted that I would be presented like everybody
else when I grew up.' So at the age of eighteen Olive Pakenham
Mahon prepared like any other debutante, some in remote corners
of the Empire: South Africa, India and Australia, for their first
London season. Mothers pored over copies of *Vogue* streaked
yellow in a tropical sun and instructed local dressmakers to match
couture evening dresses in glossy magazines. Their pale daughters
wilting in the shade of banyan or Moreton Bay fig trees, longed for
the cool of the bright green pool at the Bath Club in London where,
wrapped in bathtowels, gossiping and giggling, they would order
strawberry ice-cream from Gunters.

Olive Pakenham Mahon caught the last of the elaborate Edwardian 'courts and feathers' era, though it was the beginning of the reign of King George V and his redoubtable Queen Mary. A contemporary recalled: 'The King gave you lots of lobster and champagne, a frightfully good supper.' Later with that earthy directness, Olive Pakenham Mahon would chuckle, saying what she remembered best about being presented at Buckingham Palace was the sight of 'forty big pos laid out in a row' and a lot of doubtful dowagers wondering whether they would patronize them or not. There was 'only one loo in Buckingham Palace,' she told them back in Strokestown, 'in spite of the gorgeous red brocaded walls and the lovely pictures'.

It was an exciting time to be a debutante; the girl from Strokestown was launched on a season exotically sprinkled with Russian émigrés fleeing early rumblings of the Revolution which would topple the Tsar, revitalizing the socially jaded as Chaliapin sang and Pavlova the great ballerina sprang toe-first out of baskets of roses at an extravagant private party.

Olive Pakenham Mahon, like the other fashionable bright young things, danced prettily till dawn most mornings. 'My mother, poor old dear,' sat on the bench until 6.30 am. Every night there were parties and these delicate creatures nibbled quail, lobster and hot house peaches and were eyed by 'elderly men' in their forties, 'dear old prancing partners, jangling with orders and decorations and coat tails flying'. Lady Diana Cooper made them sound like lovable old walruses.

However good the season, 'You got out of London as if you had been stung by a bee after the Eton and Harrow match; most people went to Scotland for stalking and things.' But Olive went back to Ireland for croquet on the lawn, tennis on one of the three courts and to fall in love with Edward Stafford-King-Harman, heir to Rockingham with its private chapel, one of Nash's most beautiful houses and the only one grander than her own. Between them this young couple would briefly own 75,000 acres, considered a great deal of land in a small country like Ireland.

It was a perfect match, there would be a huge London wedding on 4 July 1914. Olive Pakenham Mahon was the bride of the season.

The newlywed Stafford-King-Harmans honeymooned at Hindhead with chauffeur and a lady's maid in attendance then home to Rockingham, where even the stables, the old coach houses with great wooden doors with shining padlocks and the French clock tower had the air of an Oxford quadrangle. Gleaming broughams, landaus, phaetons, governess carts, motor cars and dog carts were lined up for anyone's pleasure.

The handsome limestone house stood in ornamental parkland and not far away was a gentle lake called Lough Key dotted with wooded inlets. In the meadows, Ayrshire and Kerry blue cows with names like Nanny, Pookey, Darkie and Bawneen side-stepped buttercups and thistles.

Life was dreamy at Rockingham during those soft summer evenings just before the war. Lilac lolled palely purple over crescent lawns; creamy button roses and rambling honeysuckle brimmed competitively over the open windows as the sky turned rosy at dusk. It always seemed to be that colour in those late pre-war August evenings. At dinner talk would be of the Crown, the season, racing, Ascot; of the villagers, their humour, their feckless-ness, their simplicity, quirkiness, their magic with horses and how when they said, 'I'm charmed for ye' they meant it; and how they were much too idle ever to rebel.

Ascendancy families always seemed set apart. David Thompson, who was English, a tutor moving between Strokestown and Rockingham, would complain in his book *Woodbrook* that 'however kind and friendly they might be, their public school manners and clipped English . . . toneless speech makes it difficult for them to communicate even with each other. Its lack of rhythm does not suit warmth of feeling.'

On 21 September 1914, Olive King-Harman's dashing young army captain husband left for the front and she went to London to see him off. Her description of that farewell at Liverpool Street station on an autumn day would have an almost unbearable poignancy even seventy years later; 'I can see him now, putting his hand out of the train window and sort of half opening the door to come back to me . . . and then pulling himself together and shutting himself in and going away forever.'

The young wife returned to Rockingham to await the birth of their child. One afternoon in November, in a tranquil mood after a favourite walk along a path under giant beech trees soughing and shaking off the last of their leaves in a flutter of melancholy gold, she climbed the high steps leading to the extravagant Ionic portico. Her mother-in-law was waiting for her, in her hand a telegram which had just been delivered by a boy in navy uniform with red livery; a sight people would learn to dread in those Great War years.

Edward Stafford-King-Harman was reported missing. Now there was a devastating time of not knowing whether he was dead or alive, 'a frightful lull'. Both families used all their connections: 'German Princes and the Vatican', in the hope of even a strand of news from the front. But he never came back.

It was only three years before her own death in 1981 that Olive, by then widowed twice, would discover what had happened to her first love. Sitting in the mouldy drawing room at Strokestown with an 'elderly female friend' she remarked out of the blue: 'You know, I have never known what happened to my Edward,' and the friend said, 'Oh my goodness, I could have told you, my brother was at the other end of the trench. He was blown to bits by a shell and there wasn't anything to find.' These hunting women put things bluntly.

'And so you see,' she would say, 'he was whisked away from me and killed almost at once at Ypres in November 1914.' In less than five months, Olive King-Harman became a wife, widow and expectant mother.

Somehow, by her staying on at Rockingham with her husband's family, they all believed that because there had been no definite news he must be still alive; but after six years, she gave up this wistful hope and went back to Strokestown.

Their child, a daughter called Lettice, was born in April and now lives in Zimbabwe with her second husband. Olive King-Harman, who had taken up the social threads again, acquired perfect French and was much in demand at Viceregal Lodge in Dublin.

It was a time when Ireland was on the threshold of becoming a Free State and the start of the Troubles. Many people in her circle realized that their lives were changing irrevocably. Those who lived for hunting or playing cards and croquet all day, or enjoying week-long parties, now heard alarm bells ringing. They poured out of Ireland taking their treasures, leaving their houses as gaunt symbols of Anglo-Irish occupation, empty and ripe for burning.

Olive King-Harman could have gone to England, and lived in more comfort than most, with a house in Mayfair, but hers always was an endearing and courageous spirit. 'The London house,' she would say, 'is fun, but this place, Strokestown, why, it is the whole of myself.'

Once eight gardeners had cared for the croquet lawns so they looked as if they had been trimmed with nail-scissors; now they were overgrown and the huge sweeping long grass walks bushy with weeds. She would stay on in Ireland where she would meet her second husband, Major Wilfred Stuart-Atherstone-Hales, when he was quartered at Strokestown.

During those delicate, dangerous, volatile times, he had fallen in love with the young widow – whose home he was protecting – and with stirrings of gallantry, proposed. They were married in 1921 and she would be called Hales for exactly a month. Then her grandfather died; he had stipulated that if she were to enjoy Strokestown, her heritage, she must revert to her maiden name of Pakenham Mahon. Her new husband adopted his wife's name and their children, Nicholas with his twin Denys and another sister, Elizabeth, were all Pakenham Mahons.

For the next three decades life was fun again at Strokestown, but never on quite the same original *folie de grandeur* scale. At first the family had moved back to England because of threatened Sinn Fein attacks. By the time they could safely return to Strokestown, Nicholas was three. Prep school in England and then Winchester would come as a dreadful shock to this little boy. His early days in Ireland had been spent swanning about in a rattletrap hauled by a willing English nanny or urging recalcitrant donkeys along the flat turfy midland roads; where rain clouds sat blobbily against blue washed skies until bursting over sweeps of peaty bogland, giving it the colour of bitter chocolate. By the warmth of a turf fire in the harness room he and Denys, who died when they were seven, listened to stories of how 'Old Collins', the groom's grandfather, had laid out Major Mahon's body on an oak coffin table the night of his assassination during the Famine.

Whatever the political climate, their mother was welcomed back in Strokestown, and always appreciated. In the village they thought some of the Ascendancy were dull old sticks, 'as dry as they'd fart dust', but Mrs Pakenham Mahon appealed to them. With country people's perception, they admired her beauty; she turned heads, they liked her sense of fun; but most of all it was her courage and her spirit: 'She'd jump wire.'

They respected her and shook their heads over the day when she threatened to shoot a crowd of idle stable lads and her four-year-old granddaughter, Henrietta, looking up brightly, had asked 'Shall I get your gun, Granny?' They had all dissolved in helpless laughter.

She could be wonderfully bawdy too, something only a really elegant or confident woman can get away with. 'Fornication', she would say, she knew all about from her thirteenth birthday present, a pack of frisky hounds.

Strokestown was like any other big house up till the Second World War and even in the early fifties, full of bustling maids in starched organza pinafores and hats, valets, footmen and butlers, sometimes merry but always in charge. But by the early seventies the vast house was being run by 'Miss Bessie' and Massie the erratic manservant, who would confide in guests arriving for hunting tea or dinner that he was expecting a baby in July. He also became convinced that figures astride horses clattering into battle in armour in family portraits were gossiping about him. Poor Massie had to be put away in a rest home in Castlereagh, but not for long.

The Pakenham Mahons then advertised for a new butler, but Ireland had been generous with her young men, exporting the cream in two World Wars and the response was poor. In the end, and in desperation, Massie was brought out of the home and given a reprieve. This is not uncommon in Ireland today, where the people who open the door of the old houses often seem to be in a strange twilight world, on holiday from an old folks' home. If he got agitated, the major would just shake a stick at him, and say briskly, 'Now Massie, quiet.'

Bessie and Massie had their own 'home rule', symbolizing a peculiarly Irish above and below stairs relationship, at once delicate, mutinous, sly but devoted to the family. There was complete understanding of each other's foibles. House guests from England were often shocked by the informality.

Now Strokestown had begun to deteriorate, due to a combination of things, the First World War, the feeling against the Big House in the 1920s, then the savage wealth tax of 1974. Gradually the walls began to run with water; mice felt liberated; sheep were on the lawn munching the last of a once well ordered demesne. Mrs Pakenham Mahon began to sell off more furniture and paintings, putting up copies instead and laughing when they fooled people. When the electricity bill came she would storm into Carrick-on-Shannon, the nearest big town, and say it could not possibly be right.

'Ah there she goes again,' the venerables standing at the crossroads would grin and watch her striding up Lord Hartland's dream street with her walking stick, about to confront Jim Callery, the owner of the local garage, about the awful bits of rusty iron and old jalopies littering the pavement. For years, this village boy had been Mrs Pakenham Mahon's *bête noire* but secretly he had always loved Strokestown.

To save on heating towards the end of their days, when there was no longer any staff to light big turf and wood fires in the bedrooms, Mrs Pakenham Mahon and her husband had their beds moved to the drawing room. Decanters of sherry and brandy on sofa tables also kept out the cold.

Then one day in 1979 Paddy Garvey, the factotum, whispered, 'Madam, I'm afraid to tell you the major is dead.' Hales had been bedridden for some time and they had become crusty in each other's company. As it was lunchtime and between courses, the old lady asked, rather bewildered and like a child: 'What shall I do, Garvey?' After a moment's consideration the manservant sleekly advised, 'Continue you with yer dinner, Madam.'

Their son, Nicholas, confessed that it had been very hard not to be able to go back to Ireland when his father died. But the Irish police, the Gardai, had warned that they could no longer protect him. A lifelong serving officer in the British Army, his life was in danger from the IRA if he returned to his village. His crime was not so much that he had been a Colonel in the Grenadier Guards, but that he had commanded a battalion in Ulster.

When a woman deploring a violent demonstration in Londonderry said, 'You must think us a lot of savages,' this gentle man, imposing in his colonel's uniform, replied with a slight smile: 'I am Irish.' By following the service-to-Empire tradition of the men in his family, he had lost his inheritance. His mother, who had willed Strokestown to him in 1969, was shattered. 'It absolutely blitzed us,' she confided.

Her son slipped into Ireland a few more times, always incognito. This worried the life out of the security men. He was so easy to spot, so tall, alert eyes, polished shoes like black mirrors, obviously a military man, whether bending like a willow to talk to a Guards widow at a Buckingham Palace garden party, in Ulster or his mother's village; they could not wait to whisk him back to Dublin airport and get his plane airborne over the green fields.

Strokestown was up for sale and by a strange irony the buyer would be Jim Callery. It was his, with 300 acres and for less than half a million pounds. He protested that he had only wanted three acres of land for a refrigeration plant but had become fascinated by 'this indomitable woman'. In turn she was drawn to him, his engaging buoyancy and bags of charm.

'None of the rest of the family had the kick of the auld one,' Callery says admiringly; 'she was gas.' With a shake of his head, 'I always liked her;' he would visit her in Berkshire and found her the best imaginable company.

But Callery never told her how, one day, he would open a wing of the house as a Famine museum and go to America 'not to do the family a disservice' but to tell an emotional history of the Strokestown tenantry during the Great Famine of 1845.

The yellowing letters from tenants under glass are on show to the public. In upright handwriting, they tell in a simple way of struggles against starvation and eviction; 'I Joseph Gillan, north-yard, starving all this year has not a potato to eat this day.'

At Rockingham tenants who resisted eviction were forced to carry manure to the fields in creels, fitted on their shoulders with hard and spiky ropes. Manure dripped on their backs and then they were taken to the house, flogged and locked up for a day without food.

The Pakenham Mahons still smart over the implication that Denis Mahon was assassinated by some of Strokestown's destitute tenants inflamed as they watched grain being sent to England while they were hungry. Colonel Pakenham Mahon believes they really had planned to kill the over-zealous Strokestown agent, responsible for 6,000 tenant evictions, and not Denis Mahon.

'The wretched Denis was expected to pay for everyone,' his great-great-grandson argues reasonably, and points to famine crises in the world today. 'Take the Sudan; governments step in and help.' He has the table his assassinated great-great-grandfather was laid out on in his Wiltshire farmhouse, where it is correctly known as a hunting table. He has no bitterness, just nostalgia and honeyed memories of an Ireland which was safe enough until the early 1970s, of a charm, how when he wanted to borrow a boat to shoot snipe he was told: 'If it were a ship of gold ye'd be welcome, never mind.' He grinned. 'The fact was it had a great hole in it.'

There was something touching about this retired army officer, this Holder of the Order of Menelek of Ethiopia, sitting in the Cavalry Club in London on a windy June day recalling 'lovely children's parties' where lifelong friendships were made: with George Walpole who worked for King Hussein of Jordan's father, Emir Abdullah – now when he came back to Ireland, the estate workers would shrug and laugh, 'You can't treat us like them blackamoors'; the presents – the china greyhound from Jimmy Reid at the gate lodge; the shillelagh from Paddy Garvey who never stopped talking about the time he went to America; the Christmas parties when this small boy stood with his father at the top of the stairs in the stables to hand the servants – some had waited all day in the yard – their Christmas presents, 'perhaps a ten shilling note, it was medieval,' a deprecating laugh.

For security reasons, the final dismantling of Strokestown had to be left to his wife Jennifer, who spent weeks sorting through old letters dating back to the seventeenth century, selecting furniture and selling valuables. Earlier her mother-in-law had sold off a large yellow coach which had belonged to the Duke of Wellington to Tom Pakenham, Lord Longford's son, with whom the family has a 'tentative kinship'. After a long courtship, due to shortage of funds,

Arthur Wellesley was able to marry his beloved 'Kitty', Lady Katherine Pakenham, the second Lord Longford's sister, on 10 April 1806. It was her nephew Henry who married Major Denis Mahon's daughter Grace.

Retired from the army, Nick Pakenham Mahon was for a time President of the Grenadier Association, but these days he is busy on his farm and on parish councils. 'Getting involved is quite novel, you see, as the Anglo-Irish didn't touch anything like that.'

For Callery and his cousin, twenty-eight-year-old Luke Dodd, a slim young man entrusted with the restoration of Strokestown, he has nothing but compassion: 'They have a great hill to climb.' But Dodd, who read History of Art at Trinity and won a scholarship to America to the Whitney Museum, dreamt for years of saving a grand house.

In spite of the gallant attempts by this young idealist, Strokestown is still largely a shell, a clutter of wooden skis piled in cupboards, yellow and blue faded croquet balls; a Victorian laboratory, mahogany tables with circles of damp where nobody bothered to move the stain left by a leaky flower jug of inexpensive daisies. In the nursery unopened packets of babyfood left over from the twenties; nanny's ancient valve wireless set and in the playroom a Robin Hood costume.

Dodd tries desperately to match fading wallpapers and hunts for eighteenth-century velvet; he has surprising finds in old country drapery shops. And at the end of the day he makes rhubarb jam to sell to the visitors. As this small, intense and humorous man wanders round the vast sparsely furnished rooms you sense that he too is drawn to its last owner. 'She is always in the house, I like that; it is a happy place, it was never pompous.'

In 1987 Dodd invited the old housekeeper, Miss Bessie, back, by now a tottery but still mischievous ninety-three-year-old. Sitting at the kitchen table having lunch, head cocked on one side, she cackled . . . 'I can't hear ye coming now, Madam . . .' 'The place,' he said, 'was her life.' She died two years later.

Until recently the Irish have not been great country house visitors. Strokestown opened to the public with a huge fanfare; house and visitors met in a tentative embrace. It struck a special chord. After three centuries the family had come to a sad slightly ignominious end. As so often happens, the departure was not that sweet: a disappointing flat feeling. But justice had been done, in this young democracy; of course it was right, they said, that the Big House should go to a local garage proprietor, 'a fair man too'.

But some of the old people miss the old days and the wild sport of the hunt balls. Nobody will admit it but a spark has gone; they miss the sound of that booming voice, the way if anybody was in trouble Mrs Pakenham Mahon would walk into their cottage and help them out; that terrific poise; her carriage, her seat on a horse – that counts terribly in Ireland.

Olive Pakenham Mahon had stayed on at Strokestown, courtesy of Jim Callery. But when her son visited her in the spring of 1981 he was shocked by the deterioration in her health.

The three Irish nurses looking after the elderly widow at a cost of £35,000 a year to her son kept feeding her diabetic patient forbidden sugary cakes and drinks. When Nick Pakenham Mahon remonstrated, their reply was faultless in its impeccable insolence: 'If Madam asks.'

The only comic relief was the rivalry between the Catholic priest and the Church of Ireland parson looking after his mother. But in the end the old lady asked to be buried in the Catholic graveyard and not in the family mausoleum at the edge of the demesne, the only bit of Strokestown which still belonged to her son. 'I don't want to be left on the shelf,' she joked, realizing it was a decision which would upset her staunchly Protestant family.

It was unthinkable that Olive Pakenham Mahon would ever leave Strokestown, but then quite suddenly she asked her son to take her back to England. 'Of course,' he replied, moved by this sudden vulnerability. That was in March 1981.

Four months later, Olive Pakenham Mahon was dead. 'It is a huge meditation on loss.' Luke Dodd puts it well, but in the village, they are in no doubt: 'Madam,' they say, 'died of a broken heart.'

2

ASHES AND CARCASES

There were three kinds of people in Ireland in Richard II's opinion; our enemies the 'wild Irish'; the 'old' English who have shaken off any allegiance to the crown; and the 'obedient English'.

The Gaels crossed the Channel from Britanny before the birth of Christ and were considered an argumentative people, drinking moonshine and living in stone quarries.

The Romans never came to Ireland. But a culture full of mythology, a sophisticated literary civilization, would develop in Ireland far removed from the Roman Empire.

Ireland never experienced any of the formative 3Rs; the Romans, the Reformation and the traumatic Industrial Revolution which so changed the face of Britain. The Republic with its windy, obstacle course boreens would never be blessed with those fine straight Roman roads like the Fosse Way in Gloucestershire. Ireland's earliest roads appear to date back to 1250 BC with excavations recently of wooden trackways built across stretches of bogland in Longford.

Christianity came to Ireland with St Patrick, an Englishman who had been kidnapped as a boy by an Irish raiding party and kept as a slave in Antrim for seven years. He escaped back to England where he became a priest, but perhaps he had taken a shine to his captors, for he returned to Ireland in 432 to convert the pagan Gaelic kings to Christianity.

During the seventh and eighth centuries Ireland would become 'the island of Saints and Scholars', cultivated, and a literary and artistic beacon for Europe with the creation of finely illuminated manuscripts like the Book of Kells, which can be seen in Trinity College, Dublin.

Early Irish jewellery, sun discs found in the roots of an old oak tree in Monaghan, gold pendants buried in a bog in Co. Kildare, have a romantic and magical grace. They show the delicate craftsmanship of early Irish goldsmiths who created crescent-shaped collars, ornate cloak fasteners, delicate half moons from thin hammered 'repoussé' sheets of gold panned from the unsullied streams of Ireland. Delicate abstracts, ornate trumpet scrolls and animal motifs reflected too, from Britain, a Roman culture.

A typical early Celtic Adonis warrior had fair yellow hair and a glossy curling beard, and wore a green cloak with a bright silver brooch at his breast. He had a brown-red shirt interwoven with threads of red gold next to his skin and descending to his knees.

The women wore charming gold collars, long basket-shaped earrings and elaborate sunflower hair ornaments in twisted gold.

The peace of this gentle island was shattered with the arrival of the Vikings from Norway in the ninth and tenth centuries, in their beautiful curving open boats with 'bloodbeat prows'. James Joyce's onomatopoeic description in *Ulysses* would capture these marauding Danes 'riding low on a molten pewter surf' as they landed at Lambay off the Dublin coast, an island now lived in by a reclusive member of the Behrens family, Lord Revelstoke, who used to sell seagulls' eggs to day trippers.

The Vikings plundered and ransacked monasteries rich in gold where monks had worked creating exquisite manuscripts. They seized much of Ireland, a country bitterly divided, and strong only in native culture. They had a dramatic effect on Irish life. They settled, established the first towns in Ireland, introduced coins and so became more prosperous. Every ship coming up the Shannon had to pay a tax of 1,000 oysters to the monks and Ireland was attractive to particularly rapacious Breton and Spanish pirates.

The Vikings would finally be driven out in 1014 by Brian Boru, one of Ireland's favourite High Kings who was killed in the struggle at the Battle of Clontarf. Another 150 years of self rule and squabbling amongst Ireland's many minor kings followed until the Norman invasion in the twelfth century.

Some Anglo-Irish, inordinately proud of their origins, would boast that their ancestors arrived with Strongbow. But it was not until much later that the Ascendancy took shape in Ireland, when Elizabethan and Cromwellian soldiers, administrators and courtiers would be rewarded with great estates, for loyalty to Crown and Commonwealth.

A few did arrive with 'Strongbow', the Earl of Pembroke, who, mustering a band of sturdy acquisitive soldiers, sailed from Wales, arriving in Wexford on 1 May 1170, in response to an invitation by the Irish King of Leinster, Dermot MacMurrough, who was faring badly in a feud with his High King.

When Strongbow captured Dublin, his reward was Eva, Dermot's daughter, whom he married. His soldiers were given gifts of land and would spawn the first of the Anglo-Irish. His triumph brought a wave of marauding Norman adventurers, who built great castles all over Ireland.

They intermarried with the Irish, exchanged their Norman French for Irish, 'became more Irish than the Irish themselves' and would be known as 'the degenerate English', greatly worrying the English kings, who were beginning to be shrewdly alarmed by the threat that their own power might be diminished.

In addition, when MacMurrough died, Strongbow became King of Leinster and, with rather inflated notions, began to see himself on a level with the English King. This stirred London's interest in the small island, one which would continue for seven centuries.

Henry II, uneasy about Strongbow's growing power, and not hoodwinked by protestations of loyalty from Leinster, took up Pope Adrian's suggestion that he should go across to Ireland, conquer it and in God's name keep it. The Pope also suspected that Ireland was becoming lawless and altogether too pleased with itself.

The King based himself in a specially built wooden palace in Dublin, which became the capital for the whole of the country. The Anglo-Irish later gave it its character during the time of their supremacy in the eighteenth and early nineteenth centuries when

Dublin Castle was the centre of the season. Successive Viceroys would invite them to levees at the Castle, and as they danced through the decades it was with a warm feeling that this was the ground on which the first English king had asserted his authority over Ireland.

Henry left Ireland on 17 April 1172 content with the woolly agreement he had made with a few Anglo-Norman barons about trying as far as possible to run the country on English lines. Nobody seemed to be in charge and Henry would never return. It was his son John who would establish Irish law courts and a Mint in 1210.

As the worrying integration between invaded and invaders continued, the official English colony began to be at risk. In a feeble attempt to legislate against this cult of Irishness, the Irish Parliament drew up the Statutes of Kilkenny in 1366. But nobody took the slightest notice; these lawless 'Gaelicized English' went on wearing Irish hairstyles, clothes with distinctive Celtic embroidery, obeying Irish laws and speaking the language of the Gael.

In a feeble attempt to strengthen its position, in 1500 the Royal Government created an enclave called the 'Pale', a pleasant strip of land on the east coast twenty miles from Dublin. Within this area, now the site of a Jesuit public school called Clongowes, English customs would prevail. It was a desperate attempt to keep power and the expression 'beyond the Pale' is still used to describe outrageous behaviour.

The arrival of the Tudors would herald an abrasive new spell for this obstreperous little island. The Reformation, which had made England a Protestant country, had not really succeeded in Ireland. Henry VIII broke with the papacy in 1534 but many of the Old English in Ireland, as well as the native Irish, had remained Catholic. There was lip service to the idea of the King being head of the church, but really only in the Pale. It had been a difficult message to spread. Although Ireland had a population of no more than a million people, they were scattered over boglands and many spoke only Irish. For several leading Irish families the Reformation would be insidious, driving a wedge between brothers, and creating bitterness between fathers and sons as some changed faith.

A cleverly conciliatory approach was made by Sir Anthony St Leger, Henry VIII's Lord Deputy, who in June 1541 suggested to Irish landowners that they should give up their estates to the King on the understanding that he would restore them immediately with new English titles. Before they could say 'God Save the King' their lands were seized. Henry, now in complete control, declared himself King of Ireland as well as King of England.

Henry VIII died in 1547. The task of really subduing Ireland would be left to his daughter Elizabeth I (1558–1603), a woman who claimed to have 'the heart and stomach of a King'.

Her advisers worried that Ireland's determination to remain fervently Catholic might encourage strong Catholic countries like France and Spain to answer appeals for help against the English oppressor. The fear was that Philip II of Spain could, while ostensibly backing Ireland, actually cross the Irish Sea and invade England. But his Spanish Armada venture ended in disaster; the ships crept back to Spain, slowly by way of Valencia on the west coast of Ireland, where there are some fine dark Mediterranean skinned men and women to this day.

The Elizabethan ideal in Ireland was to ensure the 'rooting out' of the indigenous population and resettle with English Protestants. The mood was strongly anti Papist. Founding Trinity College in Dublin in 1591, defiantly built on the remains of an Augustinian monastery destroyed by Henry VIII, Elizabeth I spoke against 'foreign universities of France, Italy and Spain . . . infected with Popery and other ill qualities' and fostering 'evil subjects'.

Resettling Ireland with Englishmen may have been a good idea in theory, but Ireland was unlike feudal England, where the king virtually owned most of the country and the law of primogeniture prevailed. Irish chieftains valued ownership of the land. They believed in the 'free family', the 'derbfine', whereby all adult males, whether or not legitimate, so long as there was a common great-grandfather, had a share in the estate.

This would be the start of the fierce Elizabethan wars in Ireland. Apart from shiploads of troops, a couple of favourite courtiers were sent to Ireland. Sir Walter Raleigh was given the town of Youghal, 42,000 lush acres by the River Blackwater, Lismore Castle – owned today by the Duke of Devonshire – and a knighthood. Edmund Spenser, who wrote the *Faerie Queene* in Ireland, found his poetic soul shocked by the apparent brutality of his far from ethereal monarch's resettlement programme and was often moved by 'the pitiful sight' of people chased from their homes and off their land.

'Out of every corner of the woods and glens they came creeping forth upon their hands,' Spenser recalled '. . . for their legs could not bear them; they looked like anatomies of death; they spake like ghosts crying out of their graves; they did eat the dead carrions, happy when they could find them; and if they found a plot of watercresses or shamrocks, there they flocked as to a feast for the time . . .' Yet loyal to the Queen, he too appreciated that a wholesale clearance programme was the only way Elizabethan rule could be established in Ireland and would draw up an even harsher one for Ulster.

But it was in the reign of James I when the really large effective plantations began with the 'Flight of the Earls'. Two of the Gaelic aristocracy, Catholic Ulster noblemen O'Neill, the Earl of Tyrone, and O'Donnell, the Earl of Tyrconnell, broken by attempts to survive under English rule, fled into exile on 4 September 1607 in a ship flying French colours. James I immediately confiscated their estates and moved in Protestant settlers, and also resettled parts of Donegal, Armagh, Tyrone and Derry.

This paved the way for the Ulster of today. These English and Scottish settlers would be the catalysts for partition, as Ireland begun to form her unhappy modern shape and never would lose her religious acne.

During the Plantation of Ulster, Derry was colonized by the City of London in 1608, divided up by wealthy City companies, Haberdashers, Fishmongers and Drapers, and given to Scottish and English settlers who were forbidden to take Irish tenants. By 1632 there were about 13,000 half–English, half–Scots settlers, but it was not a huge success as they were still surrounded by Irish people.

During the reign of James I and Charles I, the exodus from Ireland which has bedevilled the health of the country ever since would begin. Many of the dispossessed fled to Virginia, and thousands to the West Indies. Ships sailed from Kinsale and Irish servants on board were exchanged for West Indian sugar and tobacco. Irish Catholics and Protestants would make up a large, if unsatisfactory, part of the servant population in the West Indies, where in 1667 it was reported that they were '. . . derided by the negroes and branded with the Epithite of white slaves'.

It was Oliver Cromwell who, after his victory in the Civil War against Charles I in 1625 would ensure a Protestant dominion in Ireland, for the Royalists had been supporting the Irish Catholic rebels. He arrived in Ireland in 1649 and there was carnage at Drogheda. No priest, on his own admission, was left alive, and there was a massacre of Catholics. Sir Arthur Aston, an English Catholic defending the garrison at Drogheda, when finally trapped with his men in a high tower, was clubbed to death with his own wooden leg.

Cromwell, believing he was doing God's work, rampaged through Ireland with his diligent Puritan army. His success has remained a traditionally classical example of 'English frightfulness'. Progress reports announced '30,000 people, dead of starvation in Munster', where soldiers were cutting down corn, and killing cattle until there was virtually nothing left but 'ashes and carcases', and in Wexford another 2,000 'were put to the sword, of whom 200 were women and children'.

By 1650, Catholics driven off their land were sent to the beautiful but bleak and infertile west coast of Ireland; 'to hell or to Connacht' was the option. Ever since, one of the worst things you can say in southern Ireland is 'the curse of Cromwell on you.'

By 1658, only 22% of Irish land was left in Catholic hands, the rest had gone to Cromwellian soldiers and adventurers who had financed the army, Protestants whose loyalty was unquestioning. This would result in three-quarters of Ireland being in the possession of Protestant landlords, some remaining in England but living on rents provided by tenants.

The Restoration of the monarchy in 1660 meant Catholics everywhere could go to church again. Although Charles II had an early military baptism when his father Charles I made him commander-in-chief of western England at the age of fourteen, he had been defeated several times by Cromwell and the Parliamentarians. Harassed and humiliated he fought bravely, but succeeded only after Cromwell's death and was crowned on 23 April 1661.

With the accession of James II in 1685, Catholics were no longer excluded from public office. Now it would be a time of uneasiness for Protestants, hounded by Papists who had been harbouring bitterness since their lonely exile to far corners of the west.

For the Ascendancy, the Protestant upper classes and the 'Castle Catholics', a golden age was beginning that would peak towards the end of the eighteenth and beginning of the nineteenth century. Yet when in 1720 Jonathan Swift, the Protestant Dean of St Patrick's Cathedral, Dublin, urged the people to ignore Westminster and 'burn everything English except coal', they became inflamed with the idea of independence. It is ironic that these early rumblings for an Ireland standing alone should come from the Protestant Ascendancy, a small group with a tremendous belief in its own ability and superiority. In the gilded atmosphere of the eighteenth-century Dublin they had a growing self-confidence and political ambition, the dream of an 'Irish Protestant Nation', and were spurred on in this ambition by the breakaway of the American colonies in the 1770s from the mother country. In 1782 their leader in the Irish Parliament, the lawyer Henry Grattan, announced a Declaration of Independence from the British Government. Halcyon days were here again.

They would dominate the Irish Parliament, an elegant building still distinguished today as the Bank of Ireland and not far from the peat-tinged River Liffey, and keep it Protestant. This lasted until January 1801, when the Irish Parliament was dissolved by the Act of Union and power transferred to Westminster. But as Irish members, they would continue to have influence and enjoy an even greater feeling of importance as decision makers sitting in the House of Commons or the House of Lords. In three hundred years of English rule, the privileged Irishman was nearly always defined as a Protestant of English origin.

For the pleasure-loving, landowning Ascendancy the eighteenth century was a period of stability and elegance. Theirs is Georgian Ireland; they commissioned the finest architects, James Gandon who designed the still handsome Customs House and Kilmainham built as a home for retired soldiers like Chelsea Hospital in London. The German architect, Richard Cassels, came to Ireland, designing Carton for the Earl of Kildare and Lord Powerscourt's house in Wicklow, which burned down in the 1970s. In 1745 the Duke of Leinster built Leinster House, today the seat of the two houses of the Irish Parliament.

They built early neo-classical houses like Glin Castle in Limerick and Strokestown in Roscommon; Early Gothick Revival included Birr Castle in Offaly and Slane Castle in Meath. Between Dublin and the Shannon the Royal and Grand canals ribboned effectively.

The Ascendancy produced their own fine writers: Swift, Edmund Burke, Oliver Goldsmith and Richard Brinsley Sheridan; they were patrons of the arts, of music and the theatre. Half the year would be spent in their country houses; the rest in Dublin and London for the season.

'Yours was the first country house in which I stayed . . . and since then how many pairs of linen sheets have received my pampered limbs in what fine mansions,' John Betjeman wrote in 1972 to Pierce Synnott, owner of an eighteenth-century Irish stately home in Naas, County Kildare. The Poet Laureate loved Ireland, its grand Palladian houses with delicate plasterwork ceilings dotted with exotic Minervas, cupids, lyres and luscious fruit.

Their prosperity and wellbeing would be shaken by the French Revolution, the Act of Union, the Famine and the struggle over land in Ireland towards the end of the nineteenth century.

Ireland had no middle class, no diligent bourgeoisie; this would for centuries be her joy, and her undoing. There were only two classes in Ireland, the Ascendancy and the peasantry, each in their way inept.

The Ascendancy were mainly brave, hospitable, some cultivated and rarely duplicitous, but they would be baffled by the Irish national genius for 'reservations, loopholes, wordy discrimination . . . anything on earth and under heaven except a clear statement of simple fact or intent' as Sean O'Faolain, one of Ireland's finest writers, mockingly describes his people.

In the end they would be defeated by the Irishness of the Irish. Lord Salisbury compared the Irish to 'Hottentots'. The Ascendancy found the Irish as foreign and impenetrable as Africans or Indians under British rule along great stretches of the Zambesi or in the Deccan.

The Irish used to cherish an exaggerated picture of the Ascendancy as a loud, horse-mad people with braying English accents which you rarely hear anywhere today, striding about at gymkhanas worrying about the royal family and their relatives in South Africa. Their role would become ambivalent, claiming to be Irish on the one hand, but wanting to be treated by the British as an equal.

In little more than 200 years out of the 5000 during which Ireland had been inhabited they would leave an indelible impression, distinguished architecture; but their critics say the Anglo-Irish were untenable, giving the country a schizophrenic personality. Today few of the 'auld' stock are left. Those lovable, irritating, quirky spirits are dying out and being replaced by Ireland's practical and hardworking architects, doctors, businessmen, teachers and hoteliers, a middle class at last.

3

A WILD AND WOOLLY LOT

A head pokes out from a top turret, 'psst.' It is Desmond Fitzgerald, the Knight of Glin. 'Come round the side,' and mouths, 'I'll be down.' He is in exile.

The door to the Castle has a fanlight shaped like a butterfly and protective grey pillars, but no doorknocker as the family believe in the superstition that three knocks by an invisible hand could mean a death. But it will open on the dot of five to a party of creamy upmarket Americans, three couples who, for £2,000, will stay in this Irish stately home for a week. They think it is good value and so does the owner.

As they arrive in the late afternoon, the sun is a scarlet red over the Shannon estuary and beyond the Labasheeda peninsula is watercress green. This gently battlemented castle in Limerick is mellow and confident, overlooking two of Ireland's finest counties, Clare and Galway.

Beginning life as a large plain house in 1780 built by Colonel John Bateman Fitzgerald, it was crenellated into a make-believe castle at the start of the nineteenth century and now is really a Georgian house with a sugar icing of Gothic detail. Sheltered by swooping woodlands, it has a window for every day of the year. You never tire of the Shannon and its tranquillity as it makes its way to the Atlantic and how it seems to snuggle close under the soft Clare headlands, lemon yellow with gorse. You want to jump out of the car without putting the brake on and shout for joy; this is how Ireland used to be, should be.

The Fitzgerald children have to be quiet when they have American guests. One was nicknamed 'Mrs Rats' because she used to shout at them; others have been more fun, like the Texan couple who dressed in ceremonial fur-trimmed robes each evening and asked to be called King and Queen during their stay.

In trainers, and faded stitched denim jeans bleached to a trendy white-washed blue, the twenty-ninth Knight of Glin (a title granted in Norman times) is tiptoeing slightly on the run. You feel he is escaping. Almost pixie-like, he conspiratorially darts round the grounds past a scarecrow done up like a Nazi, and stops by some bushes brimming with loganberries, raspberries and currants, a good spot where he can look up at the Castle. The Americans are just settling into some of the upper turrets.

'It's the women who save these places,' the Knight says, moving on and perching on a garden seat. Desmond Fitzgerald, who is fifty-two, can on a good day be very expansive.

The family have owned the castle for nearly 800 years. The present Knight inherited when his father died in 1949; Glin was a huge burden for a twelve-year-old boy. Had his widowed mother not married Ray Milner, a rich Canadian industrialist, Glin Castle with all its history might well have slipped into the luminous navy blue Shannon, another 'derelict pile'. Instead it was saved by Milner money in the late 1950s and cherished, enabling Desmond Fitzgerald to be the twenty-ninth generation to live on in this charming old house.

One American couple have been given the yellow bedroom with its Irish political lampoons and cartoons and fuchsia coloured *chaise-longue*. The brass taps are being turned in the old fashioned bathroom and, wrapping themselves in huge fluffy towels, they admire the old apothecary jars with gold labels, rosy pink jugs and bowls and blue and white Chinese and Delft plates.

Husbands think it is time for some pale gold Bourbon and wonder if Una 'the wise', the housekeeper and backbone of Glin for fifty-four years, could bring up some ice to the chintzy suite. 'Ah dahlin',' the seventy-year-old retainer who brought up the Knight and calls all the children 'dahlin'', asks someone younger to run up. It was against her warm presence that the Fitzgerald daughters, Catherine, Nesta and Honor, measured their height. Their mother remembers the shrieks: 'I'm up to Una's third cardigan button' until a jubilant 'I'm up to her chin.' In winter, an illuminated Gothic bird cage would light her up the back stairs. It is hard to know whether her charge loves Glin, which has been in the family for 800 years, or not.

Knights of Glin belong to one of the few last 'Old English' families, direct descendants of the Lords of Desmond who had ferocious struggles with Queen Elizabeth I and, though on the losing side, always fought with bravado. One Knight of Glin kept his nerve even when his six-year-old son was tied to the mouth of a cannon and the Elizabethan commander threatened to blow the small boy to pieces if there was no surrender. But the Knight replied that he was virile, his wife fertile, and 'it would be easy to produce another son'; the boy was saved.

Their women were resilient, one Countess of Desmond lived to be 140. A striking woman with high cheekbones, she had up to the time of her death all her own teeth and could walk four or five miles without being out of breath. Married in the reign of Edward IV (1461–1483) to Sir Thomas Fitzgerald who became twelfth Earl, she set out when she was 100 to petition Queen Elizabeth I.

She had no money, went by boat to Bristol and pushed a handcart to Windsor, helping along a daughter who was a bit infirm. At court she had a dance with her friend Sir Walter Raleigh, her plea was heard and she left happily. She died in 1604, in no way infirm, but had fallen and broken her hip climbing a cherry or a nutmeg tree. As the Countess herself might have said: 'The tree was immaterial.'

Today's Knight of Glin is fifty-two years old and a grandson of Lord Dunraven. A Harvard graduate and former assistant curator of furniture at the Victoria and Albert, this international man, who much enjoys his work representing Christie's in Ireland, never needed Glin.

Mention his name in Ireland and people smile; they like the way he can strike a bargain with the gypsies. 'I am off to see a man at Rathkeale about a picture,' he will say. When asked what they should put in the catalogue about the owner of this important picture, colleagues at Christie's will be told, 'A gentleman, of course.'

On party terms with the Princess of Wales in London, he is amusing about the pseuds in the fine art world, doing a devastating impersonation of some unfortunate widow being turned away by a Bond Street saleroom. 'So nice, but don't you think if you kept it in the family . . .'!

'We struggle.' The Knight looks out across a hazy green stretch to the water's edge. He still finds it rather miraculous that the Castle has been saved and winces about the 'awful sadness' of the auctioning of the estate of his cousin the seventh earl of Dunraven. More and more these old houses are becoming 'shattered hulks by the side of the road,' he says.

'These estates won't survive; there is a hideous disrespect for their heritage in Ireland, we will just have a collection of famous ruins.' Mournfully he added, 'This is a cow economy.' A realist, he admits there were times when as his plane took off from Shannon he would pray. 'I wanted to be dropped in the water; Glin had become such a burden.'

He has no false sentimentality about Ireland either. A shrewd farmer – with only 400 acres left of the original half a million – he has black and white Friesian cows and says the only time he got any sympathy in the village was when the whole herd was nearly killed off by brucellosis. Fruit and vegetables are sold by one of the Castle's pepperpot lodge gates.

Suddenly it is time to go in and meet his Americans. His wife was once overheard saying when he was about to begin his tour of the Castle, 'With one little match to these old curtains, we'd be free.'

The Americans, the women immaculately groomed, slim in late middle age, no spare fat beneath their sleek separates, join their jolly florid husbands. Two of the couples are from Virginia and the third from St Louis; already they clearly adore the Knight.

They blink at the delicate artistry around them, in the cornices, on the ceilings: harps, wheatsheaves, circlets of pale green leaves, while the Knight, glass in hand, a good host, stands in front of the fireplace.

It is cleverly done, as if they were such enchanting guests he suddenly felt impelled to tell them things about the house and the history of the Fitzgeralds. There are warm chuckles as he adroitly begins by claiming kinsmanship with Buffalo Bill and Texaco Jack.

The *Alice in Wonderland* title, the 'Knight of Glin', he explained, dated back to the fourteenth century; the other major titles in this widespread family are the Knight of Kerry and the Duke of Leinster.

The first Fitzgerald – the Fitz means son, often of Anglo–Norman extraction – was Norman Maurice Fitzgerald, who came over with Strongbow in 1169, settled in Limerick and married a raunchy Welsh princess called Nesta. 'A redoubtable lady, quite a girl, she had a son by King Henry the First of England.' At this there were polite titters. 'She was known as the brood mare of the Normans, she had so many children.' 'Ma word,' one of the Americans muttered softly.

'We were,' he said, 'an improvident wild and woolly lot and spent a lot of money.' Here indulgent smiles from the Stifels from Virginia and the Whitmans from Missouri, glad that the present custodian has been more sensible. The Knight is proud of one ancestor, old Cracked Jack, who had a collection of twenty chamber pots. He liked to wear one on his head and, as in those days it was illegal to carry a sword, he would challenge passers-by to crack the pot with their blackthorn sticks.

The Knight leads them into the hall with its Corinthian columns, past a Siena marble fireplace where, staring boldly out from a Georgian gilt carved frame, is another intrepid ancestor – Hilda Blennerhassett, the only female member of the notorious Hell Fire Club, haunt of a decadent group of Freemasons.

On through rooms of gleaming mid-eighteenth-century intriguing Irish mahogany furniture with strange gargoyles, animal heads, grotesque goblin masks and almost lifelike long taloned claw feet. Softly the Knight let it be known that he was now doing Irish furniture in America 'so long neglected'. 'Yes it would be possible to buy some,' that low Chelsea voice, a diffident interest, 'well'.

Clustering round him in the Orangery, they have seen beautiful things and may have been entertained by the Knight's urbanity. Unlike many other owners of stately homes in Ireland, he is less anglicized, an easy European. Now they want to know about his family, not how Thomas Fitzgerald was hanged drawn and quartered in 1567, and his mother seized his severed head, drank his blood and carried off the dismembered body followed by a large keening mob, but about his wife Madame Olda Fitzgerald. The title conjures up a matronly figure in shiny black with a formidable bosom, somehow making her sound like Madame Lupescu and her amazing parrots. In fact she is a whizzy blonde who writes with honeyed pen about old Irish houses and castles and is in London. They have three daughters and he is teased unmercifully.

Distractedly, almost talking to himself: 'Really must cut the grass for croquet,' he takes in the next question bubbling on American lips – about his children. His three daughters are being educated 'in England' and ruminatively, he adds: 'yes . . . spawning more ambivalent misfits'. When Catherine, the youngest Fitzgerald daughter, was asked by her headmaster to tell him about her ancestors, she replied, 'Oh please don't ask me about them,' and hid her face in her hands.

The Americans troop off to dinner in the dining room where the table is formally laid with crystal and Georgian silver. The Knight confesses he really has no idea why they found Glin so appealing. 'Perhaps it's not what they're used to,' he says, tongue in cheek.

Supper for the Fitzgerald family is at a charming bleached wood table with china candleholders and fresh flowers in the kitchen in the servants' wing. It has a pretty dresser with nineteenth-century French plates showing birds, butterflies, fish and flowers, a service once used for shooting-lunches. The windowledge is faced with blue and white tiles and the walls are a sunny yellow and the views are of the Shannon.

Nancy bustles about. She started working at the Castle when she was fourteen. Her great-grandfather was gamekeeper at Glin and her grandfather was coachman. The cook would throw pots and pans at her, so young Nancy left and went to Shannon Airport, at that exciting time when flying boats were landing on the River, and learned to cook for a generation of intrepid wealthy American travellers. But when she was nineteen she came back to Glin and cheerfully worked a day which began at 6 am, feeding the hens, cooking staff breakfast at 7.30 for the butler, the chauffeur, the steward, the ladies' maids, three housemaids and a kitchen maid. Then she would carry full nursery breakfast to the top of the house for Nanny, the governess and Una Burke, who was then a nursery maid. Then at 9 o'clock she would do breakfast for the Knight of Glin and his wife and earned £1 a month in 1936 with one shilling kept back for her stamp.

'She may have the smallest hands and feet,' Olda Fitzgerald says, 'but she can perform miracles. Her soufflés . . . rise like angels to the top of the oven . . . sponges dimple at the touch of a finger.'

Nancy twinkles and cooks artichokes, sorrel soup, lamb steaks and mange-tout with flair, followed by raspberries, brown bread, cheese. 'You must try crubeens in Paris,' the Knight explains. This is the true Irish name for pigs' trotters but he is chivvied by his youngest, 'Oh Daddy, you are so pompous.'

In the Castle, skittish, happy voices waft down from the double flying staircase with its Venetian window and the ceiling above with its pretty flowery plasterwork; sprays of fluting blossom and wheatsheaves send gaiety cascading down. At last they find their host, and in one voice these sophisticated travellers chirp, 'Night Knight.'

As they go back up the wooden staircase – it is Robert Adam's design and seen in houses on the Bosporus, the idea of the 'flying staircase' being that it rises on two ramps one on either side and creates an air of walking up into space – the Americans stop only to admire the lacy transparent Hussars banner, delicate with a gauzy opalescent antiquity, before meeting their four-posters.

Low-voiced, the Knight says dryly: 'Glin can be a testing mistress.' He tends to colour up if he has said something particularly mischievous.

4

THE ANTURRAJ

'Hurrah, hurrah, the dahlias are dead.' Jorrocks the red-faced squire and the whole Ascendancy are off for a winter of what they like doing best, hunting.

Ireland has always been a horsemad country, and the horse dominated upper-class life. Any philandering, squandering or drunken excess could be excused if you rode well, 'showed bottom'. It was a passion, a way of life, so many hooves across the boggy land. Hunting was essentially an upper-class pastime for gentlemen, yet it would bring together the big Ascendancy landowner, the lovable Flurry character captured in Somerville and Ross's *Irish RM*, the poachers and the sly peasant farmer, but above all a special breed of woman providing a complete vignette of Anglo-Irish life.

These hunting Ascendancy women in skintight extremely well cut breeches, crisp white jabots and bowlers, moved like dancers, with the bravado of Cossacks, their bodies bending with the horse. Sharing their natural buoyancy, they galloped across bright green fields and over tumbling stone walls, through hazel and hawthorn shadowy copses and coverts. Stopping to pick a blackberry, popping one into a vividly red lipsticked mouth, they cantered on to metalled roads then back to bridle paths, the liberating chase. Hunting was dangerous and they were brave. They rode like Genghis Khan.

Christabel, Lady Ampthill, rode with Garboesque flamboyance, occasionally hunting in fishnet tights and quite a short skirt. Master of the Ballymacad Hunt from 1956 to 1959, she and her horse once fell on the way to the meet and she lost several teeth. But nothing was allowed to interfere with a good day's hunting; she put them in her pocket, hunted all day and that evening flew to London and had them replaced. Lady Ampthill was respected as a shrewd horse dealer, was a match for the country people and made a hard bargain.

A great beauty, always surrounded by admirers, she married the third Baron Ampthill in 1918 but declared she was not ready to have children and is understood to have refused to have marital relations. Her husband, whose family motto was 'What Will Be Will Be', gave her a book on 'Marital Happiness'.

On a holiday in Switzerland in 1920, she sent her husband ('Darlingest old Thing') a letter letting him know that his 'little wify was being very naughty', was 'so happy she is almost bursting,' and that there 'had been no sports yet owing to the weather'; she had a vast following of young men, 'slim silky Argentines . . . admiring Greeks' and one 'Dago young man with hair beautifully Marcel waved'.

A year later, a fortune teller told her that she was pregnant. A doctor confirmed the prediction, while adding that the lovely Christabel was still technically a virgin. There were dark mutterings about an attempt at marital rape. A son, Geoffrey Russell, was born in October 1921.

It was not until 1976, in a highly controversial case at a House of Lords Committee of Privileges, that his entitlement to the title as fourth Baron Ampthill was confirmed. His father had died in 1973 but another son, Sir John Russell, born in 1950 by a third marriage to a vicar's daughter, contested Geoffrey Russell's claim. One of the arguments advanced in the complicated and costly case was that the third Lord Ampthill had been sleepwalking when he wandered into his wife Christabel's room. She never married again and, apart from hunting, ran a dress shop and worked as an electrical fitter during the war. She died in 1976 before the Lords hearing.

It was the seat on a horse and recklessness in the hunting field which earned most praise in Ireland and liquefied any resentment against the Ascendancy. These landed families who hunted could not have been more appreciated had they written odes to Brian Boru.

At the end of the afternoon, one Master of the Galway Blazers recalled, 'We would gather at a pub. That's where you usually ended up because the horse boxes and the hounds would be there.' 'Champagne certainly gives one werry gentlemanly ideas,' the bibulous Jorrocks remarked, enjoying the absence of all class distinction at the end of a good day's hunting. A sporting grocer, Jorrocks was the creation of the writer R. S. Surtees in the first half of the nineteenth century, who used him to express an amused satirical view of the hunting set's social ambition and snobbery.

These hunting women could hold their drink, they were admired for their elegance, one leg over the other, a glass held by bright-red-painted fingernails, which might enthusiastically stub out a cigarette in the dregs, laughing so much at 'a good yarn'.

They were uncomplicated. Once when a farmer asked a celebrated Master of Hounds why her horse was sweating so much, the reply was more than he had anticipated. 'Well!' she said, looking him in the eye, 'so would you if you had been lodged between my thighs for three hours.'

Good conversationalists, they were brittle and amusing, with a keen sense of what was fashionable. Men found them stimulating; they had usually seen the latest in the theatre in London and Paris; could speak French or Italian or both; and even talked in hunting parodies: 'The private detectives were hard at my brush,' earthy laughter and, for something they disapproved of, it was definitely 'tails down'. They had a robust attitude to sex '. . . you know, after a day's hunting.' Affairs were airily discussed, with detached amusement.

They married well: 'My husband didn't do anything.' They talk about husbands and lovers as if comparing packs of foxhounds. 'There is a photograph of my husband, and there is one of my lover,' and from silver frames in need of a polish men with clipped hair and moustaches, in uniform, stare back unsmilingly as if about to put down some disorderly behaviour, a wild woman or a horse.

Their homes are filled with Snaffles prints, classic Irish hunting scenes of half a century ago, and crotchety small dogs.

The Ascendancy woman on a horse could never be accused of lacking courage, compassion maybe. Her children had to ride no matter how timid, and as they faced a notorious fence would ask each other apprehensively: 'This is a real rasper, do we jump it or face Mummie?' So many of Molly Keane's novels deal with these beautiful, emotionally careless mothers forcing children into the saddle and coldly dismissing any misery and bruised ineptitude as they dressed for dinner.

Analysing the breed in her book *In the Pink*, Caroline Blackwood described the 'orange cream on their faces', but this never applied to the Galway Blazer girls. What is remarkable is how their complexions remain so unweathered, no broken veins, but then they always spent a great deal on themselves.

They bought couture clothes in Mayfair when they were in their twenties. Today their waists are still as slim, their incomes too but they can get into the Balenciagas and Diors bought half a century ago when their hair was always fashionably cut.

By night there was no trace of heartiness. These Ascendancy women would be transformed, luminous jewellery glowing against a skin soft from a day in Ireland's moisture; brightly made up, they had graduated long since from the Elizabeth Arden introduction to makeup for girls of good background, perennial blue eyeshadow and pale pink lipstick. Hunting Ascendancy women tended to be handsome, not always a flattering word implying a lack of softness.

Accomplished pianists and good dancers, brisk and cultivated; with a confident ease, they were not at all averse in the elation of a good day's hunting to a little dalliance but not before a decent dinner, hunting would keep their figures in shape and their livers lively.

'Sorry, darling,' a hunting woman at a cocktail party in Dublin broke off her conversation immediately on seeing a beautiful young man arrive. 'I have just seen my supper and a lift home,' and pounced. They are no simpering, vulnerable creatures and years ago were flattered when lunching in Quaglinos to be mistaken for smart 'ladies of the night' and asked as they left the restaurant, 'how's trade today?' A compliment, they thought, on their style and innate friskiness.

There is nothing the Irish like more than a character. They may not be too impressed by tidy gardens and good housekeeping but for someone like Lady Mollie Cusack Smith, when she swings into the local pub in Tuam, voices do not go down to whispered malevolence; she is admired, 'a fine figure of a woman,' they say; her conversation is peppered with words like 'bugger' and 'bloody' but when she raises her voice to sing *camalias*, mournful Irish folk songs, there is a headshaking hush. She has been seen cantering home at midnight and in the village they have crossed themselves and sworn it was John Dennis, the ghost of her ancestor, a great hunting figure and the founder of the Galway hounds, later known as the famous Blazers.

Over the years they would serve her horse a white drink, 'Guinness and stuff', and for Lady Mollie if it was really hot a large brandy and pint of cider. Her photograph hangs on the wall today alongside other celebrities. Molly Keane is one but she gets an unspoken 'tails down' for her ironic parodying of hunting women in novels like *Time after Time*.

'Oh you're going to see Lady Mollie are you?' Still the village lad in Tuam was a bit apprehensive: 'On your own head be it' as he gave directions to Bermingham House, a few miles away.

Lady Mollie Cusack Smith, formerly Huntsman and Master of the Galway Blazers, is sitting in the conservatory of this stunning pink-washed Georgian house with great windows looking out towards Galway and the west of Ireland.

She is wearing a large straw hat, toning shades of amber yellow and soft tweed culottes and trendy thick-knit stockings. She was rather cross to be there at all because she was meant to be in 'bloody Sri Lanka' where she had been hoping to buy some silks for her dressmaker but a '. . . bloody strike' had put an end to that hope.

A challenging cacaw of laughter – her breath had a slight whiff of garlic – she fixes you with immensely bright eyes of Dresden blue. Her image is as an elegant shocker in the cream of the world's hunting country but really she is quite shy. She cooks divinely; dresses with élan; gives the best hunt ball in Ireland and probably the last in a private house serving oysters and salmon to 300; her hounds are the celebrated Bermingham and North Galway.

Augustus John called her 'The Tulip of Tuam'. His portrait captured this wild, spirited young woman with her white skin and black hair whom he first met in the west of Ireland. They had in common a friendship with 'Fireball' Francis MacNamara, roistering landowning poet and believer in free love, a naughty Bohemian notion in the twenties. Lady Mollie was seventeen and had already sailed in rough seas with MacNamara, climbing, she said 'thirty-foot waves like a cat going up a wall'. The painting showed her in a white Irish wool sweater and orange skirt, a toreador hat perched fetchingly on the side of her head. 'But nobody cared for it very much. It was rather chocolate boxy.' Still she feels it was rather 'stingy' of her mother not to buy it at the time for £700.

Later Mollie O'Rourke would get to know Augustus John well when she was studying grand opera in Paris, 'same time as Melba'.

'"Gus" and I were great friends, he was terribly interesting. We used to sit together in French cafés and draw on the tablecloths. I wish I'd kept those tablecloths, everyone who came into the room used to be caricatured by us.'

Her house, not surprisingly, is full of good paintings, one by Louis le Brocquy, another of Lady Mollie, looking svelte, by Norah McGuinness. In the large bedroom a fur coat is thrown over the unmade bed, she has a superstition about making beds; on the walls Russian icons; a tiny beautiful piece of Evie Hone's stained glass and a picture of a Connemara woman praying.

She never did sing opera, instead her expensively trained contralto was used in the hunting field. 'I'd just roar at the hounds and they'd stop in their tracks. I am madly in love with my hounds.'

Her conversation has the innocent raciness of her vintage. Still pretty, her robust language comes as a hilarious surprise, also the fact that she was terrified of horses as a child when even her adored father, a brilliant rider himself, could not teach her to ride.

She was the only child of a distinguished old Galway family, motto 'Don't let Anything Surprise You'. The O'Rourkes had princely titles and links with Russia. Lady Mollie was about two when she was first put on a pony and even had her hands tied behind her back in an attempt to make her a competent horsewoman. Not to be able to ride in Ireland would socially be almost as unacceptable as saying 'pardon' or asking the way to a 'toilet'.

'I was terrified. You see I don't like horses, and I subscribe to Oscar Wilde's view that they are danger at both ends and uncomfortable in the middle.' Her later skill as a horsewoman is a triumph: 'I hated every minute of it and I am not in the least interested in horses.'

Meanwhile a couple of governesses came and went. Amusement for Lady Mollie included tobogganing down the backs of the maids Ellen and Mary; she learnt accomplished French but her marks for arithmetic were a consistent two out of a hundred.

When her father developed asthma, she was twelve years old and had to hunt his pack of harriers along with the Galway Blazers and East Galway. If he had any anxiety about her, he was reassured one crisp winter's day when everyone was out hunting. He went into the local pub and there met an old woman who told him with glee, 'I met Miss Mollie yesterday and she was cursin' hard . . .' and he smiled at his daughter's courage on the hunting field, sometimes falling headlong into a badger's sett, swearing, tumbling, picking herself up again and yelling at the hounds.

But her life was not all spent on the hunting field. After she had a row with her father about a horse, she left in a huff and drove to London where she set up a couture house in Mayfair, a tiny Jacobean building in a corner of Bond Street. 'Claridges was my pub . . . and we used to dance at the Four Hundred Club.' Then she moved to a haunted house in Berkeley Square; 'It was absolutely divine; it belonged to Lord Carnarvon, you know the one who dug up the thing,' a casual reference to the peer who helped discover Tutankhamen's tomb in Eygpt '. . . but there was something wrong with the bloody place. I never saw a ghost but I could not go on living there and went to France.'

Her business partner was Russian so she met 'lots of Russian émigrés' and, because of her age, was 'allowed to have two goes at drinking vodka instead of knocking it back in one'. They confidently set up next door to Molyneux.

But by 1936 she was back in Ireland. 'Don't ask me how old I am, I don't know anything about age,' when her father became seriously ill. Then there was the war.

'I cried salt tears in the bar of the Hibernian at the outbreak of the fucking thing . . . no more anything.' But Ireland being Ireland there were ways of having plenty of everything, and there were so few people about. 'The hunting was brilliant.'

Interestingly, she did not marry until 1946, the year her father died. 'I met my husband in Dublin at my flat. I was upside down on the floor getting out ice for a cocktail party.' The marriage ended after six years and the birth of a daughter who married a local electrician. Mother and daughter did not always see eye to eye, except on the hunting field. 'There was never a word, we were smashing together,' Lady Mollie said emotionally. 'And I have three lovely grandchildren.'

Her husband died in the middle of the divorce which was 'extraordinarily uncomfortable because I couldn't get any money at all.' But with the right priorities, she held on to her hounds, sometimes commandeering paying guests into using their Rolls Royces to take the pack to the meet. She also cracked a Crown Derby plate over the head of a 'bloody fool', another paying guest who had the temerity to suggest that she really was a West Briton. 'He asked if I thought of myself as Irish. I am Irish for Christ's sake . . . Jesus . . . But the eejut did come from Northern Ireland.'

Hunting to her has always been 'an intellectual exercise which one enjoys, and also killing the fox', not the inferior business it is today in Ireland running round boreens trying to avoid electric fences.

For someone who has followed the Pytchley, hunted boar in Brittany, had 'cracking falls' and stayed in some of the best châteaux for *la chasse*, the Ball at the Royal Dublin Horse Show, for years the social peak for the 'horse Protestant' and where bread rolls were thrown at the Waterford crystal chandeliers, is tame and she no longer bothers to go.

In the evenings as the rooks make their distinctive cawing over

Bermingham House, it looks vulnerable and lonely but Lady Mollie is inside enjoying her own company, and re-reading Walter Scott: 'all that romance of my youth. I am fascinated by *The Betrothed*. I won't have television in the house, can't stand the bloody thing.'

Like the most loved person in Britain, she always changes for supper even if on her own, but unlike the Queen Mother, it has to be more than scrambled eggs: 'Oh no, that is for breakfast.' Some little piece of game or fish will come out of the enormous kitchen with its old copper saucepans and chipped wooden draining boards covered with bunches of herbs.

For years Lady Mollie was in love with a man who was married and lived in England, the romance of darting over to London for intimate dinners and then on to a nightclub – 'My lover and I used to dance twice a week' – possibly suited her better than the restriction of a marriage. 'Thank God I am far too old for antics like that, I couldn't bear it.'

Today the really chic hunts are the Limerick, the Tipperary and the Galway Ward Union, although a lot of young Anglo-Irish hunt with the West Waterford. But the Galway Blazers is still the ultimate in terms of an interesting and stylish hunt. It has had some remarkable Masters.

Mrs Melosine – 'It is French for a very nasty fairy' – Daly was Master of the Galway Blazers, but was drummed out of Ireland by Catholic bishops disapproving of her third marriage. 'Nobody,' she remarked a little bitterly, and sourness is not in her nature, 'ever objects in this country if you live with someone, but if you marry them . . .' she shrugged.

Born in Galway in 1911, the daughter of General Cyril Cary Barnard, 'Melon' Daly, as she is known, complained: 'Daddy did not approve of girls being educated.' Her father, who had retired from the army in 1910, returned to command the Royal Wiltshires in Dublin in 1922. 'It was the time when we were handing over to the Irish Free State; there was a bit of trouble and Mummie had her throat cut.'

Her mother, Mrs Rita Cary Barnard, had been to an auction and was being driven home when 'three young terrorists tied wire across the road which cut the lamps of the car, and then the windscreen and then Mummie's throat; she also had a fractured head and her ear was cut off.'

The adjutant, 'a chap named Monty', thought she was dead so 'he put her upside down in the car and sped to the nearest cottage so he could leave the body while he went for help and an armoured car.'

But a daughter in the house was a trained nurse home on leave. 'This woman isn't dead,' she told the adjutant. 'By standing her on her head you have saved her life; if she had not been upside down she would have drowned in her own blood.' An amazed Monty sped the General's wife to Portobello Hospital, where this remarkable woman, after two years on her back and being tubed sixteen times, though she kept pulling the tubes out, would survive to live to a considerable old age. Her voice and larynx gone, she spoke in a whispery voice and lived on a diet of oysters and stout.

'The family then took an action against the King and won. I think it is called a Petition of Right which 200 MPs signed. The King wrote, "Let right be done" and Mummie was awarded about £3000.'

Mother and daughter were extraordinarily resilient; this nerve and stamina are qualities of the typical huntswoman.

Life now for the Cary Barnards had to be cramped by stringent security; it was a time in Ireland when you could be shot for singing the wrong songs. So it was slightly embarrassing for the General when his schoolgirl daughter developed Republican sympathies. At a dinner party, a voice was heard from behind the curtain singing 'Up de Valéra, he's the champion of the right.' The General, apoplectic with rage, ordered that Mary, the cook, a well-known Republican and singer of rebel songs, be sacked immediately, until he looked behind the curtain and discovered his daughter's green parrot.

At thirteen Melon Cary Barnard was the first girl to showjump in England. Officially no child under sixteen was allowed. 'Did you know I was the first woman to judge at the Royal Show?'

A few years later, Melosine was presented at Court. Poised, defiantly assured in her long pearls, feathers and lace trimming, her dress was considered too short for the Court, and she accidentally tumbled into an outraged Queen Mary's lap.

When her father retired in 1927 the family moved to Africa, a place he had always loved. At an impressionably early age, she was catapulted into the Happy Valley set in the White Highlands of Kenya.

In this colonial playground young Melon managed to escape the three 'As', alcohol, adultery and altitude, and would run away but not before innocently remarking to a guest at lunch, 'I hear you are a very good shot.' This was the Comtesse de Janze, known as the 'wicked madonna' and notorious even in the Happy Valley set. She had attempted to kill her lover, Raymond de Trafford, a friend of Evelyn Waugh's, as his train was about to pull out of the Gare du Nord in Paris! Even in that moment of high drama, when de Trafford was badly wounded in the heart and his mistress had peppered her own stomach with bullets, her concern was for a friend's German Shepherd dog brought along for the farewells.

Alice de Janze's marriage to de Trafford was disastrous and after several attempts she would eventually succeed in committing suicide.

For 'Melon' Cary Barnard it was all rather heady and hedonistic. She met the stunningly beautiful Diana Coldwell who later became Lady Broughton. This was before her lover Josslyn Hay, Earl of Erroll, a glamorous figure brilliant at polo, bridge and seduction, was found murdered in his Buick in 1941. Her husband, Sir Henry 'Jock' Delves Broughton, would be found not guilty of the murder. In those days Diana was flouncing round the Muthaiga Country Club with a millionaire. When asked by the ingenue Melon where she had found him, she replied, 'under a bush'. This may have been the spark which set the young Melosine off on a life of adventure. Others talked to her of meeting rich husbands on traffic islands in Piccadilly.

For those who never indulge in any greater excess than another violet cream chocolate after the Queen's speech on Christmas Day, Diana's sparsely attended funeral in Kenya provided a grim satisfaction.

Not long afterwards Melon Cary Barnard left home and tramped through the bush at night with only an oil-lamp. 'I thought the glowworms were rather noisy. One said ". . . aaargh" and I realized it was a leopard.' When she was finally rescued, she had sunstroke and malaria, refused to see anyone except 'nanny' and developed a mastoid making her deaf for five months. 'You have to have a sense of humour about deaf aids, fucking things.'

Her father immediately made her a ward of court, but soon she would marry Guy Trundle, a farmer in Kenya. 'He once said to Mummie, "Why did you marry the General; he has no sense of humour?" *in vino veritas*, I suppose.'

They came back to London and wherever Melon Trundle went her pet fox called Freddy came too on a lead. In the evening she whizzed round with friends like Mollie O'Rourke in her little roadster, in the style of Mrs Stitch in Evelyn Waugh's *Vile Bodies*, bumping into any 'fucking Rolls' which got in the way.

They drank at the Savoy, danced at the 'Four Hundred' and dined at Quaglino's and the Ritz. It was a raffish time with lots of penniless charmers: 'Old Chatty' who was always trying to inveigle them out badger hunting; minor aristocrats and phantom majors cashiered out of the army for dud drinks cheques, 'such fun', hoots of laughter. Invited for cocktails at the Ritz by a glamorous peer, they found when they got there that he was in an old chambermaid's room with grey green walls, an iron bed and a basin. 'But it was a very good address for which he paid a pound a week and of course he could use Ritz writing paper.'

Her second husband, Major James Hanbury, was Joint Master of England's Belvoir hunt; they had met in Cairo when he was in the Greys. The Hanbury family had been fiercely against the romance. His mother 'said I was too old, and I would never have a child. She was married to this little solicitor person and they put their heads together and offered me £10,000 to stay away from James.'

'I can't marry and I can't live without you,' he told her. She tells stories well and dramatically. 'So there were 700 people at our wedding and breakfast at the Ritz. We were to fly to Paris but before that we went to the Mirabelle and there was Guy who had been saying "Don't marry him, don't do it", so we all had dinner together.'

Life with James at Burleigh was 'wonderful', hunting three days in Ireland and in Leicestershire with the Belvoir.

But the marriage would not survive. Melon Hanbury came

home to Ireland in 1947 after six years in the war 'driving lorries from Benghazi to Baghdad and working in Anglo-Egyptian Censorship'. Home again, her daily reading naturally included *The Horse and Hound* where she spotted an advertisement: 'Wanted, a Joint Master for the Galway Blazers'.

Ideal. On her mother's side she was related to Atty Persse, one of the most famous names in hunting. The Blazers had been started by her great-grandfather, so she rattled off intelligence about him, how a Reverend Persse came to Ireland in 1600 AD and was given land in Galway, how the Co. Galway Hunt 'the Blazers' was a private pack; how another Persse, Robert Parson, put his hunt servants into 'orange plush with mother-of-pearl buttons three times the size of normal ones'; and how when he was entertaining the Ormond, a hunt from across the River Shannon in County Offaly, to a convivial dinner in a hotel in Birr it was burnt down and the hunt got its Blazers name. Others say that it was because most of the leading riders had red hair.

The job was hers; she became Master of the Blazers in 1945–6. Her cousin, Denis Bowes Daly, was Joint Master. They fell in love. He was known locally as 'the pompous' but he won the Military Cross, and was a distinguished polo player and served in the Blues.

'His family claim an almost distinct line back to Adam, certainly before Christ,' his widow assures you, quite something amongst the Anglo-Irish who are fiercely competitive about their pedigrees.

Mrs Bowes Daly was truly happy. The hunting was excellent and she would be chatelaine of the elegant, ancestral Daly home Dunsandle, with one of the largest and most splendid private libraries in the country.

Her happiness was short-lived. Catholic priests were outraged by her appointment to the Blazers. Although she was a Protestant, and divorced from Hanbury in England, she was denounced from the pulpit as several bishops preached fiery sermons about 'This woman . . . unworthy of the honour of being Master of the Blazers'. Hunting is almost sacred in Ireland.

It was a glorious scandal getting international headlines. But it is doubtful if there would be such uproar in Ireland today where in a

1988 survey one in four young people claimed that the Church was unimportant to them. But those were the days of the ferociously intolerant Bishop Brown of Galway who led the campaign against the Dalys. He even objected to couples bathing on the beach and those unfortunate enough to be caught cuddling under a bush after an exciting day at Galway races were whacked by priests with the fanaticism of mad mullahs.

She was backed by the entire hunt 'and they were all Catholic', but local Catholic farmers had to boycott the hunt and, Melon Daly confesses, 'It hurt.' This went on for about six months. 'Life was intolerable; I resigned and ran away with my joint master to Tanganyika.'

Every three years they came home to Dunsandle, but found they could not afford the house any longer; it had to be sold. There was the stinging indignity of seeing beautiful things, two of the white marble fireplaces in the Georgian drawing room salon, ripped out and shipped off to the South of France, to 'Somerset Maugham, you know . . . the writer fellow'. An elaborate brass and glass chandelier was scooped up by 'some embassy in Paris'.

Dunsandle is now a ruin; weeds shoot out of plasterwork; on damp windy days the water in the lake turns a moody inky blue.

During twelve years in Africa, where their daughter was born, 'I was the oldest woman, at forty-two, in Nairobi to have a child,' she also produced a simple *Cookery Book* in English and Swahili. They came back to Ireland in 1972. Her husband collapsed and died from a heart attack just before their daughter's marriage and after his own eighty-fourth birthday, but Melon Daly still insisted that they go ahead with the wedding in the Guards Chapel, followed by a cocktail party.

After all the disagreeable intolerance she experienced in the name of Christianity, she now feels that the Moslem faith is best. 'If we have a God he is everybody's not just Catholic or Protestant. He is God, too, for the trees and the dogs. The four-legged must never be forgotten.'

Like all those hunting people in Ireland who complain about the cost of maintaining stables, there is always enough money, rustled up from some old bonds in South Africa, for hunting, for clothes, something decent in the decanter, some game, salmon or beef, no wholemeal pasta or primrose wine for the very social Galway Blazer set. While struggling to get a pension Mrs Bowes Daly confided; 'I went mad and bought my daughter a yacht, she is a pretty girl living with her husband in South Africa.'

The last four years have been hard. 'It is the first time in my life I have been utterly alone.' She may look indomitable, like an elderly Cambridge don bending over her desk as she peers at a tribute to her husband from the Duke of Beaufort. Her grief was compounded when her step-grandson, Anthony Daly, was one of those soldiers murdered by the IRA in Knightsbridge when riders and horses were killed and wounded by the terrorist attack, among them the gallant horse Sefton.

Her home has been an isolated pleasant farmhouse in a swooping farming valley in the west of Ireland, where the windows are dark with ivy; in the lonely hills around the house a different sort of hunt was going on for a wanted IRA terrorist.

Living alone and so far away from any town, she resourcefully put out a 'terrible fire' in the house, recalling wryly how when the Fire Brigade eventually did arrive an hour and a half later, they congratulated her, took nine bottles of beer and left. 'So that was a great success but left me a bit shook. It is no good waiting for other people to do things, you have to learn to put a spade in the earth yourself, nobody wants to work anymore.' Lately she moved to the model village of Adare, County Limerick, near lots of hunting friends and people like the Earl and Countess of Dunraven.

Instead of moping, she is doing some rather exciting paintings. Obviously popular, her social life is healthy, 'staying with people ye know' in Dublin and London. Shopping in Harrods is no longer much fun; she finds it 'disgusting these days, nothing but black servants. Fortnum's is much better.' There the shop assistants tend to be white.

Still a cocktail party enthusiast, she was amused by the young man who talked to her about eating budgies and working for Mother Teresa in Calcutta because it looked so good on his c.v. This veteran of Happy Valley was not shocked or hoodwinked, appreciating that he may have been high on something other than gin and tonic.

Stirred by memories of good parties, she raced upstairs and reappeared in an old Worth black evening dress and jacket. 'I wore it the other evening, not bad, have had it for sixty years, now where did I put my Chanel?'

Desks and sofa tables are a clutter of hunting calendars, old photographs, dried hydrangeas in shades of jaded eau-de-nil, racing fixture cards and pictures of herself as a girl, exuberant in jodhpurs, hair flying, turning hearts.

Today she is spry, auburn hair curled in the forties way, lips strong red, long nails painted to match and fingers studded with emerald rings, her tweed trouser suit, the zip gaping understandably because her food is so good, salmon mousses, pheasant casseroles, elderberry and blackberry crème brulée; the lapels are leaping with jewelled brooches and her vitality at lunch made her seem younger than her old friend, eighty-one-year-old Olive Partridge, still a fine boned beauty. 'Bowes,' she said in a booming voice, she is virtually teetotal, 'always said I got drunk on conversation.'

These two old ladies giggled like girls as a wintry sun filtered through to the claret walls, remembering how Olive used to ride an Arab pony, how the previous summer they had been on a yacht in Cannes, still a racy pair, chortling over their affairs and the difficulty of renewing driving licences at their age, how best to answer the questionnaire. 'Do you hear well, badly or not at all?' they asked each other mockingly.

As the widow Malone confided in one of Colonel Barrow's hunting cartoons – he used a cavalry *nom de plume* 'Sabretache' which appeared in the *Tatler* in the 1920s – 'It's not the horses that are fascinatin' about the huntin', it's the anturraj.'

5

TENACITY OR STUPIDITY?

Amiable, rangy, little moustache, shoulders back, profile stuck into the damp Irish air, Randal Arthur Henry Plunkett, the nineteenth Baron Dunsany and eighty-three years old, could not be anything but a vigorous former soldier. Hands clamped behind his back in military stance he looks up at the Dunsany battlements. This pretty Strawberry Hill, Gothic castle in County Meath has been in the family since Elizabethan times.

Both have worn well. He roars with laughter. 'Came home to die, ye see.' Bright eyes challenge, but there is no need for soothing 'surely nots', 'too young'. He is almost apologizing for still being around. 'I was a bit too early.'

'Plunketts,' he says, 'go out into the world but one son always comes back to die.' He and a friend, Ambrose Congreve of the same vintage, watch each other with interest: 'One would be very upset if the other one was slipping.'

He addresses you in the way of elderly peers and politicians. 'When one has lived all over the world in a peripatetic manner, one tends to come back to base.' It is not really a conversation, but a hugely entertaining shooting of staccato facts: 'We are all descended from the Afghans.' Iran is referred to meticulously as Persia. 'Hear they booed a Jew at the Eton Harrow match recently,' adding, 'You know years ago Balliol always had darker intelligent students from the Empire, Trinity had sporting Anglo-Irish. "Trinity, bring out your black man," would be the cry at the Balliol-Trinity match. They would reply: "Balliol, bring out your white man," always been a bit of racial discrimination.'

Any hint of fierceness is masked by a drollery, and snuff sits on his tie and lapels, rarely making the ascent up the fine Plunkett nostrils. He will unexpectedly sing Irish folk songs, a rather savage ballad with all the rural resonance is about the Waterford family who were cursed: 'Old Lord Waterford is dead . . . and he'll get a warrrum seat by the side of a special grate where his father bakes in state.'

He marches round the billiard room with its chronological charts in bright colours, yellows and reds tracing the origins of every member of the Irish peerage.

The Plunketts: 'We go back to Noah,' have been in Ireland longer than most. In good times a Dunsany ancestor commanded the cavalry defending that exclusive Protestant area known as the Pale under Queen Elizabeth. But there was a temporary hiccough when the family sided with the Stuarts and were forced to flee to Holland, 'Got back to base in 1781.'

Most Ascendancy families boast a distinguished soldier or two but are not well off for poets or saints. However there is a resemblance between Dunsany and his godly seventeenth-century ancestor, Oliver Plunkett, Bishop of Dublin, who was hanged, drawn and quartered at Tyburn. The sainted Oliver has brought the present Dunsanys 'great kudos', particularly when they went to Rome and met the Pope. Dunsany has astutely kept the colour photograph of that meeting on view 'to impress the faithful. If you are seen talking to the Pope,' he observed, 'you must obviously be all right.'

The likeness is round the eyes. Lord Dunsany is not surprised – 'After all, what is twelve generations in a persistent type?'

Pious grannies making a pilgrimage to the Castle to kiss the episcopal ring, believing it can work miracles, were desperately upset to hear it had been put in the bank.

Dunsany explains. 'At the time of the Hunger Strikes in the late 1970s, early 80s' – the castle is not far from the road to the North – 'I felt it wiser to put some "goodies" away, things like the ring, important pictures, especially as a house near here which had belonged to Victor Sassoon was burnt down.'

He does not mock this fervent Irish passion for placing pursed-lip kisses on the feet of statues and on bishops' jewels, being a stickler for protocol himself, thinks kissing a Cardinal's ring 'is merely good manners'.

In an attempt to cheer up these disappointed coach parties, Dunsany will take them round the Castle himself: 'I give them bullshit. I endeavour to make them laugh.'

The Medici marble Venuses, the gold troika with its small gold cherub and glimmering amethyst, an Easter present made for Catherine the Great and a replica of the state troika in Leningrad; the decorative Chinese Chippendale chairs with their *petit point* dragons worked by his mother Beatrice and the gentle pale blue and gold porcelain begin to make up for not having 'a rub of the ring'.

Irishmen all over the world call their houses Tara. The sacred Hill of Tara, seat of the ancient High Kings of Ireland, is on one side of this medieval castle. In the pale apple green entrance hall, there is a portrait of Brian Boru, the last High King of Ireland, playing a harp and looking rather coy in a crown of gold. 'Expect he is watching an execution,' Lord Dunsany remarks.

The castle has thirteen staircases, five secret doors and a ghost. It is sometimes heard going up the grand parade 1780s staircase to the drawing room on the first floor. Perhaps it is Brian Boru who drove the Vikings out of Ireland. 'Had he survived this would have been his home farm.' Dunsany glances at the acres of parkland, the huge oaks, and there is a mournful rustling of beech trees.

The Dunsanys were Vikings, 'But we must have bred like rabbits, infesting the country from Drogheda to Ulster. Then the Normans came. Seeing they couldn't win, the Plunketts 'married them and became their bishops and lawyers.' However eleven Plunketts were hanged by Oliver Cromwell in the seventeenth century and the castle was defeated.

Moving into the library, a favourite G. K. Chesterton belief is trotted out: 'A man of intelligence travels only in his own library.' Lord Dunsany's has a honeycombed ceiling, famille rose pots above the doors, and with a fire flickering at dusk, and Gothick fish-scale shaped windows hidden by heavy swagged curtains, it is invitingly mellow. The softly lit rich gold silk damask walls make a sympathetic background as he sits at an ormolu trimmed desk peering intently at a piece of yellowing paper in his father's handwriting.

He is intensely proud of his romantic literary father who was also a soldier and a Professor of Greek. He refers to him as the 'Boss' and in low voice reads his last poem:

> When the world has come to its end,
> Because we were overskilled,
> Will the moon look down like a friend
> With a sigh for what we have killed?
>
> Will the moon look down from the skies
> Upon the desolate scene
> That will show we were not so wise
> As what we ought to have been?'

'My father was always concerned about the nuclear threat,' Lord Dunsany explains as he puts away the gold-bound book.

In the 'Boss's' lifetime, artists and writers, Yeats, Shaw, Lady Gregory, George Moore and AE Russell gathered in the medieval castle, entertained by the poet peer and his wife.

Although an aesthete, he followed all the country pursuits. He was Master of the Tara Harriers, hunted with the Meath and the Ward. Snipe he considered 'food which gourmets were given' when they had 'been good to the poor', and should always be cooked for 'five minutes' – 'quite long enough.'

In the days before Ireland became a Free State, excellent cricketers from British cavalry regiments stationed at the Curragh would play at Dunsany; their host was one of the elite Na Shuler cricket team. But by the 1930s these young army officers who also danced well and were an asset at parties and hunt balls had gone. 'What a team I could raise if from the mists of time eleven of the best men with whom I have played on this ground,' Lord Dunsany would lament.

When he died in 1957 aged fifty-nine, after an appendix operation, Tennyson's *Crossing the Bar* was read at his memorial service in Ireland at his own request. 'I hope to meet my Pilot face to face,' he had said.

His son and only child, the present Lord Dunsany, who left the army in 1947, had been a professional soldier: 'Wellington was a local boy made good.' In 1926, he joined the 16th/5th Lancers and transferred to the Indian Army and the romantic Guides Cavalry.

In Delhi, he became ADC to Commander in Chief, Sir Philip Chewtwode in 1933, and the fervent hope was that he might appeal to their daughter Penelope rather than that impecunious 'fella' John Betjeman, the future Poet Laureate, whom she would later marry.

One night in Delhi when Penelope crept out for a secret midnight tryst at a Moghul tomb, her mother, sitting innocently in the drawing room, hearing a car driving away at ten o'clock was alarmed and, turning to her husband's ADC, exclaimed; 'Hist! What's that?' to which Randal Plunkett replied, all Irish charm, 'Tis but the wind,' calming the Commander in Chief's wife temporarily.

It is easy to imagine him in different mood barking peremptory orders spurring on the Indian Cavalry. He is also remembered by some of the memsahibs for staying in his tent for about three weeks, worrying that he was about to get mumps and avidly reading *Gone With the Wind*.

Afterwards, in the war, he found the family motto 'Hasten Slowly' very apt, telling with deprecating humour how he led his men so slowly in the withdrawal at El Alamein where he was commanding the rearguard that they got back last. 'The enemy shot past and I had no casualties.'

In 1947 he married for the second time, a baronet's daughter, Sheila Phillips. Her family owned Picton castle in Pembrokeshire. Her first husband, Baron de Rutzen, had been killed in the war three years earlier. His first wife, a Brazilian beauty, a 'bit of a bombshell', had caused a flutter in the cavalry dovecots in remote hill stations in India with her black satin sheets. Their son Edward Plunkett lives in New York and had just been to stay at the Castle with 'the little angels', as his children are besottedly called by their grandfather.

'My wife,' he says with pride, 'is a blonde Celt.' Suddenly the second Lady Dunsany appears, a bright, birdlike creature who is funny and shrewd and believed to be very rich. Her arrival in the billiard room has quite put him off a favourite lecture on the Basques: 'They are the aboriginals of Europe.'

There is an elaborate game between them. 'My wife talks too much,' her husband grumbles. 'Darling, can I have a few of these for Peggy?' Lady Peggy Nugent is an old friend who has arrived early with her dogs from the Isle of Wight. Lady Dunsany scoops up a couple of chicken and cucumber sandwiches and he pretends to be furious.

'Now I have lost my plate. I have nothing left except some parsley . . . the crumbs will go to the floor – oh deah. I like a good homemade soup, that's what I usually have.' But a cousin in India told him 'Gentlemen do not eat soup at lunch.' Humph.

The sandwiches are like gold bullion. 'Is there no one to do it?' Lord Dunsany asks mournfully. A manservant puts his head round the door, a solid middle-aged figure, and closes it quietly.

Pulling his lips back, showing gums in dry observation, Lord Dunsany shakes his head and feels his chances of ever persuading this one to dress up as a satyr as he once did with the butler at the Castle are unlikely. 'He is good enough but not very chicly dressed, and refuses to wear a uniform.'

His wife is disappearing: 'No, we will not join you – we are on fact not blether.' Already he was explaining how 'The "Boss" inherited from great-uncle Horace Plunkett, an unmarried philanthropist.'

In spite of founding the co-operative movement for Irish farmers in 1889, attracting Catholics and Protestants, northerners and southerners, with a turnover of two million pounds by 1900, Sir Horace Plunkett was never quite accepted. He was always thought of as an Ascendancy figure, but saw himself as an 'improving Conservative'.

A poor speaker at Westminster – favourite words included 'tomfoolery' and 'shoddy makebelieves' – but when exhorted to 'let sleeping dogs lie' he replied that on no account would he let 'lying dogs sleep'.

A somewhat compulsive personality, he once rewrote the introductory chapter to a short book seventy-two times, driving his harassed staff into the ground. John Betjeman was appointed as his private secretary in 1928 and not sorry when he was fired a year later.

Always rather austere, he liked to sleep on a revolving 'hutch' on the top of his house in Dublin, winter and summer, but fortunately was away the night Republican Irregulars called with a land-mine in 1923 doing great damage. They had threatened house burnings, disapproving of anyone who joined the Free State Senate. A dispirited Sir Horace left Ireland forever, concluding sadly that he 'felt like a dog on a tennis court, despised by both sides'. He spent the last nine years of his life in quiet orderly Weybridge in Surrey and learnt to fly at the age of seventy-five.

Lots of laughter in the library. Lady Peggy Nugent, in good form, is telling stories about her late husband, Sir Charles Nugent, known as 'The Sir', who returned to Ireland in 1927 to take over the family estate, Ballinlough Castle, Co. Westmeath, which had been neglected for years. The estate had been broken up as part of the Wyndham Land Act ruling, and the castle was due to be demolished, but devotedly 'The Sir' won it back and restored the castle and grounds with its lake, haunt of dragonflies and wildfowl. This was not easy; hens were nesting in the middle of the drawing room in a beautiful but muddy Chelsea bowl; and when he called on his neighbours the farmer was in an enormous double bed with his wife and they were 'sprouting potatoes between them'. All this is told with tongue-in-check laconic humour. There are occasional grumps from Lord Dunsany – 'Get those dogs off the chairs . . . hrrumph.' The Nugents, a Celtic Catholic family, were unusual in that their original family name was O'Reilly; they changed their name to claim a legacy in 1812.

The women tease him and make him laugh, and get him to tell the story of his brush with the Gardai: 'Do ask Randal about his court case.' His first ever motoring offence is still a source of merriment in Ireland. But Dunsany's autocratic style carried the day.

'I was driving home quietly in me motor, a Princess with a Rolls engine and power steering, and I was listening to the English election results which had been filtering in but were now beginning to show a pattern. Got flagged down by the Gardai.' It was late at night and the police suggested the nineteenth Baron had been wandering consistently over the white line for some three miles.

In court Dunsany asked the policeman, 'Do you realize that this is a road which undulates?' 'Poor man,' he impersonated a non-plussed Gardai's thick brogue as he stuttered 'Whah?'

Lord Dunsany, by now in his best hectoring manner, as if addressing the troops on the eve of battle, launched into a complicated discussion on 'the laws of geometry and the tangent', concluding, 'So you see you could not have had your lights on me.' The judge said, 'Case dismissed.'

This prompts more affectionate Gardai stories of innate Irish courtesy reflected even in tense border country. Coming back from the north once, Dunsany compared 'the trooper who lurched up to the car – Sheila was driving – "That your car love?" and the Irish policeman on the border to the south, who came up and gently said: 'Lady Dunsany I think.' 'Sheila', a trained social worker and on many charity committees, 'had known him as a child in the Dublin slums'.

Like all aristocratic families living dangerously near the border they make light of incidents between the north and south, but Dunsany admits he once missed being blown up by half an hour. 'If we hadn't been indulging in stirrup talk – ' he shrugged. 'The only shot I have heard in the north is at a pheasant shoot.'

Their role in the village is slight. 'We are rather like an endangered species, and the local Protestant church is now a county library. I am not a good Protestant; we have this dreadfully boring vicar.' But in the days when the family went to church, Dunsany's father came home and a young house guest asked: 'Sir, what did he preach about?' 'Sin,' replied the eighteenth baron: The guest persisted: 'And what was his attitude?' Slightly exasperated, he replied: 'He was against it.' Although the sermons are dull, Lord Dunsany is more restrained than Lord Mayo's spinster sister, Lady Florence Bourke, who jabbed people sitting in front of her with a hat pin to relieve the tedium.

The Dunsanys flit to London, where with the same air of

authority, wearing a cloak, Dunsany will sweep into the Ladies Hairdressing salon at Peter Jones, the Sloane hunting ground, and demand that they cut his hair. An assistant will demur, 'But this is ladies only.' The Baron will not have a refusal and barks: 'That doesn't matter a damn.'

A member of the Beefsteak and the Turf, he knows everyone. He once met the Duke of Windsor at a swimming pool in Marbella. 'We were both in shorts and barefoot. I clicked my heels, bowed, said my name; he bowed back. We had a chat, he liked meeting people when he was in exile.' Dismissing a popular image of the Duke pining perpetually for England and the throne, he said: 'He was perfectly all right, you can't go through life being sad; if you were married to that woman you'd be sad, though basically she was rather a good woman but became rather a bore.'

Dunsany ambles about the Castle like an informed curator. You feel he is happiest with the warlike collection of pistols and swords, savage bronze tigers and silver hunting horns. Although priceless *objets d'art* may, for security reasons, have been removed, this still leaves a 2000-year-old terracotta lion sculpture 'from Alexander's travels in Central Asia', also an elaborate ornate enamel mug from Elizabeth I to Essex, 'when she was being nice to him'.

Dunsany is a jewel in a fairly flat but bosky part of Ireland. Superb paintings – 'well, they are all right' – include several Jack Yeats': his In Memoriam, always being exhibited, and the Flower Girl; a Van Dyck of the Winter Queen, all beautifully hung in the best light. Blinds protect them from afternoon sun; they could not be better cared for in the National Gallery where funds are low.

At Dunsany, everything is well ordered and artistically presented, an ice-blue background in the drawing room shows off a mouthwatering eighteenth-century bird-of-paradise Meissen collection in a subtly lit china cabinet, and fresh flowers everywhere. There could be no better place than this private and cherished castle for the very moving Levantine burial jars which stored the Crusaders' hearts pickled in arak.

So far Dunsany has escaped the terrorist raid. 'I expect,' Lord Dunsany suggests, 'it is because we are Irish.' He worries about Ireland, and believes the reason the Irish do not succeed in their home country is because of the climate. Asked what he would do if he were prime minister, he replied without hesitation: 'I'd resign.'

He points out that the Plunketts inherit two things, an ability to shoot, and play chess. 'We are rather good shots. "What did you do in the Revolution, Grandpa?" answer: "I survived." '

He goes on: 'The fact that we are still here, is it due to tenacity or stupidity? I don't know.'

6

TWILIGHT TIME

Robert Guy Stafford O'Brien, the seventy-three-year-old heir to Cratloe, lovable in his gentleness, claps his hands as visitors arrive: 'That's my mother,' and everyone is invited to admire the portrait of a beautiful woman who died when he was twenty.

His military father always had a tragic inability to face up to his only son's physical and mental disability. The heartbreak of not being able to pass Cratloe on to his son, the last direct descendant, was almost more than he could bear. He found it hard to communicate with the ailing boy and sent him to a special school in Dunstable. When his father died, Robert was left in the care of a land agent.

The agent died three years ago and Cratloe was handed to the next of kin, a third cousin Gordon Brickenden, an engineer. The last thing he wanted was an estate. Related on his mother's side to the Stafford O'Brien family, Gordon Brickenden lived in a large house in Arklow in County Wicklow with his wife Sylvia and children, enjoying a happy and complete life. But a benevolent god brought these loving custodians to Cratloe and into the life of "Robin" Stafford O'Brien, as they call him, now enjoying his life amongst them, though it is the twilight time.

'We gave up everything to come here,' Sylvia Brickenden says, but adds gamely: 'I like a challenge.' The house is a perfect example of the seventeenth-century Irish long house, unique in Western Europe and charmingly known on seventeenth-century French maps as 'Le Château de Cratilagh'.

Overlooking the river Shannon, Cratloe is in the secrecy of a primeval oak forest, and a she-ghost lurks in the powerful wood which provided some of the beams in the Royal Palace in Amsterdam and in Westminster Hall.

In the summer the avenue is smothered in pink and white camelias, the rich pastels of the rhododendrons and the brilliance of wild azaleas. Japanese and American tourists being whisked past Cratloe on what was once the old stage coach highway might get more flavour of Ireland's heritage if they stopped at this strange house, now filled with the sound of laughter and the smell of freshly baked rhubarb tart, instead of a four star American owned hotel at Shannon Airport.

In the house, Gothic sandstone is softened by the romantic Stafford knot emblem of shamrocks entwined with Celtic crosses at the tops of stairs and over the fireplaces. The long, low-ceilinged drawing room with its pale green walls once a fashionable eau-de-nil, its heart-shaped honey oak tables and windows opening on to a lawn, reek of the thirties, of croquet, of music drifting out on the gramophone His Master's Voice, 'Happy Days Are Here Again' and cocktails.

The aged Robin's ancestors include one of Ireland's most celebrated eleventh-century kings, Brian Boru, and through marriage he is related to brave 'Red Mary' O'Brien. When she was widowed for a second time, Mary offered herself as a wife to any Cromwellian army officer rather than see Cratloe Hall, as it was known in more splendid days, confiscated and given to the English.

The red widow's proposal was accepted by a young soldier, Cornet John Cooper. She had struggled and fought like a tigress, but looked misleadingly sweet in her jewels, her chain and jewelled dolphin round her neck and demure lace collar; but she would hang an erring manservant by the neck and maids by their hair. When one of her husbands made a slightly critical remark she simply picked him up and threw him out of a mullioned window in one of her many castles. Red Mary remained fervently Catholic, and was given the King's pardon for dropping her husband out of the window.

Cratloe was later lived in by a playboy called Lucius O'Brien who was married in 1702 to a wealthy beauty, Catherine Keightley. She was a cousin of Queen Mary II's and also one of her ladies-in-waiting. When Queen Mary was dying of smallpox in 1694, aged thirty-three, her grieving husband King William told a friend: 'You can imagine what a state I am in, loving her as I do. You know what it is to have a good wife.' Mrs O'Brien was also a cousin of the weighty Queen Anne.

The habit of a lifetime, Robert Stafford O'Brien, now respected and loved, still spends a great deal of time in his room, but will appear in tweed suit and waistcoat and smile late in the day to listen intently to talk about his lively ancestors. The Brickenden children – there are five, two of the sons married – are attentive to 'Robin' but not ingratiatingly so. The shy daughters-in-law love the old man.

Gordon Brickenden, a mild sandy-haired man with good taste is gentle and soft spoken. He wanders round the long weeping house with a pile of drawings, all the plans, but finds it hard to face the mounds of paper and unpaid bills which have gathered over many years in the agent's office. His wife Sylvia, warm, extrovert with biggish features, follows a little diffidently but then finds an album of old photographs of ancestors including Lady Elizabeth Brickenden, who, apart from making predictable but wonderful paper flowers, did caricatures; one of the nineteenth-century British workmen was particularly amusing.

Already the Brickendens have changed the outside of the house, restored and made elegant some of the interior with pale silken wood. When Sylvia Brickenden was complimented on her courage in undertaking Cratloe especially when she missed her own Wicklow home so much, her husband said shyly, 'And that's not all there is to her,' a compliment of sensual warmth which made the visitor feel like an intruder.

What makes the house so interesting is that it is not being 'done' by interior designers, but by a couple who know its history, slowly and thoughtfully. The windows are being made dramatic with

French chintz, a *chaise-longue* recovered in apricot silk, all precisely as it was thirty or fifty years ago.

In the drawing room, an album is pored over intently, being dotted with pastry crumbs as it falls open at a letter which begins: 'My dearest deare, though we did part in tears, I hope God will bring us together in rejoycinge.' How romantic and apt for the present heir of Cratloe, this dignified figure. 'Oh good,' he says, and claps his hands again not because visitors are going but in the hope that the people he has just met may return. In the past he stayed in the background; now all around him is optimism and warmth.

7

NURSERIES OF CIVILIZED LIFE

Burnt, abandoned, dismantled, the fate of many of Southern Ireland's country houses is a mournful litany with the same careless cruel ring as a child's 'divorced, beheaded, died' recital of the fate of King Henry VIII's hapless wives.

The Irish countryside has some spectacular ruins. A vast decaying portico at Kenure Castle, Co. Dublin, has a Grecian grandeur, lofty and bizarre against a white stucco housing estate backdrop. Creeper sprawls suffocatingly over the windows and Doric portico of Dromdihy House, Co. Cork. A Gothic church at the gates of Ballnegall, Co. Westmeath, has recently been pulled down by a Church of Ireland committee. At Ballynagarde, Co. Cork, a statue of Hercules survives, like a rebuke in the shadow of this crumbling eighteenth-century beauty.

You dare not explore too much, as one step could send you hurtling into a cellar to lie undiscovered until the arrival of council bulldozers. The stone turrets at Thomastown, a Tudor Revival castle at Golden in Co. Tipperary, are almost defeated in the uneven struggle to peep out above the greenery choking the stonework.

'Whatever happened to?' is a question constantly asked. Rockingham, built by Nash in 1810, was gutted by fire in 1957, its elegant ruins demolished in the 1970s; Cuba Court in Co. Offaly, built in the eighteenth century, once described as the 'most splendidly masculine house in the whole country' and where Charlotte Brontë stayed on honeymoon in 1854, was dismantled in 1946 and recently demolished. Art historians shake their heads and say sorrowfully that it may be difficult to believe but many important houses had disappeared without trace, 'simply been lost, hopelessly lost'.

Ireland's heritage is in the hands of a haphazard group: a few academics who love it; perennial optimists who have saved houses with their own money; devoted preservation societies and a government which, if embarrassed, will step in and reprieve a house or two.

Meanwhile the drips in the Ascendancy ceiling get larger; the owner, in the absence of servants, shuffles along an achingly cold stone corridor in ancient monogrammed slippers in search of a square bucket. Meissen and Sèvres bowls are filled with a thin cat's drinking water; and those joyous plasterwork hosannahs created by the Italian Francini brothers and Irish craftsmen (the most outstanding was Robert West) of winged cherubs, oyster shells, bunches of grapes and leaping Tritons lie in a heap, cracked on a rotting floorboard like the icing on the jilted Miss Haversham's wedding cake.

Who will save the old houses from being pulverized to make way for banks, hotels, launderettes, discos, Bar-B-Qs, night clubs called Floosie in the Jacuzzi?

A once fashionable seventeenth-century Ascendancy church, St Mary's in Dublin, is up for sale in spite of its classical gallery and preservation order. Soon the sound of busy feet will echo along a shopping Mall built on sacred ground. Cheeky children beg in the city's columned doorways at dusk as swans, a gift to the river Liffey and the city from Oliver St John Gogarty, glide blithely by Gandon's imperious Customs House and on under the delicate Halfpenny Bridge towards Swift's cathedral.

The lack of any real government support, and heritage comes low on the list of priorities, is partly because of the ambiguous relationship with a 'Big House' seen as a hangover of Ascendancy domination and English colonialism.

A civil servant recommending the demolition of some Georgian buildings in a Dublin street reported: 'Just one damn house after another,' dismissing houses once with fanlights so decorative they could sit on a duchess's head, first-floor drawing rooms which smelt of pot-pourri, and dining rooms with mahogany dining tables polished and twinkling under the dancing rainbowed light from Waterford crystal. Syllabub was served in special glasses with a lip to taste the cream and sherry, with a silver spoon to scoop up the froth. Fat wax candles flickered hospitably late inside tall windows until shutters closed out Dublin's night and reality.

The tragedy is that irreplaceable Irish vernacular furniture, often with unusual fetlock carving, Georgian mirrors and chandeliers are leaving the country by the container load, and being scooped up by discerning buyers in America and Switzerland.

On an average of the £40 million sales of fine art in Ireland every year, 70% goes abroad. The furniture and pictures go first, sometimes in dribs and drabs, sold by desperate owners and replaced with imitations: 'Oh, you've had your pictures cleaned,' a sly smile, 'well worth the expense.' Few family collections are left in Ireland.

One of the finest private collections is still at Russborough, the Palladian house in County Wicklow belonging to Sir Alfred Beit, one of the De Beer diamond dynasty. Sir Alfred's collection has included Goya, Gainsborough, Franz Hals, Velazquez and Murillo. In 1974 some sixteen paintings were stolen when Bridget Rose Dugdale, who had a boyfriend in the IRA, broke in to Russborough, hoping the sale of these paintings would raise funds for the terrorist organization. There was another smaller robbery in May 1986. Some of the paintings have been recovered. Others pop up occasionally for sale in places like Amsterdam.

'It is heartbreaking,' grieved Honan Potterton, who was Director of the National Gallery until 1988. 'We have neither the money,' he says, 'nor the will to maintain treasures.'

His disenchantment reached a peak when he had to shut down two-thirds of the Gallery, and in some of the rooms still open, there are depressing blank spaces where a couple of paintings have been stolen by folk heroes, 'divils they are', who just walked in and brazenly removed them. The way in which the National Gallery appeared in three different places on a tourist map but never the right one made Potterton very cross. It is the small things which madden. He resigned after eight distinguished years and now lives in New York.

In 1974 a wealth tax was introduced in Ireland. It was a charge of 1% on assets wherever they might be in the world and was not related to income. The Finance Minister at the time was Mr Richard Ryan, better known as 'Ritchie Ruin'. His tax destroyed Stradbally, a grand Italianate house in Queen's County, and epitomizes the struggle and the effect of the 1974 wealth tax in spite of an irrepressibly resilient owner in Major Ashby Cosby, who was, a cynical observer remarked, 'very intelligent, most unlikely for an Irish country gentleman; he spoke fluent Russian.' Much loved, he was laid out in the master bedroom when he died so the county could pay their last respects, but an absentminded maid switched on the electric blanket under the deceased squire, perhaps getting her own back on the major, who, when she fell through a collapsing ceiling into the dining room, had muttered, 'Damn chambermaid, silly ass of a girl.' 'Was she hurt?' 'Dunno, but the table was destroyed – suppose she must have broken something.'

Stradbally had 'such things, such beautiful things' an aesthete once drooled, but he found the unclothed Edwardian tailor's dummy always in front of the fire in the drawing room rather unusual.

When a Dutch painting was admired the Major was amazed: 'Oh that, extraordinary really what pictures will put up with. I bought it in Dublin, remembered my wife was giving a party, so had to get back, stuck it on the roof rack, didn't worry, but with the wind and the rain, the damned thing flew off . . . didn't have time to look for it for a week or so.' There is an enviable casualness about possessions. Eventually it was found behind a hedge in a boreen. 'It was perfectly all right.'

Anne Crookshank, History of Art Professor at Trinity College, is a legendary figure and another informal custodian. Capable, silver-bunned, wearing one small ring, in eminently sensible shoes the end of her pop socks showing under beige stockings; she is always ideally dressed, prepared for a tramp round old houses and castles in the hope of saving some of Ireland's heritage.

Owners rely on her advice and have been staggered at some of her discoveries, which include a Breughel painting under some hay, but admittedly, 'only a Jan B'; or once unpacking an old box to find it full of Dresden; Persian pottery tucked away with saucepans and an eighteenth-century Italian painting propped against bricks in an outhouse. Such things.

A Dublin plumber who had just been left a tiny cottage by an uncle in Killiney, a crescented stretch of Dublin's coastline, had a tingle of awareness about a painting which he thought looked valuable. 'The painting is not up to much,' the Professor told him when she called, 'but the furniture is ravishing.' The uncle had been a tailor in Dun Laoghaire in the old days when it was Kingstown and the British Navy called regularly. Instead of paying in cash, they would give the tailor a charming piece of Victorian furniture. The cottage was an Aladdin's cave, a collector's delight.

As she springs through the cobblestoned courtyard at Trinity on a crisp November day when the berries are red against the Elizabethan stone, the Professor points out: 'The decline of the big house and economics in Ireland are both extremely difficult for English people to understand because they have not experienced destructive Land Acts in the 1880s which divided up big estates and took their lifeblood, d'ye see?' End of lecture.

Decay in old houses is viewed with a quirky affection in Ireland. In the Professor's own family, a ninety-year-old aunt, a founder of the Irish Countrywomen's Association, lived in a vast draughty old house. When her niece complained that the roof in the bedroom was leaking, she replied: 'Oh yes, the dogs love the attic.' 'That night I put up an umbrella.' Professor Crookshank added proudly: 'Madness is everywhere. My aunt is now living in a prefabricated Swedish bungalow and very happy.'

Whatever their plight the Ascendancy are engagingly insouciant about survival. 'They are so very well educated, but educated to do nothing.' Matt McNulty, a cultivated man, conservationist and now Deputy Director General of the Irish Tourist Board shakes his head in mock sorrow: 'The trouble is the Anglos are not very keen on work; they think manual labour is the Spanish ambassador.' This 'paralysing atmosphere' affected James Joyce, who had to get away and write some of his best work in Paris. As a student in Dublin that brilliant mind was exercised to be: 'In time to be late for three lectures'.

The people care but seem helpless; they know that the pale pink and grey delicacy of the National Library with its meltingly beautiful great columns and flowery mouldings is how Dublin once looked, a little diamond in the Empire's jewel collection created by their ancestors. But the old houses are disappearing very fast. William Garner has established Architectural Archives in Dublin so there may be some record before it is too late. He shudders as he looks from his airy top flat with its minimalist precision, at a concrete multi-storey car park hitched to the end of a Georgian street. He complains that the house he lives in is 'rather recent: 1793'. But the view below is of a typical Ascendancy long garden and there is the whiff of a traditional box hedge after rain and a grey-haired woman and her dog are being buffeted in the wind.

There are now only about thirty major houses left in Ireland compared with some 2,000 houses in England, Scotland and Wales being lovingly restored. Before 1914 about some 2,500 families owned 1,000 acres or more in Ireland and were committed resident landlords. The Famine in 1845 meant that rents could not be paid and many Ascendancy estates were heavily mortgaged and often sold up under the Encumbered Estates Act. In this century alone some 500 houses, these 'nurseries of civilized life' as A. L. Rowse described them, have been burnt down, abandoned, dismantled or the contents taken away in pantechnicons.

' "Complacency behind their high walls" is to blame,' Professor Kevin Nowlan, a small, dedicated, academic, says. 'These great houses are part of our national heritage, but have been hidden for too long and now it is almost too late.' He too spends every spare minute peering at old houses through his spectacles, sighing over dry rot in the 'green land' as the south is lyrically known; but the dreamy Ireland of Paul Henry paintings becomes ever more elusive. Bungalows are spreading like measles.

The Quaker-like modesty and reticence of distinguished old Irish Georgian houses, or the eccentric charm of shuttered rectories, are no rivals for Ireland's 'modern dream house' in Spanish Colonial,

'Pine Irish chalet' or, for the really rich, 'Southfork', a 'Dallas' ranch house. But Ireland is such a little island, the most sparsely populated country in Europe after Finland. Birmingham alone has more people than Ireland's scattered three and a half million. It is impossible not to be aware of the unslakeable thirst for 'bungalow bliss'.

They are rarely discreet but slap on a hillside where perhaps the Atlantic comes romping in bringing a shoal of seals – the sort of place on which Irish writers like J. B. Synge based their *Riders from the Sea* – or at the foot of spectacular mountains in the west which inspired Yeats to write his classic 'Lake Isle of Innisfree': 'I will arise and go now, and go to Innisfree . . . And I shall have some peace there' – very unlikely today.

When the Irish architect Denis Anderson visited Connemara and saw the rows of flashy brutalist bungalows with aluminium windows proudly built beside abandoned thatched cottages he felt physically sick.

For years the Irish Tourist Board has rightly been marketing purple blue mountains and 300-year-old cottages thatched with reeds, which Americans may fondly imagine was their great grandparents homes before they fled during the Famine. However instead of finding a typical Irish character at the door of his cottage, the bungalow owner is inside sprawled in front of a video. There is no one to charm the visitor with lovable Irishness, telling the traveller when asked for directions 'Well, if I was you, I wouldn't start from here.'

The EEC bonanza is partly to blame. The Irish small farmer suddenly had more money than he could dream of, enough to buy a Mercedes to herd home his three cows each evening. Lying back, one muddy boot sticking out of the half open door, hundreds of children crammed in the back, a greyhound's face peeking out of the window, the driver looking like a teddy bear with his head shorn in pudding bowl cut has a word for passers-by. 'Are ye roight?' Ruddy cheeks glow under a peaked cap. The cheery reply is, 'I am so, tanks be to God.' Suddenly the car stops without any warning; out tumbles a brown tweedy rumpled figure; it has been the tradition since the days of the donkey and jaunting car to give lifts; the car glides on, disgorging any number of friendly bundles.

This newly rich peasant farmer and his wife tend to associate the traditional whitewashed cottage with a time of poverty in Ireland, the disgrace of being evicted for failure to pay the rent; so not for them walls three feet thick, a yellow thatched roof and hospitable half door. Instead they send for a bungalow. It is selected by number from a catalogue called *Bungalow Bliss*. This little manual is one of Ireland's top sellers, now in its eighth printing.

First published in 1971 it is easy to read, like a dress pattern book with pictures of eighty different kinds of bungalows. A muddy thumb selects Number seventy-nine, in multi-coloured mosaic brick. The passion is for Moorish arches, haciendas, plastic balustrades round concrete balconies, a yearning for sun. Yet this damp green island remains blissfully free of platitudes about the weather.

The local technical school teacher who has a notice on his gate 'Drawings Done Here' will do the plans. A bungalow will cost anything between £30,000 and £40,000, and in four months it will be ready.

The old farmhouse is abandoned, inviting envy in the village: 'Isn't it well for them.' A newly concreted path is made to Number seventy-nine nearby. The 'missus' puts up scalloped cream blinds which sit in a compromising half-way position rather like those in the tall dark houses in Amsterdam, but the interior is not quite Holbein; a statue of the Infant of Prague is on the windowledge in the parlour alongside another more lurid one of the Sacred Heart.

It only remains for 'Himself' to order a few yards of Doric fibreglass pillars and a nameplate 'Mary's View' or 'El Rancho'. The garden will not be a burden, a few red and yellow tulips may spring up seemingly unsupported; there will be no stone urns brimming with roses.

The author of *Bungalow Bliss*, Mr Jack Fitzimons, says: 'It is part of the Irish temperament to want to have a place we can call our own.'

Meanwhile the owners of old houses, though fairly resilient, have to put up with the indignity of seeing a Georgian farmhouse, on what was once their land, replaced by this screaming, red brick bungalow with a flat heavy black concrete roof.

'We must look after our heritage,' declared the Prime Minister Charles Haughey, and then promptly disbanded the Heritage Advisory Committee set up by a previous Coalition Government with an allocation of £750,000 a year. Now in its place, an advisory National Heritage Council has been set up with the same sum of money promised from the National Lottery. Saving old houses is just one of its tasks. It has to deal with Ireland's wildlife, green issues, geological erosion, anything to do with the environment. Although it is headed by the able Lord Killanin, who is chairman, and with members including the much respected historical architect Maurice Craig, as one country house owner observed mournfully: 'The people chosen do not belong to any pressure group and Irish Governments are notorious for ignoring their advisers.'

A few houses will be saved if considered 'historically important'. Under Section 19 of the Finance Act the owners can set the cost of repairs and maintenance against Value Added Tax, but VAT is 25% while income tax was 58% until April 1989, when it went down two points to 56%.

The hopeful news is that two houses have just been saved with public money. Newbridge was acquired by the Dublin County Council. When it was taken over, it was a wilderness of mice and rats behaving like football supporters and until 1957 had been lit only by oil-lamps. The Cobbe family, invited to stay on at Newbridge House, would by this happy arrangement help uncover an ostrich egg laid in Dundalk in 1756 and a Dean Swift manuscript and Newbridge would enjoy a lived-in feeling once again. Walking in the gold and amber corridors, marble busted ancestors looked benignly secure beneath the coronet and swan family crest, motto 'Dying I Sing'. Grace and light restored, the parkland neglected for fifteen years is serene again with 1,200 trees in elegant allées.

The restoration was done by Matt McNulty, a practical aesthete who scoured the countryside for the right sympathetic furniture, a £3,000 chicken coop dresser of old pine for holding eggs, and a tiny elm lambing chair with a heart carved on the back where once the farmhand sat on a cold hillside helping a ewe deliver.

Newbridge is open to the public. Guides go sweetly pink as, standing by the black marble Kilkenny fireplace, they explain the

'Gentleman's Comforter' a mahogany conceit holding a blue flowered chamber pot behind a flap which enabled men to 'piddle in the dining or drawing room and conversation did not have to stop', a custom which long after it had died out in Europe persisted in Ireland, where one hostess observed, 'It was done with great aplomb.' The writer George Moore complained about the 'acidities', even at Dublin Castle, the drawing room entertainment was not always of the freshest taste: 'the sugary sweetness of the blondes, the salt flavour of the brunettes . . . the garlicky andante . . . the perspiring arms of a fat chaperon'.

Tea and scones and yellow Irish cream is served in the kitchen at Newbridge, with its charming eighteenth-century hand painted wooden bowls once used for bread, and brown and white belleek mugs. There is a refreshing absence of any craft shop selling teatowels or indifferent jam masquerading under a rustic label.

McNulty grins. 'We did in four months something it would take the Trust years to do.'

'We ache for a National Trust here,' another passionate conservationist, Edward McParland, a Trinity academic in his cords and tortoise-shell spectacles who teaches History of Post Medieval Architecture. 'What is stopping us?' he asks, his grey curly hair practically standing on end, and answers the question himself: 'Ireland'.

People in Ireland prefer something new to restoring an old house, he explains in a kindly way. 'It is easier to buy a house from a catalogue than have the headache of finding slates for eighteenth-century houses where the chimney pots keep falling off,' and he adds wryly: 'I have rooms in college, otherwise I should be in a hacienda.' Unlikely.

The stately home owners in Northern Ireland may grumble about the National Trust and their choice of colours but in the south, poor Eire, the walls in stately houses are sometimes naturally green, not the fashionable Lincoln green of Georgian times but a mossy damp lichen green. A hard-pressed government Minister of Development, Tim O'Gorman, jokes: 'Occasionally families threaten us by leaving us their houses.'

But usually they are put on the market at absurdly low prices by

English property standards. Recently Tulira castle, dating back to the Middle Ages, home of the Irish literary movement, the 'Celtic Twilight', was sold by Lord Hemphill to an American, Mrs Kieran Breeden, who lavished money on it but was selling at $1.4 million. Adare Manor with 848 acres, fishing rights and cottages went for about £3 million, and is now an American owned hotel. Originally it was being bought by Canadian and Iraqi consortium but that fell through. Nothing happened for a year or two until a New York businessman stepped in – he could not resist the bargain price.

A few writers fell in love with the idea of living in Ireland but they do not stay long, though some wives have done all the right things: committed adultery, run away with the groom. Frederick Forsyth's case was different: he was defeated by the telephone system. It may be charming on holiday if the taxi does not arrive, and how Irish to be told there is a boat in a couple of hours. But this is not good enough if you are flying to America for a breakfast meeting: 'Ah well, ye didn't miss the plane by much.' J. P. Donleavy stayed on, however, and lives like a hunting squire, his ex-wife recently married Desmond Guinness's younger brother.

Sometimes the Ascendancy owner may move to a cottage in the grounds and watch the old house become an agricultural college, an hotel or old people's home, in which case they may go in themselves eventually, glad of some heat.

In some of the draughty mansions with well earned names like Ballyseedy and Ballyruin the owner is hanging on, with very little money, relying perhaps on a military pension and not much else. But you still find, without any conscious effort, an undeniable distinction. A hall maybe of Irish oak with a clutter of Wellington boots, mackintoshes, tweedy hats, walking sticks, dog leads, bone-handled whips, old newspapers and binoculars. There may be a bit of sacking under a mahogany table, a shopping basket, a barometer, a clutter which makes it all so attractive, so uncontrived.

It is all a bit doggy, slightly smelly chintz curtains, springless sofas claw you down to cavernous depths, plum mouthed ancestors stare down, the women's decolletage makes you shiver in the chill of the vast drawing room where three sods of turf and a few sticks picked up on 'Wellington's' walk – the smaller the dog the more impressive his name – fuse damply in an engraved brass Irish grate. In a murky light from under an old standard lamp with its deep deep parchment yellow shade with hunting scenes, it is just possible to read *The Field*.

A piece of canvas cut from a husband's Indian army kit catches drips unsuccessfully above the fourposter; there are rings round the bath. In the library the parchment Elizabethan deeds of the estate held with a great big seal may be just wedged unceremoniously between a couple of books on butterflies.

In huge kitchens, a sick lamb or a grizzled Jack Russell terrier has the best spot near the Aga. There may be a harmonium in the kitchen or an eighteenth-century plate warmer with a hole in it. Egg whites may still be whisked with a birch twig or branch of rosemary; it only takes an hour – what is time when you are Anglo-Irish?

In these kitchens which once smelt of roasting sparrows and blackbirds, where herbs and spices were hammered with early walnut Queen Anne wooden pestles, whatever the owner's plight you still find a heavy pot of genuine game stock, a whole salmon sits on the wooden draining board ready for a court bouillon with parsley, a lemon and the remains of a good bottle of Pouilly Fumé.

In the laundry room there are polishing stones which once gave linen its shine and old mangles where tweenies got red hands pushing through the gentry's bed linen.

These old families tend not to express a view about bungalows. They rarely see them unless they have to take the Peugeot estate car into the village to get a sheep's head for the dogs. They have always had much more feeling for the servants anyway, the farm workers and the grooms; it is Ireland's new middle-class they cannot bear: the managers, the Common Market businessmen, the dance hall owners, road haulage contractors, beef truckers and timber traders. 'Miss Twinkle O'Reilly seen at Leopardstown races, Mr Finbarr O'Dea at Dublin Airport': these people replace the earl and countess in today's social columns. The Porsche has become an absurd status symbol on Ireland's quirky roads.

Ireland's new gentry, with their riot of pink Dralon and velvet moquette; fringed silk lampshades but few pictures; German designer kitchens, pristine, nothing must sully the gleaming mock marble finish; an electric sandwich maker turns out toasted cheese and ham. The new owner chortles as he opens a letter from the taxman, not usually a flatterer but he has put 'Dallas, Co. Tipperary' on the envelope; the addressee is thrilled.

Until 1967 only two Ascendancy houses were open to the public in Ireland, Bantry and Westport. A few owners have now joined organizations like the Hidden Ireland; Historic Castles and Gardens and Elegant Ireland, a superior stately home guide, the brainchild of Geraldine Murtagh. Some are businesslike and professional but are not very good at being organized; they remain individualistic and advisers are chosen for the wrong reasons like having the right background. An agent may be selected because he is unbeatable in the saddle, or was at Eton or in the same regiment as the owner, an ideal companion, but a trained manager in a suit might be more effective even if one of the abhorred middle-class.

The good ones have agents they trust; the Duke of Devonshire relies on Paul Burton, an experienced, humorous man who has run Chevening and Mountstewart and is virtually in charge of Lismore, which is visited infrequently by the Duke and his son.

Opening their houses to the public as a way of surviving is an option which fills them with dread. Many of the Anglo-Irish almost welcomed the law passed in the 1940s which did an inconceivable amount of damage and hastened 'the great crumble'. It was attractive in its simplicity and negative suggestion. If you owned a house, you paid rates, but if you did some major alteration which involved taking the roof off you did not. So Ireland's great houses became even draughtier.

In Ireland there are surprisingly few people willing to take an old house by the rafters and lovingly restore it. Dublin is full of these tall houses with raggy but real old lace curtains, proper shutters and crumbling lintels which nobody wants. But Harold Clarke, a distinguished bookseller with an alert discerning eye, bravely took on one of these old derelict Georgian houses not far from O'Connell Street, a sort of Dublin Camden Town arrondissement. However by 1987 the upkeep had become impossibly expensive and he was forced to sell for around £85,000, not much for a house so lovingly restored. When chivvied about his selling to a religious sect – the buyer was believed to be one of the Moonies – Mr Clarke, chairman of Easons, suavely replied: 'It is not usual to ask a buyer about his nationality or religion.'

Desmond Guinness is a heroic figure in Ireland's conservation struggle, stepping forward recently with his own money to rescue Castleton, one of the country's finest Palladian houses. Built by William Connolly, Speaker of the Irish Parliament, it had been gaily sold in 1965 by Lord Carew to property developers who built a housing estate in the grounds.

The old house was abandoned and Guinness was appalled as each night scrap merchant gangs drove out to Kildare. 'They were rolling up the lead from the roof at Castletown to sell for scrap and there was nothing anyone could do.' Unable any longer to bear this indecent vandalism, he bought the house for £93,000. 'I needed this like a hole in the head,' he said, taking on also the surrounding 150 acres.

Dignity and elegance restored, Castletown reopened with a party in the green silk-walled drawing room for the Irish Georgian Society and a good sprinkling of rich Americans – 'those lovely American ladies' purrs Desmond Guinness – knowing that, without their contributions, little could be done. But it is not a bit like a real Ascendancy house; you could never go straight into the drawing room in your gumboots.

8

THE TABLE WILL GROAN ONCE MORE

The lodgekeeper, a cheery Breughelish woman resting on pink arms, checked the car number plate and then nodded permission to go through Birr Castle's iron gates heavy with heraldic emblems. 'She said you'd be comin,' and flashed this arrival time intelligence to the Countess of Rosse.

Leopards' heads on the Rosses' scarlet standard flutter wildly from the castellated battlements. The flavour is seventeenth-century Bavaria, except this is Birr, a tiny place in Co. Offaly, the flat part of Ireland, on the borders of Tipperary. It is quite elegant with its distinctive Mall of Georgian houses. Tenants once had to be vetted by a Rosse agent; a traveller from Ulster admired 'the red-coated soldiers' from the barracks near the Castle, who 'looked such gentlemen in comparison with the local inhabitants'.

Today in the library in the town a leaflet urges the Many Adults in County Offaly who cannot read and write to get in touch. 'Their inquiry will be treated in the strictest confidence.' A famous pub called Dooly's gave the Galway Blazers their name, when the old coaching inn burnt down after a particularly lively hunt dinner. It has been revamped or 'modurrunized' with its pink Emmet dining room. Further along 'Zandra's Cake Shop' is for all occasions, even a royal visit.

'Please call it a town,' Lord Rosse pleads in his cultivated

'Oirish' accent sounding quite unlike his half brother, Lord Snowdon.

On the doorstep in front of the Castle's great iron-studded door, the butler, William Connors, apologizes for being improperly dressed. He is getting in a bit of sweeping before the arrival of an American horticultural group.

Courtly and amiable, he politely asks, 'You will excuse my clothes.' He is one of the family treasures. 'Nobody,' he says, 'has butlers now. You do everything today.' This is not a complaint, just a matter of fact as he went off to help the Countess arrange the flowers in the hall.

There is no talk about 'Her Ladyship'. The Countess of Rosse, 'Ally' to her friends, short for Alison, thinks: 'Being titled in Ireland is a little like being a dodo.' But not so long ago in Irish villages bishops, aristocrats, Resident Magistrates, Vicereines and countesses whatever their title might in nervous panic all be addressed as 'Yer Worship' or 'Yer Honour'.

The present Countess of Rosse is far from intimidating with her dark oval face and diffidence. She seems as young as her eldest child Lord Oxmantown, a strapping nineteen-year-old, as she springs into the freezing drawing room in sneakers, her arms full of lilac. Slightly abstracted, she is trying to finalize plans to join an archaeological dig in Iraq. She speaks Persian, but finds Irish more difficult. Her face is much more interesting than the camera allows, fey and artistic; she also has a gentle aloofness that is invaluable at a huge house party for Italian deer stalkers or excitable Japanese botanists.

Lady Rosse believes in Irish fairies: 'They are not always good and do take children away.' She also is susceptible to castle ghosts, talks about black ravens and the French governess burnt in a fire at the Castle. 'They never found any relations.'

Her husband, Brendan, the seventh Lord Rosse, thinks it sad that neither Viscount Linley nor Lady Sarah Armstrong-Jones, the Snowdon children, unlike their mother Princess Margaret, has ever been to Birr.

The Snowdon children's paternal grandmother, Anne, Countess of Rosse, was a celebrated beauty, a sister of designer Oliver

Messel, and the grandchild of Linley Sambourne, a *Punch* cartoonist. Married first to Lord Snowdon's father, Ronald Armstrong-Jones, she then fell in love with Lord Rosse, who was so handsome he was known to contemporaries as the 'Adonis of Oxford'. If the Countess of Rosse with her inimitable style, wore a Sybil Connolly outfit even once it was worth millions to the Irish couturiere, better than any fashion show with the best models on the catwalk.

This stunning pair married in 1935 and he proudly took her home to what may have struck her as a rather gloomy little Gothic castle huddled under the lowering Slieve Bloom mountains at the spot where the Camcor and Little Brosna rivers meet. It had a statutory resident ghost; dungeons, hidden passages; and a china cupboard which converted into a secret room.

It had been in her husband's family, the Parsons, since 1620. An ambitious ancestor, Laurence Parsons, was an acquisitive Elizabethan who succeeded Sir Walter Raleigh as mayor of Youghal and then seized the boggy land in Offaly which had been forfeited by an Irish family, the Ely O'Carrolls.

Here he built Birr Castle and the style of Birr today is to his credit, but he was stern and decreed that any woman serving beer as a barmaid should 'bee sett in the stocks by the constable for three whole markett dayes', and if anyone threw 'dunge rubbidge filth' in the street they would be fined 4d. However his eldest son Richard did not follow at all in his footsteps and was an enthusiastic member of the notorious Hellfire Club famous for orgies and satanic rituals.

As a family, the Rosses were unusual; they were much more interested in music, science, literature and travel than many of the stately home owners in Ireland, who tended to study the horse. Beautifully bound editions of Balzac in gold and tan leather and Gibbon's *Decline and Fall* in the library were not just decorative but were taken down and read. Sir William Parsons, the second Earl, loved Handel's music and it was thanks to his patronage that the first performance of the *Messiah* was heard in Dublin. He would be given an engraved walking stick by the oratorio's appreciative composer.

The third Earl of Rosse, determined to outdo Sir William Herschel, created an even more powerful telescope in 1839. A monster, it beat all records for size until at least 1915 and would be affectionately known as the Giant of Birr or the Leviathan, towering in the grounds and attracting astronomers from Imperial Russia, who made their pilgrimage to Birr to see what in 1845 was the largest telescope in the world. The tube is still inside the Gothic walls. Another Parson would invent the steam turbine engine.

Not all were aesthetes. One Parson ancestor drank so much claret that, when sentenced to death in the 'haunted room' at the castle in 1689 on a trumped-up charge of treason against King James, he pleaded gout: it would prevent him from climbing the steps to the gallows. It was suggested he cut down on wine so he could be more nimble on the day, but in the end he was reprieved.

From time to time there were injections of money when the Rosses married great northern heiresses. One was Mary Rosse, heiress to the fields of Heaton outside Bradford, who would revive the Rosse fortunes when she married the third Earl. Mother of eleven children, she would create a spectacular moat around the castle, built during the Famine as part of relief work for the villagers. She was rather ahead of her time in setting up a darkroom at Birr in 1855 and was the first woman member of the Dublin Photographic Society.

A frailer less artistic woman than Anne Countess of Rosse might have been dismayed by Birr. But with her artistic flair, she would bring to this medieval Castle not only an incredibly rare set of ten Chippendale gilt chairs and two matching sofas for the Gothic room, her gift as a bride, but also a talent part theatrical, part designer which would transform it, making it live again so it glowed like a rare long neglected precious stone.

This Countess of Rosse put her unmistakable imprint on the Castle; the rooms were lushly restored, extravagantly rich lemon yellow damask in the drawing room, a golden aura for the Aubusson carpet and a Venetian chandelier uncovered after years of dusty oblivion. In her salmon pink bedroom, a pretty screen by Carl Toms, one of Messel's assistants, of the family in a romanticized Victorian demesne, the sort of elaborate touch you do not find much in the Irish midlands.

Early slides and letters between Fox Talbot and Mary Rosse were recovered, perhaps awakening her son's talent for photography. It is certainly the only kind of fox mother and son really understood, not being great hunting enthusiasts. Mary Rosse had set up a dark room in a tower of the Castle; now Lord Snowdon's photographs are in the corridors, with a few by Lord Lichfield too.

On honeymoon in China in 1937 the Rosses would discover a rare peony and call it Anne Rosse; they brought shrubs home from the Temple of Confucius in Peking; they met the great Chinese poet and botanist Professor Hu. They explored Guatemala, the Caucasus, South America, Bhutan and Tasmania. Together they nurtured the Castle and the grounds; it blossomed into one of the prettiest in Ireland with magnolias, azaleas and an impressive arboretum. The 300-year-old boxwood hedge is in the *Guinness Book of World Records* as the tallest in the world. Down by the lake, kingfishers and wild duck disturb the stately swans and fly high above the Caucasian fir trees.

The 2000-acre demesne attracted gardeners who came from all over the world to admire a golden rain tree, the Juniper Lawn, the Secret Garden dripping with wisteria and stunning Japanese magnolia and camelias. And near the dogwood and the oriental lacquer red of maples by the lake, the statues of the Graces look today as if they are lamenting a slight decline.

The Rosses attracted other exotic blooms, the glamorous and artistic: the Cooch Behars, the Brian Howards, the Guinnesses; hospitality at Birr was legendary. 'Anne and Michael', the sixth earl and his graceful wife, from being some minor aristocrats living in boggy Ireland were sought after as Birr increasingly became the haunt of the 'Bright Young Things' who, for a lark, would loll about on the roof of the castle in extravagant poses all very *Brideshead* . . . very Sebastian. Like hippies of a later generation finding the best beaches in the world, they had a talent for nosing out the best houses.

These parties were excellent. The walls of the castle glowed amber gold; great theatrical swags allowed a sliver of mellow night light in from the Slieve Bloom mountains; porcelain monkeys looked down on junketings and, more sombrely, Mary Boleyn in her gold ornate frame, the aunt of the hapless Anne, one of

Henry VIII's unhappy ladies leading a life of anxiety and fretfulness so unlike that of a contemporary, Lady Elizabeth Parsons, as in fine, feathery whirly writing on Castle parchment she wrote her tips for cleaning silks and satins; how cayenne in soup cured seasickness, juniper berry oil eased lumbago and how to make a 'chicking frigassee' or simple Hartichoke Pie . . .

First catch your 'hartichokes . . . boyle them a little . . . take only the bottomes and season them with nutmeg, cloves, mace and cinamon and a little sault.' Then take three 'Chickings' and layer with 'hartichokes cut thin', add some sliced marons 'rowled in the yolk of an egg', then 'spoon a little sugar and spice between every lay, the like of orange, lemon peel and citron and vinager candied when it is baked, put in a caudell . . . take a pint of wine, the yolks of four eggs beaten with sugar. Stir it over the fire till it be thick, then put in ye pye and put it in the oven agen.' And incidentally, 'You may lay large mace between every lay.'

These Rosse countesses were careful, keeping dairy notes: the milk yield of Duchess, Joyful and Dolly and how at Christmas in 1908 'Bachelor Dwyer in the Forestry section' got a shirt but 'James Feigherry, being married with one child, was entitled to a vest and a flannel petticoat.' An example to us all, a record was kept of any books lent, not just a hardback, but more like 'nine volumes of Shakespeare' in 1906 at one go.

There was nothing parsimonious about the menus when Antony Armstrong-Jones, now Lord Snowdon, brought his wife Princess Margaret home to Birr, driving along the Mall to savour the smell of turf. His mother's menus outdid Lady Parsons' in deliciousness.

The hundred bedrooms in the Castle were redecorated and 'Rooms twenty-two and twenty-three' were for Princess Margaret and 'Tony' with a view of Birr's main street; Jeremy and Camilla Fry were in Number One; Billy Wallace, Lord and Lady Rupert Neville and the Dunravens in other parts of the Castle, and in the nursery wing Crocker the detective and Mrs Gordon the maid.

On their first evening, Friday 6 May 1960, turf and applewood fires crackled in the Saloon and Drawing room, though it was May, and that was unusual in Ireland where the seasons are sharply observed to save on heating. Nor was there any of the ubiquitous

Irish country house warm sherry, followed by stewed mutton, soggy vegetables and jaded rice pudding. Instead the menu started with aperitifs and delicious nibbles of 'Foie gras'.

Royal recipes tumble out of a folder written in the Countess's clear hand, the black ink sometimes smudged where the Irish cook has puzzled over some French culinary note: The table *en grand decor* with lace cloth surtout; best table cloth and silver plate served with aperitifs; silken swan tankards; pastry fingers to go with ice praline'.

To make things easy for the cook in case there were any little presentation difficulties, there were drawings for that first royal dinner party for twelve. One showed how a large melon should be scooped out and topped with large Dublin Bay prawns; then poussins sketched snuggled together on a large serving plate with knots of bacon, mushrooms, new potatoes; chopped salad on oranges, followed by Floating Angels on two dishes and a savoury chopped tongue in pyramids *en croutes*.

The royal dinner was served in the Gothic dining room, with its rich ruby red flocked walls where Parsons ancestors looked down at the English princess. Later that night, long after the guests had gone to bed, the cook and butler basking in praise suddenly heard a terrible scramble in the royal suite and the newlywed Princess Margaret appeared downstairs ashen faced.

The rare antique wallpaper which had apparently been specially put up in the royal couple's bedroom had not been pasted on thoroughly by the Paddy or 'was it Sean?' assigned to the task. The Princess, alarmed by the noise, thought it sounded like a beginning of a fire and was terrified.

Next day the Princess assumed she would be given a different suite. In an early battle of wills, her mother-in-law made it plain with great charm that there would be no moving. 'No,' she said; 'I put the wallpaper up specially for them and now they will have to live with it.'

Today's Rosses like to eat in a small antiquated kitchen in the bowels of the castle which is freezing and are fond of eggs with cream and macaroni. Simon Marsden, a photographer interested in the occult who had been staying in a lodge in the grounds at Birr, wandered in. 'Sorry Simon,' he was told by Lady Rosse with a mischievous little smile, 'there was not enough for you.' There is cream in a brown earthenware jug and a few groceries in a cardboard box – some eggs because 'little Michael', aged seven, the Rosses' youngest, likes a frizzled egg for his tea. He attends the local primary and has a lyrical Irish accent, talks engagingly about his 'Mammy' who says she hopes she can learn Irish with him. He sounds quite different from his brother Patrick and sister Issia.

His father had a traditional upbringing . . . 'very much behind the green baize door, never allowed in or out of the front door or up the front stairs; at lunch we always sat at a different table.' His mother's meticulous notes record: 'Saturday lunch for 14; children in window.' Brendan and his young brother could join the adults for peaches with zabaglione.

Educated at Eton, which he hated, 'partly because of a sadistic prefect', he then read political history at Oxford where he met the artistic 'Alison' who now has a studio in the Castle.

Her memories of her first visit to Birr to meet her future husband's family was simply of 'rooms filled with people laughing and talking and racing upstairs to change for dinner'.

Brendan Rosse dresses in bomber jackets and cords, is lean and has a cheeky slightly pugnacious chin. He bridles at the word 'settler', colouring slightly; he will look you in the eye and tell you he thinks of himself as Irish.

When his father Michael, the Sixth Earl, died in 1981 he had been working with the United Nations for seventeen years and he and his wife had been living in Iran and more recently Algeria. The only relic of eighteen years' nomadic life is a battered Peugeot – North African vintage. With a dry little laugh he explained that he was part of something called ACDC which actually stands for Advisory Council on Development Corporation. He had volunteered, and loved the work, which for him was mainly in Persia, Bangladesh and North and West Africa.

He asks: 'What could one do? We had to come back.' It helps that he is an organizer; he sits on committees though his mother used to tell him: 'The Irish always start late.'

When he first came back to Birr he thought it would never

become viable. His parents had led a sybaritic and glamorous life, but there was little left except heart-shaped cushions embroidered with the names Michael and Anne entwined.

The last to live at Birr in the grand manner, with their parties and their travels, they were not the most practical pair in the world; stretched by costly entertaining, they never had the heart to sack anybody or cut down. It was a great if extravagant love match; their chauffeur for thirty years says, 'I never once heard a cross word spoken between them.'

Not a great deal had been done to maintain the Castle and Princess Margaret's bedroom has damp. Brendan, now the Seventh Earl, also inherited a horrifying number of debts. He decided that he would do anything rather than open the house to the public but he and his wife envy the support given by the National Trust in England.

Family papers have been scrupulously kept in a small turret of the Castle. They get lots of inquiries: 'Would his Lordship's archivist be kind enough to. . . ? 'Well . . .' Lady Rosse says wryly, 'that's me' and smiles at the imagined team of earnest archivists.

Rosse is constantly trying to think of ways of making money; he has restored family treasures and arranges expensive deer-stalking parties on the estate.

Last summer there was a Three Centuries of Childhood exhibition which included Lord Snowdon's fetching small antique black pram. 'Poor Michael's nursery has been denuded,' Lady Rosse remarked, looking sympathetically at her son's Peter Pan nursery which like all nurseries in a perfect world faces the Fairy Hill inspiring Spenser's famous poem, which can look blue and appealing on a good day.

Standing in the grounds, Lord Rosse is urging a housewife to buy some shrubs, and famous Scarlet Pimpernel potatoes. In minutes he has extracted five pounds from her which entitles her to visit the grounds at Birr anytime during the next year. 'But I live in America,' she wails. He grins disarmingly – he is pushy, he has to be.

He is determined to make it pay. There is the offer of the 'bothy', a charming lodge in the grounds, at £400 a month, and some seventy to eighty cottages in the grounds, one of which was rented by Desmond Guinness's former wife, the dramatic Mariga.

Lord Rosse's diplomatic training means he tries hard to bring some accord between the north and the south – but his astutely acquired Irish accent is not always taken seriously though he is respected. He does lecture tours in America promoting Birr and Ireland. The family motto is Dieu et Mon Rege; perhaps in these prickly times in Ireland it could be watered down to Dieu et St Patrick although the Rosses are popular enough.

Whatever economies are necessary in the house, inflation cannot stem the classical beauty of the grounds.

Martin Hynes, to give him his proper title, is the Chief Propagator at Birr. He is full of charm and when you compliment him on the scent of a rose from Beijing smiles: 'Ah you'd be pourin' honey on me now.' With the head gardener he lovingly coaxes delicate cuttings and shoots into life.

The Dowager Countess of Rosse, who now lives at Nymans, the family home in Sussex, has always kept in touch and invited him to come and visit five of the National Trust's best gardens in England. Everywhere he went he was given presents, but not allowed to bring them into Ireland. He has the gentleness and humour of a true horticulturist.

Darting around among the azaleas he exhorts an old lady who has only come to buy a lettuce: 'Go under that shrub and don't tell me if it isn't the smell of France.' His face is expectant as she beams back at him from under a special lilac.

The gardeners are down to four; there are student helpers but Martin Hynes says: 'Ah . . . they will be expert at telling how much moisture a leaf retains – but they have no natural talent.'

Shooting parties in the winter, when an American, Dan Galbraith from Columbus, Ohio, takes over the Castle, help pay bills. Lady Rosse personally supervises the kitchen and in the dining room the table will groan once more under venison roasted in honey and served with red cabbage with caraway seeds and morels; roast teal and croutons; sucking pig and tangerine ice-cream and talk of the day's bag. While they tumble into bed, roseate from a brandy by a log and peat fire, the normally ascetic Countess must ensure next day's picnic when the Shoot will be in Dove Green: Mutton broth in mugs, turkey, oysters; sixteen beaters meat sandwiches; tea . . . Mrs Beeton would approve.

The staff worry. Hynes wonders if Birr can compete: 'Stag is nothin' to those rich American fellas . . . when they can be off shootin' bear in Poland.'

But the 'statelies' stick together. 'We are a close little band,' Lady Rosse explains, and when they have a party of tourists to lunch: 'I will ring Olda and ask if she is giving them rhubarb . . .' Olda is the wife of the Knight of Glin.

Meanwhile, 'Foyles say they would like a cheque.' It is not the bookshop who are used to waiting for years for a payment, but the local grocery shop. It is a struggle.

Lady Rosse may not appear to be the typical chatelaine – yet when an elderly retainer was dying in the village two summers ago and not wanting to leave her cottage to be taken to hospital, it was Lady Rosse the family turned to: 'Would she come?' Of course. She sat with the old lady, a gently comforting presence, the best of the old feudal tradition.

9

DANCING TO MAHLER

The clanging of a Tibetan bell, the slush of water from an ancient jug, a libation is being offered to the goddess Brigid, a little dithering about whether to wear a crown of snakes or stars; lunch is about to be served at Clonegal Castle in County Carlow, still no sign of Lord Strathloch.

Suddenly he appears. This is almost too robust description as the chalk pale, ghostly figure comes wafting out quite suddenly from a dark shadow of the long dark castle corridors, like a spirit. Dressed completely in black, except for a Robertson ceremonial tartan hat, but black cravat and black overcoat, he seems so slight and white, he might at any moment disappear. 'Poor Derry,' his sister says. 'He has just come out of hospital.'

His sister, Olivia Robertson, in a long black silk Japanese wraparound held at the waist with a red belt, full of a warm enthusiasm, is wearing little black shoes dotted with matching coloured circles. Her hair is bound under her crown – she has decided on the one with stars. With one slightly funny eye she takes a look in a mirror where the snakes and stars crowns and necklaces are reflected incongruously hanging beside the Staffordshire dogs.

At once touching, engagingly nice, Olivia Robertson is also rather funny and fully appreciates that 'some people loathe the supernatural.' As she fiddles with her massive necklace, she explains her own involvement which goes back to 1946 when she had a mystic experience on a train to Bolton. Her calling to the supernatural was confirmed on another occasion when she was driving out of the Castle: a mystery voice in the car boomed 'stop', and as she did so, a huge elm tree crashed down in front of her.

'I then realized I was fully psychic, had always been aware of poltergeists banging round, but most of mine were nice,' and she leant forward hoping her lipstick was not just going to be 'a pink blob'.

There is a certain professional skill; brother and sister starred in the film *Barry Lyndon*, and are not unaccustomed to the media: 'We have been visited by a terribly highbrow group from Channel 4.' On the way to the dining room, passing ceremonial halberds, knowing blond children scamper about chasing one another along the gloomy Aubussons, in and out, hiding behind the dark drapes and then, under the eye of a stark sculpture of a man with aquiline features and a lamb round his neck, disappear to the kitchen.

'Children,' their great-aunt explains, 'are aware, and still have the little grey flame at the top of their heads until they are twelve.' These are Lord Strathloch's grandchildren. Their father, David Robertson, who did the sculpture, is thirty-five and the heir to Clonegal. 'He does beautiful carving and has been studying the occult at a College of Psychic Medicine.'

The atmosphere is not particularly light; the prostate operation had made Lord Strathloch's voice very faint. There are incredibly long pauses which could be unnerving as the thinnest of smiles spread across his face registering pleasure in the eerie stillness.

His wraith-like frailty adds to this other worldly aura. As a clergyman in England, where he was known as the Reverend Lawrence Alexander Durdin-Robertson, he suddenly realized that God was a woman. He has written several books on goddesses and has a copy of the Bible from which every reference to God as a 'he' has been removed.

'The realization came rather unexpectedly.' And in delicious understatement he explained that his ideas meant, 'I became rather divergent from the official church.' The Irish, who love to exaggerate, say he preached cannibalism and was unfrocked. Not at all.

'It was in 1966. I had trained in Wells but of course seeing God as a female altered everything.' 'Gravy, Derry?' his sister asked as she wafted round a far from ethereal roast chicken, which was sent scooting in on a trolley by cheery girls from the old-fashioned kitchen with its copper pans and a wooden clothes washer. It arrived, *deus ex machina* as it were, through an ingeniously opened up seventeenth-century stone fireplace. 'Gravy . . . no,' His sister chuckled, 'Wasn't it Dickens who said it was only for the commercials?' She had been in quite a dither about carving, but after a little aside to herself about calming down, she hummed as she sliced.

Lord Strathloch's view of 'a mother God' in his Norfolk parish was rather novel for that solid squirearchical backbone of England parishioners, some friends of the royal family, solid, devout, churchgoing landowners. 'I had followers who included fearfully grand people related to the Master of Hallerton.' Lord Strathloch still felt he should resign, but his Bishop refused to accept his offer, 'So there was a spell of inactivity in the parish; I sort of stayed put but didn't practise.'

It then seemed the most natural thing in the world to come home to Clonegal Castle, to the twenty-first feudal barony, and to set up a shrine to Isis 'who began life modestly enough as the first daughter of Geb and Nut' as told by a present day Irish goddess . . . Isis would marry Osiris, a god from a neighbouring town, and together they would do great things, civilizing Egypt.

They had a son, Horus, and all was bliss until Osiris was assassinated by a violent brother Set, who cut the body into fourteen pieces and scattered it to the wilds. The inconsolable Isis searched and found the precious fragments of her husband's body –all except the phallus which had been gobbled up by a Nile crab, the Oxyrhynchid which was immediately cursed.

Isis, a sorceress anyway, full of spells and magic, had lovingly managed to put Osiris back together again and, restoring her god husband to eternal life, she retired to some swamps in Buto to be worshipped as a star of the sea, by followers as far away as the banks of the Rhine and a castle in Bunclody.

When Lord Strathloch and his sister openly became 'Children of

Isis' and established their temple, they found 'The Anglos didn't really mind what we did as long as we didn't become Catholics.'

Her view of 'Ascendancy bods' is the popular one that they tend to disappear behind their high walls. 'They say "hello"; Desmond Guinness for instance: "Hello, Olivia, how's your mother?" Well, mother died twenty years ago.' Olivia Robertson is not enamoured and explains why some of them were cursed. 'The fourth Lord Doneraile, for example. A woman could not pay the rates, and was expecting a baby. Doneraile said "Drown the brat." Curses,' she believes, 'are such energy of hatred.'

Olivia Robertson and her brother may take a poor view of some of the Anglo-Irish, but Lord Strathloch and his sister say that even talking about socialism is damaging to the psyche.

Their own background is a curious mixture. On their father's side they are related to William Robertson, the great architect who planned Dublin and Cork. On their mother's side: 'Grandfather was a gunner in India and had to choose between having another child and a hunter.' Their maternal grandmother was Anglo-Indian. Their mother grew up in India as a boy, dressed by a manservant, 'brought up as a square basher, she had a god awful temper' and shot her first crocodile at the age of twelve.

'Mummie was very masculine; Daddy adored her. She was very brilliant, shrewd and receptive. I appreciated her mind. She never carried a handbag, always stuffed things in her pockets and used to write about salmon in *The Field*.'

A rather fleshy woman looks bonny in a gold frame. 'That's Mummie; she always used lots of Indian words like wagga pagga, conversationally.'

One of the specialities at Clonegal is talking to people in the spirit world. 'If it is divine will, I leave them there and walk slowly backwards.' On one of her excursions in 1965 Olivia Robertson met her own mother again when she was in a trance.

'I was out of my body, there was a little hand, a bit of a struggle then I shot along this tremendous tunnel and there was Mummie. "How marvellous to see you," I said, and asked if she had met up with Daddy. There was this long intellectual chat, then contact started receding like a mad telephone wire.'

It was a happy experience unlike that recalled by Jessica Mitford, one of the famous sisters. When someone contacted their father in the spirit world and asked what he did all day, he answered: 'I go out, have sex, eat something, run about a bit, have sex, more food, run about, that sort of thing,' and his daughter said that this did not sound a bit like heaven. To which her father replied: 'But darling, I am a rabbit in Australia.' Caroline Blackwood, a writer and the ex-wife of painter Lucien Freud, asked Olivia Robertson to do a conducted trance.

The fame of Clonegal has spread round the world. Hallowe'en is always a busy time at the Castle; priestesses dancing to Mahler, filling a big silver basket with grapes, and waving incense. People come from all over the world. 'We had an important DOM here, a Benedictine monk who is an aristocrat, a Von somebody or other and a Jesuit priest and some Cherokees.'

Her face looked rapt, nothing to do with a sherry. 'It is a very euphoric feeling being in touch with all these gods and goddesses, and with shepherds of the starry flocks; it is the language of the angels. The other world is so much more advanced than ours with our frightful cruelty to each other and fear of the dead. A Swiss gentleman said it was all to do with strontium 90.'

They do not make sacrifices at Clonegal. Instead 'We prefer to offer friendly things like incense and water to the gods.'

'A Seven Up for you, Derry.' Her brother has been sustained by teenage fizzy drink since his illness, by reading theosophy and by frequent visits to the Castle well 'with its wonderful healing properties'. The daily visit to the temple, heralded by the ritual clanging of the bell made of seven metals is the highlight.

It is dark, studded with stars, Hindu and Tibetan bric-a-brac, tiny altars in alcoves, ornamental cats, bright red rugs made by Brigitte Bardot's sister and elaborate vivid face masks . . . 'Don't you like our fancy pussies?' and 'Here, Derry, hang on to this like a good bloke.' Olivia Robertson passes her brother the water jug; everyone has to be sprinkled and then she shivers: 'How much colder it is without my velvet bolero.'

They deserve their Isis followers and their success; they have created a happy atmosphere, one of innocence, but of vulnerability.

Ireland, they say, is the ideal place for Isis worshippers. 'The veil is thin – they say, the Greeks captured Irish girls to intercede for them at temples.'

'Oh look, this is our pregnancy chair; people love this healing chapel; it is jolly and here is a witch's broomstick from Mauritius.' There was an old Arab screen for women in purdah and a replica of a Pompeii sphinx.

'Now, Derry, where is your stole?' Lord Strathloch, a ghostly glimmering figure hovering in the background, was sometimes caught in the intrusive searing daylight from a Gothic window as he went gliding from one dark alcove to another in the ceremonial headdress of Egypt as worn by the Pharaohs.

'Let us have a prayer, that Derry should continue to recover from his experience,' and the small group is in front of an altar with snake carvings . . . 'So glad we have the proper gear.' Miss Robertson takes a feminine pleasure in the propriety of being robed in black and wearing a snake crown.

There was more lighting of candles in the temple with its Virgin Mary window and William Morris panels and not very appealing cat goddess Bast, the principal feline deity.

Ancient French tarot cards may be part of the ritual. 'I am a very red person, red is for vitality,' Miss Robertson explains; 'yellow for intellectuality; green for nature, orange for . . .' here she ahemmed for a minute . . . 'well, high spirits'. Any reference to libido is still a bit risky for unmarried ladies of a certain age in Ireland even if they are hard-working high priestesses. A rather sinister crow hangs in her office and a couple of gods in her bedroom. She says they are 'absolute smashers'.

Now it was a happy 'have a wish' atmosphere, childlike fun. 'The Force is here – let us light more candles; Derry, have you got your crook?' Miss Robertson likes to stage manage. 'Now where have I left my sistrum?' the ancient musical instrument is found.

Standing in front of some strange mirrors: 'If you look out here you can see your past – and if you look here you can see your future,' Miss Robertson urged. The trouble was the mirror for the future was like an amusement arcade glass so the future seemed very short and unpromising. 'No, no, the future goes on forever,' was the reassuring reply as Miss Robertson tightened her grip on her magic wand made of ivory: 'my ankh, the sign of life in Isis'.

There was brief prayer before the Sekhetlion goddess. 'In this game, as they say, I have picked up a few Greek words. I am very Pan Hellenic and love the cleanliness of Greek mythology.' But she is also attracted by Indian mysticism. 'For a time there was an Indian swami at the castle.' Miss Robertson, smiling, explained that the trouble was the people who worked for them did not always understand, but as long as nobody was in the nude they seemed not to mind too much.

'Now come along out here; this is the door which is meant to be like heaven.' It leads on to the lawn of the Castle. Coffee is in the conservatory. One of the women from the village appears, interrupting an exciting discussion on the goddess Ishtha who descended into Babylon: 'I saw her in a vision.' Miss Robertson was then stopped in full flow by the earthly request: 'Could I see you for a moment, Madam': and there was a soft sibilance over a piece of paper. 'Oh Derry,' it was more like a wail . . . 'another cheque . . .' His pale hand glided to a signature; it looked like £3,000. He is tired now and goes to rest stretched out on a *chaise-longue* raising two pale fingers in parting blessing.

His sister hums cheerfully, opens a door into a gloomy room where an old lady is sitting hunched in a collar. 'Derry's wife; she's had a couple of heart attacks, but is awfully keen on Isis.' Dogs were moaning.

The finer points of their belief, a love of Stonehenge, celebrating the summer solstice at the Castle, group meditation – 'Sometimes we go to Tir na N'Og, the mythical land of the perpetually young' – classical Greek dancing, wearing the flimsiest gauzy covering, performing mystery plays about Aries and Psyche and the loud playing of Richard Strauss's tone poem *Thus Spake Zarathustra* are not fully appreciated in the village.

The local priest who has chased romantic young couples with a blackthorn stick has thundered from the pulpit that 'Bunclody' with its one small street of dismal houses and very few people is 'a Babylon' and has pointed the finger at the elderly gentle aristocratic hippies at the Castle. Olivia Robertson skipped out of the temple, her good humour and feeling of 'this is heaven' changed for a minute to a sadness which clouded this sunny face with the speed of an April shower. 'Bad vibrations belong to the sexually promiscuous and there can be bad vibes with a good churchgoer; just because some white witches came here.' She would say nothing more harsh.

Near the Castle there is a sign to a place called Shillelagh. At the gates against the melancholy sound of dripping trees digesting more raindrops, Olivia Robertson says: 'Ah Clonegal, such a dear furry old place.' Down the street there is a sign which says 'Nudity is Dirt'. At the Castle gatehouse Mrs Lily Shiel protects herself and her family from hell and damnation by keeping a large leaf on a statue of a Greek god. But she does not seem to know that up at the Castle they say hell is due to end any moment now and be replaced by a rainbow.

10

A DIET OF SEAWEED

Lord Altamont, heir to the twelfth Marquess of Sligo, would happily spend part of his working day dressed up as a lifesized bucktoothed rabbit known in Westport's marble halls as 'Pinkie' but accepts the fact that: 'Men can't walk like a rabbit, women move better and more convincingly.'

His Lordship, who prefers to be known as Jeremy Ulick Browne, is a droll, coolly pleasant, lithe youngish man, who pads around in trainers and cords. His humour is laconic, and he almost defies you to laugh at his feigned delight in Pinkie: 'There is something about a pink rabbit and a stately home.' The giant Harvey figure is purely his own invention. He had not been able to sleep and then kept having a recurring dream about a pink rabbit. Pinkie, 'Ireland's favourite rabbit', is as big as a grown person, to whom you feel you should be introduced. Lord Altamont likes to be featured in its company as much as possible. 'Some people are slightly disapproving.'

Outrageously commercial, yes, but he is one of the few aristocrats in Ireland who recognizes that if you want to survive you must adapt. Westport is unique in Ireland, and one of the most successful country houses open to the public.

'We have no competition. There are only about thirty houses open to the public; the rest have been burnt down or the people have gone away.' He shrugs but is never complacent.

Twenty-five years ago, he visited Lord Montague's home Beaulieu in Hampshire – 'a nice little house, nothing special' – and the Duke of Bedford's Woburn Abbey for advice on the opening of a stately home. He has no time for titles and prefers to travel under the name 'Mister Altamont'. 'As soon as they hear a title you have to tip more and your evening is not half so much fun.'

'I am not a title person. It takes a lot to bother me but Britain is the most snobbish country where people judge you by your accent. If you are part of the Establishment in London you are expected to know only other people with titles; it is a network rather like footballers.'

Behind the understated humour, the elegant indifference, he runs Westport on smooth, sharply efficient professional lines. Part of the success is catering for children who do not want to see the Wyatt staircase or Synge's violin: 'They are the big spenders.' Ireland had been slow in the leisure field. He smiles and you get the impression he would not be above selling bottles of Mayo air and turf . . . 'just plain sods' to the visitor. 'Give them what they want.'

The road to Westport in County Mayo has warning signs 'Machines Crossing' and some wonderfully contradictory intelligence. On a fearsome bend, one side urges you to take care: 'Accident Black Spot', but on the other 'His Nibs is beckoned to Flanagan's Lounge Bar if he feels a "Sahara thirst" '. It is rather like the cyclist who, on signalling a turn to the right, tumbles headlong into the ditch on the left. In the small town of Ballyhaunus, the Halal butcher does well.

Westport, a tall Georgian house, is set in staggeringly wild beautiful Yeats countryside of pale purple mountains and huge lakes. It overlooks the Atlantic, Clew Bay and the remote and haunting Achill Island. Nearby there is the penitential stony Mountain called Croagh Patrick, haunt of pilgrims who climb the shingly hillside barefoot in the hope of salvation.

The house is romantic and famous for its appeal to women. Altamont thinks Westport is a feminine building possibly because of the family connection with his celebrated ancestor Grace O'Malley, raunchy warrior Queen of Connaught, pirate of the high seas and more than a match for Elizabeth I. Her Irish name was Graine.

The limestone house, designed by the great German architect Robert Cassels, was commissioned by Colonel John Browne who had fallen in love with Grace's great-great granddaughter, Maud Bourke, a daughter of the Third Viscount Burke of Mayo. They married in 1669.

It strikes you immediately as being more like an English stately home, with its mahogany doors from family sugar plantations in Jamaica, its good order, gleaming impressive entrance and massive locked doors.

Outside however the flavour is completely Irish as donkeys nibble the lawn. Spanish Armada guns may look frightening but do not deter the Irish visitors who have no idea about opening times and like to drop by even when houses are shut – 'Ah, are ye closed . . . we wondered,' and they wander off disconsolately looking for swans to feed crusts from their sodabread picnic.

They try to peer into the hall with its white marble mantelpiece from Welbeck Abbey; a harp carelessly resting against a seat; an Irish Elk head looks gloomy, a poor relic of these once magnificent creatures, ten feet tall and roaming the Irish countryside with wolves 10,000 years ago.

Grace's imperturbable descendant climbs the marble staircase towards a life-sized cool white statue of an angel in an alcove. He gives an almost involuntary bow: 'I feel every time I pass I should shake its hand though it is rather cold.'

In the library, perched on an embroidered gold chair, surrounded by seventeenth-century French novels, he suddenly seems rather boyish, bright dark eyes, crinkly grey hair and expressive hands which he uses a lot. There is a certain charm and restraint.

He was educated at St Columba's College in Dublin and then went to Cirencester Agricultural College, which he dismisses as 'a waste of time'.

A self-taught expert on promotion and development, he loves watching the effect of the pink rabbit on the average American tourist, 'who is harassed, has perhaps had a bumpy flight, been sick in a paper bag, is jet lagged . . . that sort of thing and been fed a rich diet of Ireland's sorrows.' He particularly appreciates the moment when the visitor is rapt in admiration of a Joshua Reynolds painting of the first Earl of Sligo, or the engravings from murals once in Windsor Castle, a James Wyatt ceiling or the exquisite Chinese wallpaper. When the rabbit taps them on the shoulder, 'They are afraid to react.'

The rabbit does not stay to hear about the second Marquess of Sligo, though a Regency buck. He was a friend of George IV's and of the poet Lord Byron – they were at Cambridge together. A vivid character, he once drove a coach from Holyhead to London doing 270 miles in thirty-five hours. Then he went to hunt treasure in Greece. As he sailed into Phaleron Bay he spotted his old friend Byron lolling on the beach. Byron was scathing about 'Sligo' and his brig with 'fifty men who won't work, 123 guns that refuse to go off, and sails that cut every wind except a contrary one. He has en suite a painter, a captain, a gentleman mis-interpreter (who boxes with the painter), besides sundry English varlets.'

The Marquess seized a couple of columns from the Treasury in Atreus and decided to return home, but realized his friend Byron was right about his crew. He stopped a British warship and bribed a couple of sailors who navigated his brig back to Ireland. This exploit outraged the Admiralty. The Marquess was tried at the Old Bailey, sent to Newgate Prison and fined £5,000. His mother thought the judge Sir William Scott was wonderful and the judge was so moved by her plea on behalf of her son they got married as soon as he was released after his four-month prison sentence. The columns lay in the cellars at Westport until 1906 when the sixth Marquess uncovered them and presented them to the British Museum.

The Library holds some 10,000 documents relating to the Famine. It is a respectable family history. Marquesses of Sligo starved with their tenants during the Famine, faced bankruptcy and total ruin. Perhaps this is why the family have always been liked. Not so long ago the guard on the train from Mayo would unceremoniously throw people out of first class, saying: 'Shligy's on the train. Howt with ye now! Howt ye all get' as the Marquess started his journey back to London.

Altamont would like to see the family papers displayed in a Document Room but there was no helpful financial response from the government. Naturally guarded, 'These days,' he says, 'you have to be wary of people allegedly coming to research,' and even deliberately puts out things for kleptomaniacs.

A natural cynicism is not allowed to intrude on the product and Westport is well done. It is quite an achievement for the west of Ireland which is so remote. There are cottages in the grounds for 12,000 holidaymakers; a Slippery Dip, a huge slide; wallabies and deer; 'a 'Kiddy ball pond' all designed to attract 50,000 visitors a day. In the basement is an amusement arcade with one-armed bandits; in the walled garden llamas and beavers, and a monkey house which Lord Altamont built himself getting step-by-step instructions on a cordless telephone from the man who designed the Cotswold Wildlife Park in Gloucestershire. By the gates there is a charming restaurant on the shore of Clew Bay where they serve fresh warm prawns and mussels in cream, decent white wine by the glass and the walls are covered with paintings by local artists.

Standing in front of a painting of his ancestor Grace O'Malley in the hall, Altamont warms to the story of her meeting with Elizabeth I and to these two 'strongminded women'.

Grace, who had been raised like a man, was like Catherine the Great of Russia, another doughty Queen, enjoying a vivid love life. She had several homes, one called Hen's Castle, married twice, first a warrior called Donal of the Battles O Flaherty and then a Burke, one of the distinguished fourteen tribes of Galway. 'The Brownes are part of this clan.' Her son was created first Viscount Mayo in 1627 by Charles I.

After the defeat of the Spanish Armada, Grace felt unduly harassed by Elizabeth I's henchmen, and by her son's being in jail. Sir Richard Bingham had assiduously hunted down enemies of the English Queen, reporting with satisfaction that in Connaught '. . . my province there have perished at least six or seven thousand men.'

Although in her sixties, Grace could stand this no longer and in the Year of Our Lord 1593, gave the order 'Prepare my galleys' and set out on treacherous seas round the west coast of Ireland to sail to the land of the English 'she-king'. She cruised up the Thames and came ashore, where she jumped on a chestnut mare to gallop to

Greenwich Palace for her audience with Elizabeth I, who she referred to disparagingly as that 'Tudor woman'.

A liveried servant in black velvet and white ruff led her through tapestried halls of dark oak past carved bureaux, some holding the odd death warrant, under ceilings elaborate with carvings and plaster swirls until she was in the presence of the pale red-haired Queen dressed in white silk, studded with coral, pearl and black onyx, and sitting on a gilded throne beneath a scarlet canopy.

A flamboyant figure herself, Grace swished her cloak around her shoulder. She had survived on a diet of seaweed on the voyage. Some velvet pantalooned courtiers such as the Queen's secretary, Sir William Cecil, in white silk hose and silver buckled shoes, turned up their noses thinking Grace none too fresh in the crowded warmth of the Elizabethan court.

Queen Elizabeth I, resting her long fingers on the arm rest and sometimes toying with baskets of cherries, nectarines and apricots, was faintly intrigued by the wild, striking woman before her. She had a certain royal bearing in her saffron overdress, with traditional red and green Celtic embroidery, her greying dark hair held with a jewelled bodkin from the Spanish Armada.

The courtiers held their breath as Grace spoke to the Queen: 'I apply to you as one chieftain to another . . . you rule here, and I am sovereign in my own territory.' The formidable pair had already begun to have a respect for one another, but having no language in common, one speaking English the other Irish, communicated in Latin.

Elizabeth I listened intently. Sipping wine mixed with three-quarters water, she remarked that she had met no one quite like Grace O'Malley before. The Irish Queen smiled and suggested that they were both unique. Grace was invited to stay the night while Elizabeth pondered, 'What is it you want more, Grace of Ireland? Your ships released to you, or the freedom of your imprisoned son?' Grace replied that it was a cruel choice. Elizabeth melted. The next day Grace was handed an olivewood casket; the scroll in Latin gave her everything she had requested.

'She was much better than the men and was a survivor.' It is a word Altamont uses frequently, but thinks it a pity so much energy was dissipated as the clans squabbled fiercely amongst themselves after her death in her late seventies at the end of a rumbustious life.

He is a quiet contained man who reads a great deal and is happily surrounded by five women. His wife Jennifer is a former model and still looks striking. They escape by going to a city somewhere in Europe, always as the anonymous Mr and Mrs Browne. They have five daughters, Sheelyn, twenty-four, who has an honours degree in History of Art and wants to be a book illustrator; Karen, twenty-three, a nurse; Lucinda, eighteen, who is cooking in Spain; Clare, twelve, and Alannah, aged seven, at the village school.

'There are vicious rows and I sometimes feel that they think of me as a male chauvinist pig but I consider women to be as important as men.' He said this twice. However, having only had daughters does create a problem over the title and inheritance which irritates Altamont greatly.

'The United Kingdom is glued to the horrific hereditary titles system even when a sister is more capable than a son of taking over. Look at Grace.'

Westport is such a commercial success, a visitor once told him she had nearly cancelled her visit because she hated the rich. Altamont replied, 'I hate them too,' and added, tongue in cheek: 'Everyone has seen now how the other half lives or does not live' and shooed away a donkey from the front steps.

He loves the place, is rarely away and mischievously enjoys the nuances of the local dialect when 'a powerful woman' means a lovely woman though she may be sticklike and glossy. In his own case, the highest compliment he has been paid on the estate is to be called 'a great auld whore', pronounced 'whoer'.

He invites loyalty, has 400 acres and employs sixty people including a cheery highly efficient secretary Mrs Mary McNeela who finds him very funny. 'Have ye taken her to the dungeons yet?' and looked disappointed when he shook his head. Visitors flock to the ice-cold seventeenth-century dungeons built by Grace O'Malley for her enemies, but they are, Lord Altamont says, 'only for those with nerves of steel'. You hear the most frightful wailing, but it is all done by recording. 'People like to be terrified of something,' Lord Altamont suggests, 'something which can't hurt them.'

11

PLENTY OF GRASS

For Irish Presbyterians the Restoration of Charles II provoked serious doubts. He seemed increasingly drawn to High Church showy Catholic ritual rather than their own dryer Puritan practices. His deathbed conversion to Catholicism in 1685 came as no surprise, and the accession of James II, who was openly Catholic, added to their anxiety, as did the alarming increase in a popular 'Distroy all Prisbiterans' mood afoot. In the first half of the eighteenth century, some 250–400,000 emigrated, driven out by what they saw as a burgeoning Catholic majority growing in 'strength and insolence'. Their dread was the kind of religious persecution which had driven the Puritans to New England. Irish Protestants would also favour North America.

In their haste to leave, they could not have anticipated the arrival of the Protestant Dutch King William of Orange. His overwhelming triumph over King James II's Catholic army in 1690 would have made their lives and their faith secure. King 'Billy', riding his white horse, speaking halting English and controlling his army of 35,000 men, would become a dazzling symbol of Protestantism, the architect of the Orange faith in Northern Ireland.

For Protestants in Ireland, the Glorious Revolution was a turning point. They had held out in the city of Derry under siege conditions for four months, fending off troops of the Catholic king. They were starving, surviving on a diet of rats and candles, but would not suffer the same ill effects as the Russians during the German siege of Leningrad in 1941–2, who in the famine aftermath became almost totally infertile.

The relief of the city of Derry by King 'Billy' has been celebrated ever since on 12 July, with drums, pipes and enthusiastic emotional marches. 'Darrey' as they pronounce the name of this much loved city in the north would become the new Jerusalem, a holy city, a glorious example of Protestantism triumphant. The victory was seen as a potent symbol that God had been on their side, God being a Protestant.

Even with his French and Irish allies, James II had been no match for William of Orange and his Protestant fleet. On 1 July 1690, after a daylong battle at the River Boyne, in the heart of Catholic farmland in County Meath, he suffered humiliating defeat.

The Catholic King, allegedly one of the first to leave the battlefield, arrived in Dublin at ten o'clock that night, where he remarked sourly to Lady Tyrconnel as he mulled over the day: 'Your countrymen, Madam, can run well.' But his hostess replied swiftly: 'Not so well, Your Majesty, for I see you have won the race.'

Under the leadership of a cavalry officer, Patrick Sarsfield, the Catholics fought on until a crashing and ultimate defeat at Limerick. Even with this 'final victory' for King Billy, Sarsfield irrepressibly suggested it was a pity they could not 'change kings and fight it over again'. James II had by then galloped south to Kingsale, boarding a frigate for France and the sumptuous safety of the court of the Sun King, Louis XIV.

Catholics in Ireland would feel even more vulnerable with the introduction of the Penal Laws in 1695. Already stripped of their estates, Catholics were forbidden to practise their religion; they could not vote, join the Navy or the Army, hold any office of State, practise at the bar, stand for Parliament or buy land in Ireland.

Mass had to be celebrated secretly under hedgerows or in fields. If the priest was caught, he was likely to be hung, drawn and quartered. 'We shall never be safe and quiet till a wolf's head and a priest's head be at the same rate,' declared a Roscommon magistrate, making one of those wild, swingeing statements that are still a perk of the legal profession.

Catholic children were taught in secrecy at 'hedge' schools. All this subterfuge is blamed for an Irish inability to give a direct answer, being 'ingratiating' and 'masters of deception'. 'I have no treasonable information,' an old man once told the writer V. S. Pritchett in reply to a straightforward question.

A plan to castrate priests insisting on vows of celibacy – it had been standard punishment for Jesuits in Sweden – was vetoed by the English Parliament. And the wise old House of Lords blocked a plan to brand unregistered priests with a P on the cheek.

It all seems bizarrely repressive by today's tolerant standards when there is a mosque near London's Regent's Park and, a few miles away, a pleasant golden temple holding a roly-poly Buddha in Battersea Park. Some of the Penal laws could verge on the absurd and would seem almost comic if not so sad.

Any Catholic owning a horse could expect to be stopped by a passing Protestant and compelled to hand over his RC horse on the spot. In return, he would get, regardless of the creature's worth, only £5. One Catholic farmer shot the horses drawing his carriage and walked home rather than hand them over. He later drove about drawn by a pair of bullocks.

When people shake their heads over Ireland's inertia today, perhaps it is with a short memory. These laws left a legacy as enervating as that caused by the excesses and hedonism of the Boyars in Tsarist Russia and resulted in the same sense of fatalism and procrastination in the Irish and the Soviets.

The reign of the devout Protestant, Queen Anne (1702–14) was not marked by much enlightenment or religious tolerance. Grossly overweight, often moving only with the aid of pulleys, the Queen preferred to concentrate on her prayers rather than reforms in Ireland, a country which had become so impoverished and desolate that Benjamin Franklin was shocked, reporting on a visit in 1771 that he had never seen such 'sordid wretchedness and extreme poverty' as on his journey from Dublin to Belfast. It made him 'thankful for the happy Mediocrity' of America.

By 1714 barely seven per cent of land in Ireland remained in

Catholic hands. By the middle of the eighteenth century, the time of the land war, a network of secret agrarian societies, the 'Whiteboys', who allegedly protected the peasantry from middlemen and unscrupulous landlords, were particularly notorious.

In England there were other preoccupations, the loss of the American colonies and a king prone to bouts of madness. George III would occasionally attack the Prince of Wales at dinner, hammering his head against a wall; or he would talk to an oak tree believing it to be the King of Prussia. But in his clearthinking moments, he got terribly agitated at the thought of Catholic Emancipation. Both he and his son, later George IV, felt it unthinkable to have Catholics sitting in parliament, seeing it as a violation of the sacred coronation oath.

Fear of any increase in Catholic power was partly responsible for the founding in 1795 of the Orange Order in Armagh, ostensibly commemorating Boyne Orangeism. In reality it was a self-protective organization for Protestant farmers, landlords, city workers, tenants. These Orange lodges would be the spark igniting an Irish Protestant 'nation' while the spirit of supremacy they represented provoked in 1798 a peasant rebellion which after four months left the country desolate and 30,000 dead.

Dublin, with all her grace and elegance, would no longer be important in Europe when the Irish Parliament was abolished by the Act of Union in 1801. Now Ireland would be ruled directly from London. There were those in the Ascendancy who were flattered by having a seat at Westminster, not appreciating the long-term damage to Irish culture they had created. Sophisticated and literary Dublin would become a provincial city.

In 1803 an abortive rebellion was staged in Dublin by a young man, twenty-five-year-old Robert Emmet, son of the Lord Lieutenant's physician. He hoped to seize Dublin Castle with an army of 2,000 men; instead he had a ramshackle band of no more than eighty carrying pikes and blunderbusses who were keener on a bit of rioting and looting.

Emmet, a dashing figure in a green cloak and cocked hat, fled to the Wicklow mountains, but was caught and hanged in Dublin a month later, although not before an emotional speech from the dock: 'Let no man write my epitaph . . . when my country takes her place among the nations of the earth, not till then let my epitaph be written.' The Irish like to compare his sacrifice with that of Christ.

Ireland remained in a state of 'smothered war' in the 1820s. The country was dominated either by huge Ascendancy houses, barracks for English soldiers, workhouses or asylums. Thackeray was struck by the size of the lunatic asylums. He saw one in Ballinasloe in 1842 and thought it so magnificent, he compared it to a palace. Today, on the main road into Cork city, a vast, gaunt institutional Victorian building still proudly overshadows a bosky hill and overlooks the tranquillity of the wide river below.

Anticipating Catholic Emancipation, many of the landlords moved to England. It was granted in 1829, a triumph for Irish Catholics and for the statesmanlike lawyer Daniel O'Connell who had campaigned for twenty years for the removal of all discrimination against Catholics in Ireland.

If Catholic Emancipation meant the lifting of a burden, a cross which had been imposed by their faith, a far heavier one awaited, this time physical, as the Irish people staggered towards the ultimate disaster, the Famine of 1845. 'Famine's wasting breath would touch everything,' Kerby A. Miller, Professor of History at the University of Missouri, says in his *Emigrants and Exiles*.

Ironically, the summer before the Famine had been one of the best the old people could remember, ideal growing weather. Young potato plants were strong and green, billowing with white flowers. Potatoes were the country people's staple diet; they ate on average eight pounds per day, and a man working in the fields could manage about twelve pounds.

Inexplicably one summer's evening, the potato crops were suddenly shrouded in a sinister mist. By morning the white flowers and perky green leaves lay crumpled and rotting, black with the sudden decay from a relatively unknown fungus *Phytophthora infestans*. One farmer poignantly recalled going out that bright July morning and seeing his crop 'crumbling into ashes when touched . . . the air was laden with a sickly smell of decay'; the aura of death was in a potato field.

The people watched 'the putrifying vegetation', helplessly 'sitting on the fences of their decaying gardens and fields wringing their hands', or wandering about 'cowering wretches almost naked in the savage weather, prowling in turnip fields and endeavouring to grub up roots . . . little children . . . their limbs fleshless and their faces bloated, yet wrinkled and a pale greenish hue', who would not live to the end of the year.

The small farmers desperately struggled to hold on to their tiny three- and five-acre farms and sent their mothers, wives and children to poorhouses where the sight which met them was of other Famine victims dying against the granite walls too weak to go inside for dignity in death.

By Christmas 1846, fifty-six workhouses built to cater for 100,000 were hopelessly overcrowded; within a month, 108,487 women and children were crammed inside these inhospitable walls.

Many children died from dysentery; others suffered from eye infections and over 1,000 lost their sight, partially or totally.

The Irish were convinced that the British Prime Minister, Robert Peel had a smile 'like the brass plate on the lid of a coffin'. He had dismissed some Famine reports as histrionic, saying the Irish tended to exaggerate, but was instrumental in ordering the Repeal of the Corn Laws in 1846, lifting all protectionist duties on grain imported into Britain and Ireland and thus making bread cheaper. But the starving could not afford bread anyway. Indian corn arrived from America; it was so unpalatable it was known as 'Peel's brimstone', but it was cheap. Not long afterwards a list of food sailing from Ireland to England revealed 300 bags of flour, 147 bales of bacon, 1,996 sacks and 950 barrels of oats, 9,398 firkins of butter and 542 boxes of eggs, was seen as insensitive.

Westminster was not deliberately uncaring; communications were difficult and the English government could not understand why the landlords were not able to deal with the disaster. It was a sorry tale of ineffectual mismanagement that would reflect badly on the British and also on the Irish themselves.

A relief commission was appointed in Dublin. The Victorian ethic applied: even in time of Famine relief should not be given except in return for work. So roads would be built in Ireland, and weak and hungry road workers would be given a bowl of porridge in lieu of a wage and would appreciatively call the road Stirabout.

A handful of bigots saw the Famine as God's chastisement on a rebellious Catholic peasantry, but on the whole there was a huge caring if inadequate effort to help. Constructive aid came from several British charitable agencies, particularly the Society of Friends with their soup kitchens.

Queen Victoria, who had come to the throne in 1837, personally sent £2,000 to the British Association, a group of prominent people in England who, horrified by the Famine, collected for aid.

Landlords, often for philanthropic reasons, paid their tenants' fares to America, the West Indies and other new lands. Lord Lansdowne spent £14,000 in this way.

Those who stayed were lucky if they had landlords like the Gore-Booths in Sligo, who almost bankrupted themselves in their efforts. But others were extremely irresponsible, having parties for three or four days while their tenants were starving. Lord Barrymore at Fota hired a coach from a Russian prince and chased off to Eastern Europe.

More compassionate landowners who had helplessly watched the tragedy unfold, waived rents and raised funds to provide food; these included the Duke of Devonshire, Lord Erne, the Marquess of Ormonde, and Lord Rothmore in Monaghan. The Leslies at Glaslough Castle kept a cooking pot on the fire for tenants and found work for 200. The Moores of Moore Hall ran a horse they owned called Corunna in the Grand National at Aintree which won the £10,000 race; with the prize money, they bought everyone on the estate a cow.

Unscrupulous landowners found the Famine an increasingly attractive excuse to clear the land of deadbeats, especially when there were arrears of rent, and would persuade tenants of small-holdings to give up their land and emigrate. Some of the ships were not all that seaworthy, earning the name 'coffin ships' for the death rate on board was more than fifty per cent as they foundered in rough seas.

Driven out by this latest in a series of disasters the involuntary exiles felt like the 'children of Israel'. They would never stop pining for the smoky smell of peat in the mud-floored thatched cabin, 'the smoke of their owne Cabbin if they can but beg neer it', even though often enjoying a better way of life, particularly in North America.

Ireland's decline had begun, and this slow haemorrhaging would go on until the 1960s. The Famine has been blamed for every misfortune in Irish history.

Ireland had her blessings, with potentially good farming land so close to Europe, but lacking the Protestant work ethic of her neighbours. Work came after play. Whiskey houses always had an appeal even in the more industrious north where master weavers would walk away from their looms and go out and buy a pack of hunting dogs. The sport was the thing, 'the good crack'.

In the spring, they could make money again; labourers turned 'spalpeen' and went to work as far afield as the Newfoundland fisheries, making enough to come home with arrears of rent sewn into their clothes. It is a custom which still exists – as the Paddy-Mikes and Finbars join the building trade in England for a lucrative few months each year.

In the eighteenth century, before the Famine, the Irish population had quadrupled; during the nineteenth a population of eight million would be cut in half. The Famine laid seeds of resentment against England: a feeling of hurt, and this in turn prompted a movement for national independence fuelled by sons and daughters in America where it has never ceased being a haunting tale, no matter how often it is told or by whom.

Ireland is not unlike India in its acceptance of disaster, but in that vast sub-continent the heat, persistent drought and paralysing poverty conspire, making almost palatable a life impossible to change. Ireland became a republic about the same time as India, in 1949. Both suffered partition: in India the creation of Pakistan set Hindus against Moslems; in Ireland the border to the north separates Protestants from Catholics and Catholics from one another.

'Between Ireland and England the memory of what was done and endured has lain like a sword,' Cecil Woodham-Smith concluded in her distinguished book *The Great Hunger*. Ireland's neutrality in

World War II was a retaliation, she argued. Her fair and balanced view has never been disputed. She painted a heartbreaking picture of Petty Officers and Able Seamen in the British and Merchant Navy killed off the coast of Ireland because Irish harbours were closed to British ships. 'From these innocents,' she explained, who, in all probability were ignorant of the past, 'who had never heard of failures of the potato, evictions, fever and starvation, was exacted part of the price for the famine.'

The overwhelmingly generous Irish response to the Ethiopian famine appeal is thought to reflect the potent memory of the Famine. It may also have had something to do with Bob Geldof, a young Irish rock singer who cursed and swore and used television and radio to tell the world to get off its backside.

But in nineteenth-century Ireland, news arrived weeks late. An ironed copy of *The Times* read in a leather armchair in the Kildare Street club might carry a disagreeable story, but having read it, there would be no further intrusion, no bombardment of horrifying television pictures crashing in on complacency.

'Everyone knew' the Irish could live on anything, the Duke of Cambridge remarked, and suggested helpfully there was plenty of grass in the fields.

There were vegetables in Ascendancy gardens – artichokes and asparagus. The Anglo-Irish brought to that green damp land a flair for creating flowery arbours, waterfalls and romantic gazebos, a talent for gardens sadly without appeal to this day in Ireland where a tired geranium will sit on the concrete 'hacienda' while in the overgrown rickety old Georgian farmhouse garden Gloire de Dijon roses, lavender and lilac still thrive in bushy profusion – grown from cuttings imported long ago to flourish alongside Ireland's natural wild, purply pink fuchsia.

12

THE NEXT PARISH

Bunratty Castle is fifteenth century, and once belonged to Lord Gort. But this evening a bewildered American, James Minto, a mechanical designer from California, is being made honorary Earl. 'I am just regular folks,' he says, staring myopically through pebble glasses as a crown is pushed down on his head of thinning hair.

A candlelit banquet, 'heady mead', an evening of 'Irish culture, music, history and folklore', a quick look at the Brussels tapestry and everyone is sent home moist eyed after an emotional chorus of 'Danny Boy'.

'My lord there is a scoundrel in our midst who has been trifling with the ladies of the court.' A local schoolteacher, Paul Davis, dressed up as a minstrel, appears on stage. A plump American boy in a navy blazer becomes 'our gallant prisoner, three cheers for Marty Holleran, a student from Washington, DC.' He is hurled to the castle's cellars, the medieval tableau has begun.

The banquet, indifferent soup and chicken, is presented for 'My Lord's approval'. A red-haired violinist with a vulnerable face, wearing pink and purple, joins the Lady Deirdre to play a haunting O'Carolan concerto. The noble Earl is blowing his nose, he has never had snuff before. Suddenly, a large black lady jumps to her feet and cries: 'Praise the Lord,' and soon the rafters of Bunratty tremble with voices chorusing: 'Lord ain't got time to die . . . Amen.'

'Three cheers for our group leaders and the Riverside Choral outing from Southern California.' They beam and sit down again. The prisoner has been released; more cheering.

A white-haired old man is moved by the Irish music. James Biglin, aged seventy-five, once from County Clare and now living in Pennsylvania, shakes his head; a grandson puts an arm round his waist. Outside an American asks if the castle shop has any books on fairies; the rest flock hopefully to Durty Nellie's, to this seventeenth-century village inn which does well on its name alone, disappointing those who hope for something a bit risqué, only to find it is the name of the old woman who took the toll from soldiers, aristocrats and petitioning tenants crossing the small bridge over the Owengarney River to the castle.

At Dunguaire Castle near Galway Bay the mood is gentler. It is not far from the rocky Burren landscape full of rare flowers and the 700-foot cliffs of Moher beyond. 'You gotta take a coach ride or you're nobody,' one American confides. Another introduces her husband: 'He's good in bed.' Tales of Celtic mythology unfold and the story of the Cladagh ring, worn in the west. The small gold heart held between two hands is turned inwards after the wedding, showing that the bride's heart now belongs to her husband; it is worn more proudly than any family crest.

When Desmond Guinness was married to his first wife, the volatile Mariga, they became concerned about the decaying eighteenth-century houses and formed an Irish Georgian Society in 1958 to protect them. Now there are branches all over America: in Arkansas, Georgia, Florida, Massachusetts, Maryland, Kentucky, Colorado and Washington. Americans love to think they are saving Ireland's heritage. In return for a life membership of $1,000 they tour stately houses led by the 'divine Desmond', who also lectures in America in places like Moultrie, Georgia; he even receives them at his home in Leixlip Castle, where they are never discouraged from buying sets of laminated coasters and tasteful prints of the Rotunda, Dublin's Lying-In Hospital, at the Castle shop. 'In a year, we have 390,000 North Americans,' says Frank Hamilton, spokesman for the Shannon Development Corporation.

Another place of pilgrimage is the Famine graveyard in

Waterford. They sit in the corner of the Seanachai public house where there is the traditional big black pot over the fire, but it is empty. Instead little Diarmid is eating micro-waved chips – 'Finish your chips, they'll do you good.' The Americans smile and look at their guidebooks. If it were not for the Famine, their ancestors might never have left Ireland and there would be no Vuitton luggage, no world trips on which the women can show off their Oscar de la Renta evening dresses and be thanked by the Georgian Society for their patronage.

So for many there are confused feelings about the graveyard. Some emigrants had in desperation walked across the breadth of Ireland to reach a port. During the three centuries before the Irish Free State was set up in 1921–2, seven million people emigrated from Ireland to North America. 'Send us, Your Honour, where you like,' pleaded one desperate farmer graphically and succinctly. 'Only let us go. The cuntery is done.'

The crossing from Ireland to Liverpool could take up to thirty hours and cost ten pence. The passengers huddled together on open decks, terrified in case they got washed overboard. Livestock always had priority on the Liverpool steamer. The pleasure of one passenger, Mary Cummings, at arriving in Liverpool was dimmed by the discovery of a dead rat beneath her head when she woke.

Those who did get to America sent back in the first half of the nineteenth century an average amount of £1.2 million each year in the hope of bringing out unhappy relatives. There were also euphoric letters home from America. The excited Annie Gass from Armagh was delighted to discover that her family in Indiana lived in a large house 'with ritsh Carpet', 'mehogny furniture', and 'silver dishes, nives and forkes'.

Remember 'Dear Patt', wrote one mother to her emigrant son, 'what you promised . . . to take me and little Dickey for the honour of our Lord Jasus Christ and his Blessed Mother hurry and take us out of this . . . little Dickey longs and Sighs Both Night and morning.' Even today people in the 'wild west' of Ireland refer to Boston, Massachusetts, as 'the next parish'.

Although the feeling between Ireland and America is strong and supportive today it was not love at first sight. The flood of people from Ireland, particularly between 1870 and 1921, was cautiously received and caricatured as either yobbish and half-simian or, with a little more indulgence, as the comic George McManus caricatures 'Maggie and Jiggs', lace-curtain Irish struggling for respectability.

However successful the emigrant Irish, many mourned, sang Celtic songs, danced reels and jigs, and never stopped missing their country, affectionately called 'the auld sod'. Homesickness bred bitterness and, now far away and dwelling on Ascendancy ineptitude and heartless absentee landlords, they saw themselves as 'victims' of oppression. Yet funnily enough few were persuaded to return home. Unlike homesick Italian or Greek migrants who preferred to go back even to dictatorships, the Irish stayed put in America.

They complained of the heat and the 'Flies and Musketoes'. They deliberately spoke Irish and could barely make themselves understood in English. They clung together in little ghettoes in Boston, New York and Philadelphia, San Francisco, Chicago, Pittsburgh and St Louis, where seeds of Irish-American nationalism were sown.

A mischievous Anglophobia would develop at this time and remain deep-rooted amongst many Irish-Americans. Later generations who may never have known Ireland absorbed word-of-mouth stories of hardship passed on and becoming more vivid and full of pathos with each telling.

In Northern Ireland there was an outburst by the late Robert Kennedy's son in 1987, a young senator who was resentful and provoked an embarrassing incident when stopped by soldiers on a routine patrol. His uncle, on the other hand, the charismatic President John F. Kennedy assassinated in 1963, unlike his hot-headed nephew, merely paid a sentimental visit to the old homestead, a modest two-storey Irish house in Dunganestown, County Wexford. His great-grandfather, with that Kennedy family drive, had sold everything he owned to buy a one-way ticket to America where he headed a powerful family that still has glamour and retains those distinctive Bostonian Kennedy vowels.

Two of America's most successful presidents had Irish roots. President Reagan's ancestors came from Ballyporeen, a very small place indeed in the Tipperary farmlands. President Roosevelt claimed he had Irish ancestors, never an unwise assertion by any American political candidate: 'I am proud of the strain of Irish blood in my veins.' 'It had,' he claimed 'filtered through' on his mother's side, 'from the Barnwells of Ireland.'

Many other Irishmen succeeded in America with near legendary flair: the hugely successful Henry Ford, founder of the popular motor car whose mother had died of 'Famine Fever'. A grandson of Charles O'Carroll, also from the Reagan lushlands of Tipperary, would sign the Declaration of Independence. The O'Mores in South Carolina became colonial governors. Marcus Daly of County Cavan became a wealthy mineowner in the Montana copperfields and a racehorse breeder, after an unpromising start as a telegraph messenger in New York. Others became priests and policemen. Infiltration of the New England WASP Society would come later.

Yet even after sixty successful years in America, Thomas Mellon, a distinguished financier, missed his roots in Ulster. It was something to do with the first five years in a child's life, he decided, from which everything was remembered so vividly.

Now they come back to Ireland not in search of the Big House but looking for the old cottages, and are touched by a gentle hospitality in pubs called Scappa Flow where there is a smell of baking, apple pies and brown sodabread with melting salty butter; and the kindness when, if they are stopped for speeding, the young policeman puts away his notebook in mock despair when he hears the American accent.

The returning American who had just had an operation for throat cancer is restored by the soft voice of 'Mammy' Scott at her bed-and-breakfast farmhouse outside Galway. 'You are a fine cooker, Moma' – an ecstatic message has been left for her by an Italian group.

In the morning as he puts his face out to the rain to appreciate the yellow gorse and the hawthorn bent in a crescent over the low stone walls, the air is so pure and the moisture so soft on the skin. His wife joins him, sticking her head out of the window. 'Honey, this is better than any Erno de Lazlo product,' a reference to one of the most expensive cosmetic houses in the world.

Some go to Knock where the Virgin Mary appeared to some schoolchildren. A huge woman greedily gulps the water taken unceremoniously from a tap in the low wall by the shrine. Knock is the place of miracles. The Irish believe that on Thursday, 21 August 1879, a wet day naturally, the Virgin Mary appeared in a great globe of light. Confessions; jewellery; holy water; vocations; take your pick. A gaudy gold rose from the Pope celebrates the apparition.

Australians of Irish ancestry average one in four. During the Famine years some 4,000 orphan girls from Irish workhouses were sent to Australia because there was a shortage of women there. One of the most famous antipodean exports from Ireland was the swashbuckling bushranger Ned Kelly. It is now chic in Australia to claim convict or bushranger blood. Only in Adelaide in the Ladies Clubs do prim Australian matrons assure you, 'We have no convict blood here.'

Sir Henry Browne Hayes, an Irish aristocratic convict, was sent to Van Diemen's land in disgrace because he had kidnapped a Quaker heiress in 1797. Sailing through Sydney Harbour he was far from depressed, unlike Charles Darwin, who thought little of the 'thin scrubby trees' which 'bespoke useless sterility'. Sir Henry bought 105 acres of this priceless land on the edge of one of the world's most stunning harbours for £100. He called his house Vaucluse after a favourite village in the south of France. Immediately he surrounded it with a moat of turf, brought sod by sod from Ireland in the belief that it had been blessed by St Patrick and would keep snakes away.

This pretty castellated icing sugar 'cottage' which is really a mansion is in a perfect place at South Head; it has warm sandstone wide-flagged terraces, verandas hung with wisteria; bright parrots flutter about trying to pick up sponge fingers from the teatable on the lawn, and the air is scented by the casuarina tree. The gardens are a mixture of Australia and Europe, with the Sydney golden wattle, white and purple daisies and bamboos leading the way to a demure old-fashioned rose garden.

At Vaucluse there is the modest table on which the Australian Constitution was drafted, the stability of that great continent resting briefly on Irish whimsy. Pudgy cupids and Staffordshire dogs mixed with Ned Kelly hats are all reminders of a frontier civilization passing into legend and the ambitions both noble and ridiculous of what was once a raw colony.

13

RATHER MAL VU

Molly Keane is a cult figure but warns adoring fans before they meet her: 'I'm bound to be a disappointing old woman but I shall be very glad to see you.' The face peeping out above the blue half door, the little-girl slide holding back brown curls convey a vulnerability, a mask for a wicked ability to get under the Ascendancy cuticle.

Her home is a cottage isolated on top of a cliff, near Youghal the ancient garrison town created by the Phoenicians when they came to trade in skins. 'It is,' Molly Keane says, 'a perfect place to write but lonely.' Her garden in late summer is filled with hydrangeas: 'The blue always remind me of the old Berkeley.'

Most weeks she is being called on either by the BBC or by glossy magazines, *Vanity Fair* from America or *Harpers and Queen*, to be lionized: being photographed as she is whisked to literary gatherings in London and appearing on television; being conferred with an honorary doctorate by the National University of Ireland in 1989; being profiled in the *New Yorker* describing her octogenarian self as a 'great old break-awayer'. Camera crews take over; artists and photographers spend hours shooting pictures: 'Molly Keane writing at her desk', 'with her dog', 'looking at the sea'.

This glossy international group of Keane worshippers rarely go down the hill to the village of Ardmore where they would find in a pub, near the water's edge, a different camera at work: close circuit television. The locals are entranced; big wrists lift foaming pints and they nudge each other as a fat girl reappears in the street: 'There she is again.' They are purple with laughter.

Irish barmen are said to be some of the best in the world: 'We're whippin' the cream for your coffee,' he explains the delays but goes back mesmerized as the camera brings live gossip straight from the street to a hunch of shoulders. As it pans in on concrete bowls of flowers against a white wall – 'That's Trevor's whitewash,' there is more desultory chat about a wedding: 'Tony married on the Sathurda, sure after the weddin he got so fluthered that his Mammy wouldn't let him go on the honeymoon till he'd sobered up. So the wife's gone ahead on her own.' Irish mothers are possessive of their sons.

'Sons are gods in Ireland,' Molly Keane says, putting on her straw hat to pick thyme for an omelette, and carries her dog Hero with her – 'He is my hero.'

Her words are elegant and precise. It is when she buries her head in her hands that there may be the most devastating remark. Describing the marriage of a formidable hunting woman called Smith as 'the relief of Ladysmith', and of someone louche as 'coming from a long line of tarts'. Those naughty blue eyes reappear: 'What an extravagant puss,' an inimitable lovely Molly Keane thanks you for a flower or any small kindness.

Her talk is sharp and up to the minute. She is a member of Groucho's Club in London's Soho and has a wistful fancy for *Spectator* columnist Jeffrey Bernard, and worries about him and the waitress who is in love with him.

At eighty-five she has just finished *Loving and Giving*, once again capturing brilliantly this centaur class, the hunting Ascendancy, the beautiful women with their porcelain hearts and their bullied, timid gauche daughters.

'I was never anything like beautiful,' Molly Keane says, and you sense there has been a preoccupation with this primitive passport and how it can become a curse 'almost like a pain and as women grow old it fades'.

Nobody understands the Anglo-Irish better; she is after all one of them. Her family name was Skrine and her upbringing was pure

Ascendancy: no books, a lot of hunting and a remote mother in a social world with little time for this sensitive observant daughter. 'I was isolated, growing up almost alone in County Wexford.' There were no lovable aunts with ankle bones as 'many-angled as those of hungry little birds'.

'It was terribly lonely,' so she longed for brother Walter's return from boarding school. But when he did arrive home at the end of his first term, she was rather upset: 'He knocked me down.' Walter Skrine later became known as 'Sawn off Skrine'. He had insisted on having a leg shortened to match the one damaged in the war, so his balance would be right when he twice rode in the Grand National.

In her study which is more a playroom, her perch, like an Ascendancy nursery, with Snaffles prints and a koala bear on a windowsill, there is a photograph of both of them out hunting, Molly Skrine a wild girl, keen, intent, lunging towards a ditch. Hunting was a passion.

Her education was in the hands of governesses until she was sent to a French boarding school in Bray: 'I was awfully unhappy and I thought I'd be so popular.' Signs of tuberculosis meant she was confined to bed and began writing under the name M. J. Farrell. Her first book was published by Mills and Boon, and she spent the money on a party in the Shelbourne and on a pair of riding boots; to have 'a good leg for a boot' was essential in that milieu.

They were heady and attractive times for young Molly Skrine, who says now, 'It really was not done for a girl to earn a living.' A century earlier, the Somerville and Ross parents were shocked not by their daughters' closeness but because they wanted to write. All rather *mal vu*, as Molly Keane put it – this use of the snappy French phrases, the old-fashioned chic of the twenties. Molly Keane marvels at 'these two virgin ladies' writing in 1878. Supreme in their own field, she is critical of their character Flurry Knox in the *Irish RM*: 'They had no idea how a half gentleman behaved and as for Lady Knox she was so common.'

In spite of the adulation, Molly Keane remained a country girl and 'passionate about hunting'. Looking back now she is slightly shamefaced as she remembers being on a train as a young woman on her way to a literary lunch in London and wishing she were going out with the hunting men in the same carriage. 'And of course I was about to meet David Cecil,' that inspiring literary figure who used to read Jane Austen to the Queen Mother.

Molly Keane went from success to success with books like *Mad Puppetstown*, *Full House*, *The Rising Tide* and *Two Days in Aragon*. From the age of twenty-four she had written ten novels and then her husband died in 1952. 'Mol has known hard times,' her friends will tell you, and she struggled terribly when she was first widowed.

She met her great love Bobby Keane, one of a Waterford squirearchical family, soon after her London season. Her husband's cousin Sir Richard Keane lives in a stunning Georgian house at Cappoquin. He is tall with a white moustache and strides about with gun dogs and seems serious when he says 'Queers? Wouldn't have one in the house,' and 'Only the professional classes take holidays.' The trouble is that whatever your opinions they can set like concrete behind high Ascendancy walls where there is no one to challenge them except a bandy-legged old groom or a wife only interested in *gros point*.

The cousins were not alike. In the hall of Molly Keane's house there is a painting by Norah McGuinness which says much about her marriage. It is a glorious picnic; a young man with golden hair is lying on the grass and beside him a girl in a straw hat – Molly. They lived together for five years, which was terribly daring in those days, and then moved to Belleville, a house of charm by the Blackwater.

When her husband, 'a witty happy man who loved old furniture, me, his daughters, good food and talk', died suddenly at the age of thirty-six, she moved to a simple cottage at Ardmore down the lane from interesting neighbours Claud Cockburn and his wife Patricia. They owned the white nineteenth-century sea captain's house with a huge brass fish doorknocker on a blue door and inside leather chesterfields and vases of Queen Anne lace on marble fireplaces. Her own cottage was simple but transformed with the help of a local man who would have drained the seabed of sand if Molly Keane had asked. A terrace was created overlooking a sensational long stretch of Ardmore's sandy beach.

James Agate, a distinguished theatre critic, said: 'I would back this impish writer to hold her own against Noël Coward himself.' Now she would write several plays in addition to her novels. One starred Margaret Rutherford and four were directed by her good friend John Gielgud. *Dazzling Prospect* in 1961, which starred Sarah Miles, was a flop; the mood was not right, people wanted realism, plays like John Osborne's *Look back in Anger*. 'It marked one of the last times that people actually threw spoiled fruit at actors in a West End production.' There was never a time when she needed the support of her beloved 'Bobby' more; it almost broke her. Molly Keane returned from London and wept in a friend's car all the way from Dublin to the peace of Ardmore. She would shut herself away and stop writing for the next twenty years.

Molly Keane insists on giving even able-bodied guests breakfast in bed, a delicate tray with rosebud teacups, honey and toast. 'Now child don't get honey on the blankets.' Nearly everyone is 'child'; if someone is difficult or unpleasant they are 'trixie'. In the guest bathroom, where, of course, the hot tap pours cold water, there is Floris Malmaison carnation essence, and a Victorian painting, 'Love In a Barrow', of some gambolling children in white lace. 'Lascivious little devils. I am convinced young girls did it in those days, though they may have looked pure as cocoa.'

Dame Peggy Ashcroft was staying with her old friend Molly Keane and being spoilt in the pretty guest bedroom with its white bedspread and cottage simplicity and wanted something to read. Molly Keane gave her a handwritten exercise book, one of her manuscripts, sprinkled with yellow dots for corrections. Dame Peggy loved it and persuaded her to send it to a London publisher. Serendipity. There had been silence from Molly Keane until 1981, now *Good Behaviour* was published by André Deutsch under her real name and greeted by the critics as a triumph.

Loving and Giving, her latest book heroically finished when she was far from well, is about a fat, lumpish daughter named after one of her father's favourite racehorses, who turns into a beauty, but is self-destructive, leading an ingratiating, door-mattish life. There is a bosomy aunt Tossie who leaves her vast house for a mobile home

and there she lives with companionable bottles and a stuffed parrot
hanging over her bed.

Some among the Anglo-Irish wish there had not been a
renaissance of Molly Keane novels and feel uncomfortable if they
meet her at dinner, fearing, like the 'huge toppling blonde with
frightfully good legs', that they may appear in her next book.

People tell her things; she is so sympathetic. In Paris, at a dinner
party in her honour, the French simply could not imagine how this
frail enchanting old lady with a gossamer mildness could have
created anyone as unpleasant as Jasper in *Time After Time*, written
in 1983. She replied, 'But Jasper, c'est moi.' The character is
contained, remote, elegant and louche, a brilliant cook, terrified of
a large cat and of being seduced by his exotic blind cousin. He
exercises a subtle tyranny over his sisters – each of the family has a
defect. His eye had been shot out by a younger sister and he was
given the nursery wing to wash out the socket in privacy. At the
end of the day he triumphed.

In the kitchen at Ardmore, Magella, a local girl, is ironing a
purple satin shirt, an eighty-second birthday present for Molly
Keane from an old friend Baron de Breffni who died of cancer in
1988. The two women talk companionably as the girl asks if she
wants more butter and cheese for the omelette. 'Too rich,' says Mrs
Keane, who thinks thyme, parsley and chives will be enough; she
always gets the mixture right.

Stunned by an illness in 1987, after a spell in hospital, she came
home rather shaken but with her acuity undiminished. 'I thought
how terrifying . . . how preposterous.' It had made her thin and
pale and fluffy in her beige dress and alarmed when her wedding
ring fell off her finger and disappeared.

Slight heart failure makes her very annoyed with herself. She has
always been a 'self-confessed health fiend', keen on exercise and
delicious light herby food. 'It is,' she says, 'like a terrible stammer in
your head . . . but somehow it's not as bad if you have a little
drink . . .' and mixes two powerful Bloody Marys.

Forbidden by doctors to go in the kitchen, but of course sneaking
in for she is a marvellous cook. There is always something
interesting simmering on the stove and she rustles up a pudding

made with orange juice, yoghurt and orange liqueur – a Skrine syllabub.

She laughs in an exasperated way when naive worshippers say how lovely it must be to write, how easy it must be. 'It is,' Molly Keane replies softly, 'absolute hell.' She still feels she needs to earn more money and is terribly protective of her two daughters, Sally Phipps, married, gentle and kindly, a writer who lives with her husband, a tenant farmer, nearby, and her other daughter who is married to film producer Kevin McClory, who produced *Thunderball*, a James Bond film. All three are close.

The purple satin is being worn that night to a party, her birthday is on 20 July – Molly Keane says she is a Cancerian, but also a bit of a Leo: 'I am now coming out of my shell.' Any dewy sentimentality is chased away. Molly Keane with her velvety gentleness and aura of delicacy makes a classic remark: 'I am a bitter old pill really.' But still eighty-five years young.

Asked if she was working on another novel, she replied, 'Oh no, child, I am a barren old trout now.' But there was a copybook open in the study with its windows on to the sea.

14

A CLASSIC AMBIVALENCE

The road from Dublin to Slane Castle in Meath is superb. George IV had it straightened so the royal carriage could speed him to the castle to indulge a singular lust for its busty mistress, Elizabeth, wife of the first Marquess Conyngham.

It is like a Roman road, so direct and so unlike most Irish highways, the driver wishes the King had had liaisons all round the emerald isle instead of this one with his last mistress, after Lady Jersey, Lady Melbourne and favourite Mrs Fitzherbert. No longer the witty Regency 'Adonis of Loveliness', George IV with his gargantuan appetites had become a florid gross–bellied 'Voluptuary'.

On his way to the castle in the small grey stone town of Slane, the King would drive past the sacred hill where St Patrick lit the first Paschal Fire in 433, celebrating Ireland's release from paganism, and the historic river Boyne where William of Orange defeated James II in 1690.

Slane, designed by two of the finest architects, Gandon and Wyatt, is like a child's picture of a castle. You almost expect to see witches flying over the battlements and horsemen galloping out at dusk.

The King's visits were brave as this part of Meath was a rebellious corner, but in the elegance of Slane he found comfort. As he danced with his love in the ballroom with its lacy fan–vaulted Gothic

Revival ceiling, had the conversation turned to politics, he would find Lady Conyngham was no simpering royal coquette, but interested in Catholic emancipation and opposed to the death penalty. She would live to be ninety-two, a spirited old lady walking to church every Sunday and leaning on George IV's cane.

The King was generous to all his mistresses and their families. Even in the twentieth century, if a royal prince sets his eye on the nubile wife of a friend, the husband's role is difficult. While not exactly a *mari complaisant*, or toothless old pussycat, he must appear to enjoy the flattery of royal attention. The Irish say that the reason the Marquess was ennobled so often was his capacity for being asleep at the right time.

The other spin-off from the King's fancy for Lady Conyngham is a Castle which today is full of charming little royal mementoes, a Sir Thomas Lawrence portrait of George IV and many of Lady Conyngham. The present Lady Mountcharles, the second wife – 'No, I am not, in the *Tatler's* phrase, "the melon-mouthed" Lady Mountcharles, I am the new one he married eighteen months ago' – is slightly dismissive of the pouty Lady Conyngham, remarking coolly as she studies her portrait: 'She is just a shelf for diamonds.'

Her husband, Lord Mountcharles, thirty-seven-year-old heir to the seventh Marquess, treasures the King's writing desk, designed by Henry Holland and studded with ormolu, and with lion-heads gripping the desk handles between their teeth: 'A very fine piece of English furniture of interest but of less value than a royal ring,' and he shows one of the King's. With its 'rose for England, thistle for Scotland and emeralds symbolizing shamrocks', it speaks for days when the British Isles included all of Ireland.

'I sometimes say out of the corner of my mouth that the two greatest collector kings were respectively Charles I and George IV: one lost his head and the other one tried to.' Lord Mountcharles also has some of the King's diaries, but of those, will only murmur a discreet 'mmmmh'. People tend to stare intensely at Mountcharles wondering if they can spot any royal features in the smiley slightly immature face. Far from being Hanoverian, he almost invites the question: 'Who's a cheeky boy then?' If you ask him if he is rich, the answer is 'yes'.

Born in Ireland in 1951, educated at Harrow where he was nicknamed 'Boggy', young Henry was 'the most beaten boy in the school' and the butt of all jokes. After Harvard, he got a pleasant job in publishing at Faber & Faber editing science fiction.

Matthew Evans, the Chief Executive, who would become one of Mountcharles' 'seriously good friends', when interviewing him for the job wearily anticipated that his new editor would be bound to want time off in August . . . 'Why would I be wanting holidays in August?' the puzzled young Earl asked. 'For the grouse of course.'

There probably is no ideal time, but it is curious how many eldest sons have suddenly been saddled with vast estates as a result of a telephone call in the middle of the night from an aristocratic 'Daddy' speaking from a tax haven in Switzerland, Jersey or the Isle of Man.

In Mountcharles' case, the call came at 8.30 in the morning. 'I'd just got out of bed and was wondering about catching the tube, I always timed it to the last second. My father suddenly started pouring out all this stuff about Slane. For him there had been serious financial troubles, the 1974 coalition had introduced a wealth tax so he was uniquely vulnerable because all his assets were in land.

'Daddy had to contemplate a "doomsday situation". He also shrewdly suspected that his eldest son, if left much longer, "would be unwilling to take the sceptre" . . . as it were.

' "Give it five years," he cajoled. Daddy knew I wouldn't say no.'

So Mountcharles, aged twenty-five, jumped on a plane to Dublin where he and his father spent three hours wrestling with lawyers and accountants. 'By the end of it my father had made Slane Castle over to me.'

The Marquess went off to the Isle of Man and his son came back to Slane, 'terrified of being ripped off and suffocated' by his heritage.

'I am quite Sicilian,' he says with a schoolboy giggle, but those dark looks are convincing. 'Some people tried to take advantage of me, but I have a memory like an elephant. Also I learned a lot from

Paul Getty about the wisdom of caution.' He formed a company to run the Castle, employing thirty people, opening a bistro where he worked as a waiter and a night club. His rock concerts would put Slane on the map, attracting groups like U2; Queen; Bob Dylan; Bruce Springstein; David Bowie and the Rolling Stones whose music on summer nights touched the battlements.

'Anyone seen Henry?' Emer Mooney, an amiable, unflappable local girl who worked as secretary also for Mountcharles' father asks. It is the day of the Bowie concert and 65,000 fans are expected. Many are already on the road to Slane looking like early pilgrims. On the noticeboard there is a picture of a hound called Henry; old portraits are stacked against the wall alongside sepia photographs of celebrated otter packs. Outside two men are moving a mattress across a Stable Yard believed to have been laid out by Capability Brown, but he never came to Ireland.

There is an air of contrived casualness disguising an efficiency. Lady Mountcharles goes around swearing softly. She has a long mane of hair, is tall though likes to wear incredibly high heeled purple suede shoes, almost fantasy stilettos, a dream for artist Allen Jones who features women in tight dresses and sexy shoes.

The most exciting moment of the concern for her will be when she slips away with her husband and they run up to the roof of the castle and listen to the music.

How wonderful, a public schoolboy's dream to have the best international rock singers play in your own home. How exciting to fly over your land, over the woods of Slane and the river Boyne, and see thousands of people below whose money would go towards the Castle so it could be decorated in lurid theatrical pinks with jacuzzis and saunas, no mossy green walls at Slane with brownish water trickling into an old clawfooted bath. Some of the takings would also go towards the Slane Trust Fund to help young people find employment and fight drug abuse.

With her wry humour, Lord Mountcharles says his wife has the ideal temperament for Slane. They are very close, she dark, rangy, emotional and he behind the skilled charm is reserved. 'I could not be married,' he says, 'to someone who does not care about Slane.'

Lady Iona Grimston, a younger daughter of the Earl of Verulam, worked in public relations for Moët & Chandon in France as a *maîtresse de la maison*, where she met 'Henry' on a 'freebie' to the champagne house. He gave her an incredible diamond ring with yellow stones.

He had lived alone for quite a while after the breakup of his first marriage and had to get a divorce in Britain as it is forbidden in Ireland. 'I loathe hypocrisy and the religious structure here drives me bananas.' He and his first wife Juliet had grown apart – 'We were far too young when we married' – that was in 1971. They were twenty and there was parental disapproval. Their two children, Alexander thirteen, Henrietta eleven and an adopted boy Wolfe, aged nine, 'son of my wife's sister who died', live in London with their mother. At Slane Castle they say: 'Ah Juliet, she was lovely . . . dreamy.'

The sitting room in the Castle overlooking the Boyne is deserted. Organized chaos, the remains of lunch, as if everyone has suddenly heard that the bomb was about to be dropped. The radio is on; there is an enormous photograph of Mick Jagger; a painting of a tired nude downfaced on a bed; an intriguing collection of Tara brooches and a huge piece of modern sculpture.

Mountcharles is on the lawn giving a press conference. Skilled at manipulating the media, he finds it exhilarating and laughs when teased about this ability. He will pause thoughtfully at questions though he may have been asked a hundred times. He gives knowing nudges to an Irish star columnist implying he wants to confide in him as a personal friend. But really all he is going to give away is another political ambition.

'Bowie is a mega, I have been trying to get him for four years.' The adrenalin of controlling *Gandhi* type crowds is heady. 'Oh yes, the hype, it retains the cutting edge physically. I am mentally and physically fit.' He enjoys talking about himself.

Back at the castle, he leaps about taking steps two at a time, past royal ancestors, the throne where Queen Victoria once sat and a collection of what he calls 'Oirish' landscapes.

Whether clowning with his wife or driving round the estate, Mountcharles in odd socks and open shirt waving to the staff or pointing to slogans scrawled by the IRA: 'I like to wipe them off before the children see them,' is resilient. Everything he does or says is with shrewd attention to publicity and security. The Castle may appear mellow, protected by pine trees on either side sloping down to the river but it is perilously near the border.

Somehow the Bowie concert did not have quite the edge of the others. Mountcharles is defensive. 'Mick,' he says, referring to Mick Jagger of the Rolling Stones, 'told me Slane was the best gig for him.' Perhaps it was something to do with growing up. At thirty-eight maybe it was less exciting to meet yet another rock star though David Bowie, he found, 'the least uptight and an absolute delight.' But Jagger remains the idol.

'The VIPs can be so petulant,' Lady Iona Mountcharles complains jumping out of a battered blue Renault. It has been a massive undertaking with a huge private party in the Castle, invitations astutely sent to the Gardai, the priest. She may appear harassed in striped shirt and well cut jeans but it is a bit of an act, a way of getting the best out of staff, looking over a secretary's shoulder as she sends out invitations: 'Don't forget to put the *grave* accent,' 'Make sure Oisin and Finian get to the concert,' two Slane teenagers. A little smile, she scoops up her basket and is off – 'Anyone seen Henry?' 'Stupid shit' – not her husband, but some official who is making a fuss about fire safety.

Next a chat with the castle manageress, a bright skinny blonde called Sue Wade. The problem is how best to get 'eighty portions of chicken à la King' and the 'fucking' tartlets and quiches to the VIP marquee in the grounds. They decide that the food should go by helicopter. 'But what time does Henry want the helicopter?'

It is such a convenient way of entertaining friends to a summer party at the Castle. Desmond Guinness in an ecstatic note: 'We simply can't thank you enough for the three tickets,' all 'a huge success' and no disasters unlike the year when a boy was drowned in the river during the Dylan concert.

On the face of it, the Mountcharleses would appear to have everything, and, as if that were not enough, he recently inherited a splendid eight-bedroomed mid-eighteenth-century country house called Beauparc and 460 acres with private fishing rights on a 'wonderful stretch of the River Boyne' from a remotely related neighbour called Sir Oliver Lambart.

'It was a thunderbolt; he used to give me things, but I had no idea.' Mountcharles smiled as he held up an obscene cartoon of George IV. In addition to the house, the paintings and the furniture, he claimed Lambart's financial estate also, worth more than £1.5 million. When he lost the case, his wife went very pink and burst into tears. 'I have,' she said, 'just had some very bad news.'

While the inheritance was being renovated and 'toilets' – Lady Mountcharles made a face and joke at this non-U word; she likes Cockney slang – 'were being chosen' they lived in the flat in the Castle. But 'it is very much a "one dish dinner", the kitchen is in the basement and it couldn't possibly hold all Henry's family.' Beauparc is home except when they have paying guests. £150 a night, bed and breakfast.

They like Mountcharles in Ireland, his dimply smiley face, the clichéd description of him is as 'a yuppy peer'. His apparent accessibility and business acumen is admired. He would be far less of a celebrity in England.

His forays into politics have been watched with pitying kindness. Irish politics are notoriously Machiavellian but this is where he longs to make an impression. He tried to form his own party in Ireland based on the Social Democrats, had debates with Gerry Adams the Sinn Féin leader in Ulster but admitted: 'I don't think my father greeted all this with overwhelming enthusiasm.'

In November 1982 he joined Fine Gael, one of the two principal parties in Ireland then under the leadership of the scholarly Dr Garrett Fitzgerald and was subjected to a 'fairly extraordinary amount of abuse'. But two days after he joined, he had the heady success of being nominated by his own branch to stand at the General Election.

There were some rough experiences and more than once he was heckled in such a 'derisory' way – until something went snap inside this well-behaved public schoolboy who went for his critics like a 'coiled spring' and got a standing ovation.

However he did not get on the ticket. Mountcharles justifies this: 'For someone of my background as a peer of the realm with a seat in the Upper House at Westminster it would have been a little bizarre.' His father has a seat in the House of Lords as Baron Minster of Minster Court in Kent.

Each Monday, the chatelaine used to appear at the gallery at Strokestown and drop menus and rations of tea from jewelled hands to the housekeeper, standing below at a respectful distance in the stone-flagged kitchen.

Strokestown, with its neo-Palladian grace, was one of Ireland's grandest country houses. The land, originally 27,000 acres including a royal deer park, was a gift from Charles II to Nicholas Mahon, who supported the Royalist cause long after the execution of Charles I.

Above: Olive Pakenham Mahon (with her father, Henry Pakenham Mahon, in pinstripe) enjoyed a gilded childhood and was given a pack of hounds on her thirteenth birthday.

Left: Olive Pakenham Mahon's mother was such a great beauty people would stand on walls to catch a glimpse. Her daughter inherited her looks, though tinged with the sadness of becoming a wife and widow within five months in the autumn of 1915, when her first husband was killed at Ypres.

Above: An only child, Olive Pakenham Mahon was the indulged, beautiful daughter of the big house. Half the year was spent at Strokestown and the rest at the family house in Mayfair.

Right: Oh happy day! Local garage proprietor Jim Callery is now the owner of Strokestown, bought for under a million pounds. 'She was gas', he says of the previous owner Mrs Pakenham Mahon, who died in a nursing home in England in 1981.

Right: These hunting women were fearless and many rode like Genghis Khan. As a 14-year-old girl, Miss Cary Barnard caught the attention of *The Times* and *Daily Telegraph* when she made two rounds of a difficult course with a total of only six faults, riding 'Trilby', which belonged to her father, General Cyril Cary Barnard.

Left: A spirited beauty, Miss Melosine Cary Barnard has a defiant glamour and is far from demure at her presentation at Court. Reluctantly she had to conform with Queen Mary's wishes and lengthen her dress with net and lace.

Left: Lord Snowdon's stepbrother, Lord Rosse, with Lady Rosse – 'Ally' to friends – and their youngest son, Michael, and a local schoolfriend. Michael, with football, has an 'Oirish' accent, as does his father; this, and the family's liking for cords and denim, earns them local approval and goodwill in their uphill efforts to maintain Birr Castle.

Right: The stylish Lady Altamont finds it hard to stop posing as a model even in family photographs. Father of five daughters, Lord Altamont has made the property over to them; 'They are very determined, capable young women'. He feels sad that antiquated laws prevent them from inheriting the Marquess of Sligo title.

Above: The first sign of the Famine was one summer's evening in 1845 when the potato crops were shrouded in a sinister mist and by morning lay crumpled and rotting. Helplessly, the people watched the 'putrefying vegetation' in their neanderthal plots.

Left: Pride in royal favour endures. Lord Mountcharles, heir to the 7th Marquess Conyngham, enjoys the romping bucolic fun of a cartoon entitled 'Pitch in the Hole', as the gross-bellied George IV has fun with his somewhat discomfited mistress, Elizabeth, wife of the 1st Marquess Conyngham. Royal flunkies and an astonished giraffe look on.

Above: Apart from total immersion in the duty-free shop at Shannon airport, one of the delights for visiting Americans is a candlelit medieval banquet at fifteenth-century Bunratty Castle, nearby. After an emotional chorus of 'Danny Boy' they make their way to the nearby hostelry, 'Durty Nelly's', to mop their tears and think sentimental thoughts about 'the auld sod', as Ireland is affectionately known.

Left: Lord and Lady Castlemaine at Moydrum, their home in Ireland, later burnt down in the Troubles. Lady Castlemaine peers uncertainly from behind her husband's bulk, yet both manage the stern formality of old-fashioned photographs. Their daughter Evie, a wildflower enthusiast, married Sir Charles Gairdner, who became Governor of Western Australia and later Tasmania. They chose not to go back to Ireland and ended their days in Australia at their pleasant house in Peppermint Grove, Perth.

Above: Richard Grove Annesley surveys the gardens at Annes Grove. Luxuriant an[d] intriguing, they are now open to the public. Richard Grove's grandson, Patrick Annesley, has to keep an alert eye on women visitors who deftly help themselves to cuttings; some wear capacious knickers for the outing, nuns more modestly rely on umbrellas to keep the admired cuttings out of sight of the helpless owner.

His son thinks of himself as 'unequivocally Irish' and wants to 'explode' when this is questioned. He rejects the assumption that 'someone of my background is expected to live in this country by stealth and as long as we keep our noses clean and are seen parading at the Curragh or the Horse Show.'

'My father's study was a place you had to gain entry to, as a teenager, and I remember having my suitcase packed for me.' He grew up surrounded by servants but 'I never felt terribly comfortable.' He is warm about the influence of his grandmother's Irish housekeeper, 'an amazing lady called Mary Brown' who interested him as a small boy in Celtic literature.

'The way Iona and I live here is dramatically different from my parents.' She amuses him in her fey way, drifting about like a slightly lost Hans Christian Andersen princess.

English in Ireland and a 'Paddy' in England, where he is seen in the *Tatler* doing the round of art gallery openings and charity balls. A direct descendant of the Duke of Wellington, he says: 'The English amuse me with their capacity to claim for their own some of Ireland's greatest, Anglo-Irish men like Castlereagh.'

Yet for all the protests about being Irish, he travels on a British passport. This is the classic ambivalence which annoys the Irish. And he will take up his seat in the House of Lords. 'Had I been in the Upper House at the time of the Falklands, I disapproved of the invasion and would have spoken against it vociferously.'

He sees himself as a public figure. Nowadays he is to be found sitting on worthy platforms. At a debate on the role of women in Ireland, the speaker, a Ms Walsh, talks about Irish women today 'some in the poor areas stretching out the dole money' or those 'in well-heeled Dublin 4 which is full of golf widows while "himself" is out on the course looking for a birdie'. These are worlds Mountcharles knows little about and he looks faintly relieved when the intensity lifts with a story about a cannibal chief walking on a beach with his son when a beautiful girl is washed ashore on a raft. The boy suggests they take her home and eat her, but the father says: 'We'll take her home and eat your mother.'

The peace of Beauparc means more to him than flitting off to Venice or the west of Ireland. Here he can lock himself away avoiding 'events' up at the Castle: weddings, Gaelic football matches, ceilidhs and all the ghastly snobbish 'castle creepers'. His son will inherit only 'if he feels inclined.'

He sees Slane as a friendly albatross, always demanding. One Sunday morning, the ancient bell at the Castle clanged, waking up Mountcharles, who staggered sleepily to open the great studded doors. An American slightly shocked by the dishevelled figure blurted out the question which had been troubling him: 'Can you tell me,' he asked earnestly 'if this is a real castle.' The young earl, looking him straight in the eye, replied: 'It is made of polystyrene granules,' and at this the American looked at his wife . . . 'Gee this is a bit weird,' and fled.

What Lord Mountcharles says he wants now is *Lebensraum*, more room to live.

15

A LITTLE REMOTE FROM REALITY

In the aftermath of the Famine, Queen Victoria made a triumphal visit to Ireland in 1849, arriving, with the Prince Consort and her two eldest sons, at Kingstown, a pleasant port now known by its Irish name, Dun Laoghaire, just outside Dublin.

It was one of the Ascendancy, not anyone in the huge crowd which turned out to welcome this 'pleasant young woman', who almost incurred royal displeasure. The convivial Earl of Clonmell, a guest at a royal garden party, kept shaking the plump royal hand again and again in a warm Irish way, peering whiskily into those impassive features as he inquired: 'I know the face but for the life of me I can't think of the name.'

There would be more royal visits. Edward VII visited the Dublin capital. In 1899 the future George V and Queen Mary stayed at Kilkenny Castle and were cheered from the banks of the river as they sailed to a picnic. A boy refused to raise his cap, not for any political motive but because he was bitterly disappointed they were not wearing crowns and thought they must be impostors.

Ireland, weakened by Famine, welcomed Liberal pressure in England which forced absentee Anglo-Irish landlords to come to heel. In 1869 Gladstone disestablished the Church of Ireland and the 1880s Land Acts eased the plight of Irish tenants oppressed for years by grasping landlords. But it was almost too late.

The 1903 Wyndham Act meant that the Irish could borrow money to buy their own farms. This land purchase act coaxed through Parliament by a philanthropic Secretary of State for Ireland, George Wyndham, known also for his dashing good looks, was lauded by hard-pressed landowners. Those who were feckless and hopeless at administering their estates particularly welcomed the Bonus, an additional payment of twelve per cent when they sold to the Government. But in truth it spelt disaster for Ireland. With the exception of a few the great estates shrank, the landlord hanging on to a hulk of a house and keeping a few hundred acres, never more than a thousand, and the woods for privacy and shooting. Southern Ireland would become a patchwork of sad little Neanderthal plots, hardly more than scrubby potato gardens. The owners of these farms were not ambitious; despite every incentive to buy with interest payments lower than the rents most had no dream of a competitive thriving rural economy, preferring the doctrine of *laissez-faire* and the wisdom of ancient proverbs: 'Good fortune is better than rising early;' 'There is nothing in the world but mist' and 'Prosperity lasts but a short time.'

The slow-moving rural people were criticized for being lazy. These ignorant small peasant farmers were not stirred by thoughts of acquiring large farms although by 1914 three-quarters of the former tenants owned their own small-holdings. Inertia prevailed so that Ireland tends to be compared with Russia. Ireland, they say, is too small and Russia too big.

A combination of an irresponsible eighteenth-century squire-archy and a well-meaning but ineffective late-nineteenth-century Ascendancy caused many of the 'Big Houses' to decline, soon to be suitable only as the setting of a novel. Some shrewd landlords retained their land by selling to the state, being rewarded generously and then repurchasing on the same low mortgage rates as were given to the tenants. However this was often a short-term solution, leaving unfortunate heirs lumbered with an encumbered estate, the money from the sale of tenanted land perhaps recklessly spent on racehorses or in casinos. So sadly neither landlords nor the new tenant owners seemed able to bridge the gap of yawning inefficiency between good and indifferent farming; and for the latter wholesale emigration came to be seen as one solution.

'The Irish are illiberally jealous of rising merit among themselves,' the traveller Edward Wakefield observed in 1812.
Emigrants took this attitude with them to Australia, where it is
known as the Tall Poppy syndrome today. Too much success has to
be downed with a typical Antipodean 'aagh . . . it was just a bit of
luck that galah put a bit of business his way.'

One of Ireland's most distinguished poets, Seamus Heaney,
grieves over a 'guilt of achievement' in Ireland and makes a
comparison with being a successful writer in America, where the
feeling is of uniqueness and exhilaration. In Ireland, he says, it is
'part of the function of the established writer to be there to be pissed
against . . .'

More Protestants emigrated than Catholics, who, lacking a
'natural shrewdness and strength of mind,' Edward Wakefield
noticed, 'stayed home enduring degradation'. Their material
progress too was markedly different. The Protestants were not
burdened by religious indoctrination that it was better to remain
poor and had no feeling of guilt about possessions.

America would be liberating while in contrast an 'iron morality'
dinned into the post-Famine Irish made them amongst the world's
most rigidly religious and 'sexually controlled Catholics', a persuasive deterrent to Ulster Protestants if contemplating union with the
South.

Irish dynasties would spring up in America, emigrants feeling
freer to marry, escaping the gloomy old adage in rural Ireland
'marry for riches and work for love' whereby daughters were
marketed in return for a good farm. Many loveless marriages were
made in Ireland.

Today modern folk songs in Ireland still echo a bitterness about
marriage, one on Radio Eireann warns a young girl about to get
married: 'You'll end up as his dumpling . . . marriage is a bore,
better be a whore. He'll have a jam tart on the side . . . marriage is a
curse.'

A Jansenist streak in Irish Catholicism meant 'lads and lasses' had
to walk on opposite sides of the road, forbidden to speak. This
shocked Irish Protestants and travellers from abroad, who thought
the Irish a 'priest-ridden' people.

The criticism that the clergy were 'taking innocent joy from the social side of life' was not confined to Catholic priests; Protestant and Presbyterian clergy sternly condemned card playing and dancing and were upholders of Sabbatarianism. Charles Stewart Parnell, a Protestant himself, was a victim of this prudery and denied full credit for his championing of Home Rule because of an affair with Kitty O'Shea, a married woman, his standing as the 'uncrowned king of Ireland' diminished.

The Anglo-Irish were bitterly opposed to Home Rule and to Gladstone when he introduced the Bill in 1885. The very idea sent them to the Unionist ranks, not that they had ever been anything but staunch supporters of Union with Britain. Many felt that if Mr Gladstone could be hung in chains it would be too good for him. Northern Protestant resistance to Home Rule was led by Sir Edward Carson, an Irish Protestant barrister and Member of Parliament for Dublin University.

Randolph Churchill, Sir Winston's father, as a Conservative determined to undermine the Bill, adroitly chose the 'Orange card' as 'the one to play' and so attracted jumpy Protestants belonging to Orange Order Lodges in the North. In his crusade against Home Rule for Ireland he also had the support of the Duke of Abercorn, who would raise his arms and cry: 'We will not have Home Rule.' But their efforts were in vain; by 1912, Home Rule for all Ireland had become law.

Two years later, in an emotional response at the start of World War I, Irish Catholics, Protestants, Northerners, Southerners willingly joined the British Army. There were great Southern Irish regiments: the Connaught Rangers, the Munster Fusiliers and the Dublin Fusiliers. A recruiting poster showed a fetching red-headed girl playing a harp. Irish neutrality in World War II may have provoked ill-feeling, but Irishmen did not hesitate to serve in the British army; some 38,554 men and 4,695 women enlisted from the Irish Free State.

By 1916 'a terrible beauty' would be born in Ireland – Yeats' description of the group of Irishmen and women who, determined on an independent Irish Republic, openly rebelled against the British Government. This was the Easter Rising and afterwards 'all was utterly changed'. Some of the Ascendancy were caught unawares, typically, enjoying a traditional Bank Holiday Monday at Fairyhouse Races.

The rebels struck in Dublin, seizing the General Post Office in O'Connell Street and fought until they had control of the city.

Germany, lending support to the rebels, sent 20,000 rifles in a 'neutral' ship called the *Aud*. Sir Roger Casement, an Ulsterman formerly with the British Consular Service now an ardent convert to Irish nationalism, arrived at the same time in a German submarine to try to stall the Sinn Féin 'Ourselves Alone' rising. But when he landed in Kerry on Good Friday morning, although he had shaved off his beard, he was immediately identified and arrested.

By 1921 Lloyd George, the British Prime Minister, suggested an Anglo-Irish treaty, the only alternative an 'immediate and terrible war'. There was a strong British military presence in Ireland.

So after 750 years' intermittent squabbling, the more recent guerrilla warfare and bitter fighting between Catholic revolutionaries and British soldiers, a modern divided Ireland began to take shape with the signing of this Treaty on 6 December 1921.

Ostensibly it would give Ireland its own army and navy and control of its affairs. But as he put his signature to the treaty Michael Collins, the rebel leader, declared in an emotional outburst: 'I have signed my death warrant.' It gave his country the constitutional status of Canada. Ireland remained a part of the British Commonwealth.

At a General Election held in Ireland in 1922 there was, however, a pro-Free State Treaty vote, and the Irish Parliament, Dáil Éireann, approved it with a majority of seven.

This 'Irish Free State' consisted of twenty-six of Ireland's thirty-two counties. The other six, Londonderry, Armagh, Antrim, Down, Fermanagh and Tyrone, would be known as 'Northern Ireland' with its own Parliament under the Sovereignty of the British Government. In June 1921 an important royal visit set the seal on the creation of a separate state of Northern Ireland when George V went to Ulster to open its Parliament. The Six Counties would remain an integral part of Great Britain.

In the South William Cosgrave, a fair and moderate pro-Treaty politician, headed the Free State Government of 1922 and tried to keep a sense of balance and calm. But that year would mark the beginning of Ireland's Civil War between the Free Staters who supported the Treaty and the Republicans led by de Valéra who opposed it.

The Troubles had begun in earnest, an unhappy tale of hatred and heroism, of civil strife and brother often against brother that bred what Yeats would describe as the 'fanatic heart'. An assassin's bullet killed Sir Henry Wilson, a security adviser in Northern Ireland, in June 1922; he was shot down on the steps of his home in Eaton Place, Belgravia by the IRA.

Ascendancy sympathies were with the Free State, with one or two exceptions, among them Countess Markievicz and Erskine Childers, who was captured by Free State troops on a charge of illegally bearing arms. Childers was eventually shot but the Countess, a daughter of the Gore-Booth family, although sentenced to death was reprieved and released after a long prison sentence.

During the 'Troubles' there had to be the ritual burning of Anglo-Irish houses, seen as symbols of oppression. But often it was a half-hearted business, the villagers reluctant to help in this final destruction, and there was little loss of life.

Between 1920 and 1923 some 200 out of the 2,000 Ascendancy houses were burnt in Ireland. Occasionally the incendiarism was a reprisal against the Auxiliaries and the Black and Tans who had been recruited from the British Army and were greatly feared in their half-black and half-khaki uniforms for they had a reputation for brutality.

Inevitably, being Ireland, there was the occasional comic touch as the 'Big House' became a battlefield between the Free State Troops and the Republicans. Lord Waterford's aunt, Lady Susan Dawnay, was almost sorry she had missed the skirmish at her home at Whitfield Court in Waterford. The gardener later informed her that far from being depressing it had all been rather encouraging. 'There was a battle on the lawn this morning,' he reported. 'There were no casualties and both sides greatly admired your Ladyship's antirrhinums.'

When the IRA pounced on Kilkenny Castle, Lord and Lady Ossory assumed that they would be taken prisoner, but the Commandant replied in a soft voice, 'We would not like to be disturbing Herself or your Lordship at all.' As if it were a tennis match or medieval jousting, the imperturbable couple stayed for the expected siege, a servant appearing with a tray of bread and cold meat at lunchtime, while the rebels busied themselves sorting out their machine-guns, bombs and boxes of ammunition.

In the afternoon, as Free State machine-guns opened fire from a tower and the Republicans fired back, a tousle-haired rebel put his head through the coal cellar door where the Ossorys were enjoying bezique to inquire solicitously, 'I hope Herself is not frightened.' Lady Ossory, a model of calm, with a typical Ascendancy sense of priority was concerned only about her dog, a petrified trembling Peke.

As the fighting intensified, Lord Ossory, known as the 'Boss', slipped along the subterranean corridors to the kitchen to get some Stilton and a bottle of port. When the Republicans were defeated, they made a point of shaking hands with the Ossorys before being marched off to the County Jail.

Often the rebels were the sons of butlers and cooks in Ascendancy houses, both sides having a tacit understanding of the rules for Civil War. A gamekeeper working for the Percevals at Balymote in Sligo went to watch the fighting one afternoon and thought it so unprofessional he said, 'Give me that gun, I'll show you how to shoot properly.' But the young fresh-faced rebel replied, 'We can't, sir, we might hit somebody.'

Norah Perceval, whose husband was known as the Haddock, one of Rosa Lewis's adoring young officers who bought her champagne at the Cavendish, marched straight into the middle of the fighting. Apart from the gamekeeper, the rest of her staff had been too frightened to go into the town. Exasperated, she cycled the ten miles into Ballinasloe and knew she was getting near when she heard the shooting. She demanded to see the Captain on the south side and asked him to kindly stop the battle, which he did, holding up a white flag. 'Mrs P,' he announced to the north side, 'wants to go shopping.' The fighting stopped and, wheeling her bicycle, Mrs Perceval was escorted carefully by an officer, for the bridge, having been blown up, was rather shaky. Then a time was arranged for her return, after which the battle would start again.

Lady Gormanston was paid the highest compliment when 'the lads', the young village rebels, proudly showed her one of their homemade bombs, fished out from a tweedy pocket. As it began to roll about on the kitchen table, Lady Gormanston suggested perhaps it would be better off back in his pocket, but he replied reassuringly: "Tis all right, Miss. Yer could play ball wid it yerself and no harm so long as yer didn't pull this pin out.'

And being Ireland there was even a literary flavour about some rebels who called at the writer Elizabeth Bowen's house. The Bowens were away, and the rebels, exhausted after their journey, went straight to bed where they read red leather bound Rudyard Kipling stories until they dropped off to sleep.

The Civil War ended in 1923. Three years later de Valéra founded Fianna Fáil, his strongly anti-Treaty republican party. Its members had all bitterly opposed the 1921 Treaty, seeing it as a betrayal of the 1916 Rising, and despised those who had agreed to it, particularly the clause which stipulated that members of the Irish Parliament would take an oath of loyalty to the English King.

Victorious also in the 1932 election, de Valéra and his party were now drawing up Ireland's new Constitution. Many were sad; there are still small voices to be heard in the south of Ireland which say it was a great pity links with Britain had to be severed.

Even in the embryonic stages, the Vatican played a powerful role in Ireland's Constitution. Cynics in Ireland like to paraphrase Kruschev's description of India. The Irish church, they say 'is like an elephant – it won't run and it won't fall.' The 1937 Constitution was drawn up in close consultation with Rome, each draft sent to the Pope for his blessing before being presented to the people in the Dáil for approval. Ireland, where the Catholic church still dominates, remains one of the Vatican's brightest and most constant apostles.

In this Catholic Constitution, divorce and birth control would be forbidden by law. At least four thousand Irish women still set out on lonely treks to England in search of abortions each year.

The Anglo-Irish Protestants, who loathed de Valéra, denying him the courtesy of the aristocratic *de* in his Spanish title and calling him Vera, nevertheless gradually came to admire his integrity.

They found it very difficult to accept the hard line on divorce and birth control. In 1925, Yeats, 'the greatest poet of our time', according to T. S. Eliot, spoke on their behalf in his famous and moving speech: 'We are no petty people'. It was an attack on the Irish Catholic Church and a plea to allow divorce in Ireland. Yeats was a Senator in the newly elected independent Irish Parliament, one of the few drawn from Ascendancy ranks; others included Sir John Keane from Waterford, The McGillycuddy of the Reeks and Sir Horace Plunkett.

'We are one of the great stocks of Europe. We have created most of the modern literature of this country. We have created the best of its political intelligence,' Yeats eloquently reminded Ireland's new masters of the worth of the Protestant Ascendancy.

Viceregal Lodge had been shut down. There was no longer a Governor-General in Dublin but, as a sop to the Ascendancy, smarting in its new subordinate role, the first President in 1938 was Douglas Hyde, a Protestant.

In 1949, Ireland broke away fully from the Commonwealth and was declared a Republic. The Irish language had been made compulsory in 1922; it would be impossible to get into the civil service or a Catholic university without it. Catholics were forbidden to go to Trinity College, Dublin. The 'silent sister' of Oxford and Cambridge which had nurtured Oscar Wilde and Samuel Beckett was seen as a symbol of Protestant and British Ascendancy.

Dublin, a city like Calcutta designed by foreigners, the conquerors' choice, had become rather parochial and rundown. To a once subject majority, the dilapidation of many of the old houses with exquisite moulding, the tall mahogany doors and graceful fanlights, becoming tenements, symbolized a fitting end. Not everyone in Ireland mourns the crumbling of the Georgian façades.

A constant criticism of the Ascendancy has been that they played so little part in shaping the new Ireland; but in fairness they had no reply when asked the key question: 'What did you do in the war against England?'

In this new Ireland, an alien place to many of the Ascendancy, it was almost with a sense of relief that they could abandon the 'Big House'. By the 1920s land sale had become compulsory, the 'Bonus' had been spent. George Wyndham would shake his head as he recalled seeing an Anglo-Irish landowner he knew in Monte Carlo, who hailed him excitedly, beaming at the mass of chips in front of him: 'George, George, the Bonus!' For many of the Ascendancy the answer had to be a foray back to family roots in Scotland, Gloucestershire or the Home Counties, but this was depressing as their money could buy precious little. So they came back to Ireland and settled in places like Galway, Wicklow and west Cork, all exceptionally good hunting country, prompting Brendan Behan's definition of an Anglo-Irishman as a 'Protestant on a horse'.

'If the French noblesse had been capable of playing cricket with their peasants, their châteaux would never have been burnt,' G. M. Trevelyan suggested. The Na Shuler had not survived, and the Anglo-Irish could hardly take up hurley, a rather violent game a bit like hockey except you are allowed to raise the stick above the head and with it clouds of mud.

So some of the Ascendancy were happy to come back. The rich ones had never left, knowing that even in decline, nothing could change the essence of Ireland, the courtesy, the humour, they were in Ireland's thrall.

But they would find this newly independent race even more impenetrably inactive, full of the 'serpentine perversities of the Irish psyche' which allows terrorists to slip through a legal net with that deeply atavistic tribal loyalty; the smiling indulgence every time a rule is bent or a bureaucrat hoodwinked.

In Ireland today there is still an inordinate amount of goodwill towards the Ascendancy with their decaying country houses, their ruined abbeys and sometimes shamefully indulgent histories. But Ireland would be a dull place without them.

An endangered species, they invite affectionate head shakes – 'ah sure' and the implication is that anything is still possible with these hard-riding 'gentry'. If they were not so confident on horseback their quirky scarcity value might be less appreciated by the Irish, who also like the seedy wistful charm of the Ascendancy house, now faintly incongruous with its Gothic arch and entrance hall of imperial dusty splendour, sitting in the middle of grand unkempt parkland.

Sacheverell Sitwell, from a family of dedicated aesthetes to whom Ireland must have been an anathema, was yet sensitively aware of the island's natural disadvantages. In 1936 he wrote: 'Its shapes and contours make of it a paradise that is unhappy. And so it must forever remain, far away from the stream of life and with the sadness of all things that are a little remote from reality . . . This green country on the edge of the world, with nothing beyond it . . .'

16

MAJOR DOMO

Bells are chiming in the mellow red-stoned courtyard of the Plantation castle with its Adam interiors. A blissful scene, with fluttering doves. Here is all the gentleness of Ireland.

On the round pine table in the apricot coloured kitchen, an Irish crystal goblet, the rim marked with pink lipstick, a cigar band, a Pucci spectacles case and a jug of pink roses. In the larder, two huge joints of lamb, smoked trout and a huge salmon. The owners are at the Balmoral Show, a pleasant rural social event in Belfast, particularly for the landowning families and never missed, just like the Royal Show.

Suddenly a news bulletin, in this summer of 1988, brings a grim message to those at home: there has been a bomb at the Balmoral Show. Nobody killed but several injured. The house is barely fifteen miles from Belfast airport and near a road banded with sleeping policemen.

These landed families in the north, and there are only about fifty left out of 200, when asked what they do about security against terrorism, smile: 'We have a few rockets in the chimney and geese are excellent.'

They speak casually about incidents, the way other people might regretfully but unemotionally talk about a poor crop of courgettes. But the reality is that, behind all the civilized hospitality, as the host

chats engagingly by a fire lit with timber from the estate, a
Winchester Repeater and a Luger automatic rifle may be down near
the log basket, or a Smith and Wesson hidden behind an old damask
curtain.

It would be bad manners to have obvious security. There is a
feeling of delicate poise in some of these old houses in the north so
that, no matter how vulnerable, their doors are hardly ever locked.
It would be an insult to the villagers, to people they have known all
their lives, with whom there is an underlying bond as fine as silk
and as resilient. They will not allow artificial barriers created by the
tension to come between them.

When Sir Robin Kinahan, a popular Lord Lieutenant of the
County for many years, and his wife Coralie were guests of Tom
King, the Secretary of State for Ulster, at Hillsborough, there was a
sing-song after dinner.

'Tom likes us to sing round the piano' – a wry picture of the Ulster
Ascendancy singing grumpily for its supper. But Lady Kinahan, a
bonny woman who wears flamboyant Italian silks and is an accomplished painter, exhibiting alongside Annigoni, likes to sing.

Afterwards the major domo at Hillsborough approached Lady
Kinahan and congratulated her: 'I remember, Madam, you had a
fine voice when you used to sing in the bath in your aunt's house
where I was a footman' – unchanging Ireland.

The north tends to be a mixture of hard core titled ascendancy at
the top, next naval and military, and then the small landowning
class who feel distinctly upper-class in Ireland, but middle once in
England.

The even tenor of their lives goes on, an impression of
undisturbed serenity, time to read, time to paint. They have always
been a much more sensible lot in the north too, far away from
Viceregal junketings in Dublin. 'These northern families never
bankrupted themselves trying to make an impression; lives did not
revolve round the heady excitement of Dublin Castle.' As a result,
in the north you find less patched-up ostentation, fewer mothy
butlers, their boots smelling of dung. Yet when a boy from
northern Ireland was asked at school in England about his house, he
replied, 'It is very like Buckingham Palace.'

An idealized figure has been William Whitelaw, a traditional Tory with old-fashioned values, compassionate, unwavering in his beliefs and loyalty to the Crown. Links with the royal family are cherished, but there are complaints: 'We only get expendable royals here, never Prince Charles.' But in November 1988 the Princess Royal visited and openly spent a day in her courageous style in Belfast. When Killala was being included in a title for Prince Andrew, the late Marquess of Dufferin and Ava gently inquired: 'Isn't that one of ours?'

Many of these families in Northern Ireland though claiming exciting ancestry were in fact part of a scheme of voluntary emigration from the Lowlands of Scotland to Northern Ireland in the eighteenth and nineteenth centuries. Some of course had been close to the throne and were rewarded with extensive Plantation lands.

The Montgomerys, for example, one of the leading families in Northern Ireland, are directly descended from a first cousin of William the Conqueror. 'My ancestors played an outside right at the Battle of Hastings,' William Montgomery says wryly. 'Sotheby's man' for all Ireland, he also travels round the world for them in his soft leather black tasselled shoes looking at luscious property.

One ancestor, a great court favourite, reluctantly killed Henry II. 'He had an awful premonition about the King's death and pleaded with him, seeking every possible excuse not to be asked by him to joust,' but Henry II insisted. In the Place de Vosges jousting yard, a Montgomery lance would splinter the king's visor but the horrified Montgomery was pardoned by the dying king reeling from the wound in his eye.

These warring Montgomerys, who had a county named after them in Wales 'kept bopping people on the head'. Depending on which history you read, they were always either robbing, raping and pillaging or spreading peace, order and prosperity. Bill Montgomery thinks neither is the case: 'They were energetic opportunists.' His wife Lucy Montgomery, thin, animated, sits on the floor by a great fire, eating homemade pancakes and gooseberry jam and reading from an ancient Montgomery family recipe book:

'. . . for fits and convulsions . . . take the brain of a small child.'
They must carry on with their lives. She is defensive in her lyrical
praise of the arts in Belfast, and says: 'There is no crime here.'

There is another branch of Montgomerys up near the Giant's
Causeway at Ballybogey where a garden of herbs, flowers and fruit is
cherished at Ben Varden, with the letters from an ancestor, Lieutenant
Montgomery of the 5th Dragoon Guards who was at the Crimea.

'My Dear Mama, I am sorry to tell you the order came last night
to prepare for service . . . I hope you and Papa will not be in low
spirits about it . . . I enclose some bits of my hair . . .' followed by
a disapproving note from Varna, 22 August, about 'a horrid old
brute . . . who commands the cavalry out here'. His name was
Lord Lucan and the soldiers had nicknamed him Lord 'Look On'.

Hugh Montgomery put the letters down for a second and said he
knew the last Lord Lucan, who disappeared some years ago after
the murder of his children's nanny at their house in Eaton Terrace,
Belgravia. Montgomery thought his old friend would be most
unhappy if forced to live in exile: 'You see, he despised foreigners.'
Lucan loved foreign countries but was not at all keen on the people
who lived in them. The Montgomerys thought him great fun,
recalled how they always had to meet in restaurants and never went
to his home near Eaton Square 'his wife would never meet us'.
They also thought that he was so tall, so distinctive looking, he
could easily be recognized if he were abroad. Apparently the film
director Darryl Zanuck once spotted the Earl in a restaurant and,
taken with his moustache and Edwardian good looks, invited him
to be screentested for a film in which he would star opposite Shirley
Maclaine, but 'Lucky Lucan' was too wooden.

Montgomery picks up another letter, dated 3 October 1854 on a
happier note from Balaclava: '. . . this is a beautiful country, plenty
of grapes, walnuts, almonds, nuts . . .' But after the Fall of
Sebastopol, and praise for Florence Nightingale with 'her calm
quiet face' who was at the front dressing 800 wounds in eight hours,
there is a premonition which prompted the boy to write . . . 'Tell
papa he might as well get rid of the black greyhounds for me.' But
Robert James Montgomery survived to return to Ben Varden and
become the great-grandfather of Hugh.

17

A WORLD OF MY OWN

'True eccentrics are really only to be found amongst the aristocracy.' Dr David Weeks, a leading clinical psychologist at the Royal Edinburgh Hospital, has made a study of this delicious rare species and discovered only 130 genuine eccentrics out of 800 hopefuls. They are not easy to uncover; it is the breeding ground which is so important and the perfect place where eccentricity thrives is Ireland, land of fairies and crocks of gold.

Eccentrics are 'very creative, caring and invigorating people, and happier than most of us'. Elan is needed for eccentricity. The true eccentric needs an atmosphere of lightheartedness, an Owl and Pussycat skittishness and a dotty flamboyance. Ireland is in tune, a place where Lady Muskerry could deliberately take her snuffling peke to Mass and annoy fellow parishioners each Sunday, and the middle-aged woman who tried to offer herself as a virgin sacrifice by throwing herself from the top of a mountain could lead her red lobster around on a string.

Lord Northcliffe the celebrated Anglo-Irish newspaper proprietor never thought of himself as eccentric. In his newspaper empire, authoritarian messages were sent to editors and staff: 'I shall give you all hell when I get back' a thought many proprietors cherish but are not usually unwise enough to express in a telegram. Nervous young journalists of promise were chivvied by the

seventy-five-year-old press lord: 'Are you a shrimp or a brewer?'
Their career could be made or wrecked – it was either Washington
or Widnes – depending on their answer to this nonsensical question.
But if he was frightening one minute the next he would give
elaborate presents, fur coats for all the switchboard operators.

He raved in railway stations, not because trains were late but
because he was convinced that attempts were being made on his life
with a Perrier bottle, the fizzy mineral water marketed so successfully
by his brother St John Harmsworth. He would board a train smiling
beatifically, wearing a white hat and a sprig of white jasmine, and then
quite suddenly his face would cloud and discomfited railway officials
would get a final blast: 'God is a homosexual.'

On another occasion he became agitated about the moon.
'Someone has moved the moon,' he said crossly. 'What have you
done with it?' It was around the same time he expressed the view
that Jews were not liked, 'Especially in country society, as I know,'
he glowered. 'I have a house near Guildford.'

Ireland's premier baron, Lord Kingsale, is not an eccentric; he
just likes to work as a plumber poking about among rotting old
floorboards. A Hogarthian figure, this Irish peer educated at Stowe
is astute enough to know that his titles – he has fourteen – 'if I use
them people tend to think I am a firm of solicitors like that Irish firm
Argue and Phibbs' – give him an advantage over his rivals whatever
his ability to mend a ballcock. He is only too aware of the cachet of
having a peer look at your drains and runs a profitable plumbing
business from Bruton in Somerset.

He has a colourful social life, in between lucratively installing
nouveau 'country' kitchens in beautiful rickety old houses. For the
last few years this roly poly peer has been seriously looking for a
wife of childbearing age so the title can be carried on. He has a
strong sense of family, motto 'Truth Conquers All Good Things'.

The right wife 'should be half my age plus seven.' He is forty-
eight. There will be no castle for her, just a lighthouse, nothing is
left of the Kingsale estate. It is unlikely even if the Earl works
overtime, and the hourly call-out rates for plumbers can be
anything from six to thirty pounds, that the fifteen villages once
owned by the Kingsales could ever be recovered.

Extremely jolly and a little overweight, this former Guards officer is rather anxious about 'sireing' fairly soon. Otherwise the title will pass to Nevinson de Courcy, a sixty-eight-year-old cousin who works as a drains inspector in New Zealand. Obviously plumbing has caught the imagination of this family, which earned distinction when Sir John de Courcy conquered much of the north and west of Ireland for Henry II, who rewarded him by making him Earl of Ulster and Connaught. There were further rewards when the family supported Henry VIII in his wars with France and collected gifts which included a large and distinguished library.

In the hope of finding a healthy and uncomplicated bride Lord Kingsale went to Australia and set up a marriage agency in the Barrier Reef. 'Everyone was tested for Aids. I had a whale of a time, had first choice.' Michael Charles Cameron Claremont Constantine de Courcy, who has worked as an extra in *Cleopatra*, appeared on 'What's My Line', opened gourmet festivals, worked as a white hunter, admittedly only at Woburn Abbey, been a barman and was a wow as a bingo caller.

One rich Australian woman, Mrs Filinea Kennedy, offered to turn the ruins of the old castle into a shrine for world peace, and sent the impoverished peer an airline ticket to fly out to Queensland. She did not blench when he ordered a £75 bottle of wine. He likes to use phrases like 'mad as a cut snake' and she was entranced by his tales of lunching privately with the Queen Mother: 'wonderful, just like having dinner with your aunt'. 'S'truth,' said Filinea, but a marriage would not take place.

Lord Kingsale says: 'I don't think I'll bother. I am having too much fun. The title will go to this New Zealand cousin,' and he shakes his head, 'He is a tiny little chap.'

Finding an heir for a stately house in Ireland has sometimes driven Ascendancy mothers to dress up their daughters in mannish suits in the hope that wearing a collar and tie, plus fours or a bowler, might by magic turn them into a son. Sir Vere Foster's wife at Glyde Court in County Louth had two girls, but always pined for a son. As a result, his eldest daughter, with her mother's connivance, would insist on being called John, had her hair cut short by a local barber and wore boy's clothes graduating from short pants into long. It was working very well. People thought, what a nice well-mannered boy, never too rough or coarse, then quite out of the blue, a son was born. Lady Foster seemed never to get over the shock, would become extremely eccentric, and was happiest hibernating in the winter.

Cross-dressing was certainly not the rage in Ireland in the early 1900s; this was long before actor Quentin Crisp made it a voguey art form. Years later Raymond 'Tibby' Lecky-Browne-Lecky, always dressed as a girl by his mother, who wanted a daughter, was a wonderful sight sitting at a piano in soft white Donegal tweed suits made up and looking highly rouged. There were many theatrical evenings at Ecclesville, his family home in County Tyrone, when he was always stunning as Mrs Tanqueray.

'Mr Lecky-Browne-Lecky queened it . . .' Local newspapers would review these evenings in a delightfully innocent way. '. . . and at the conclusion of the party was the handing round of mince pies.' The ringed and jewelled Browne-Lecky hands would fly over the keys accompanying a friend, Miss Helen Bonaparte Wyse, on the piano. Wanting to do something a bit different to mark his eightieth birthday, this elderly spinster who liked to recall her ancestor's campaigns popped on her Bonaparte cocked hat and, tucking her hand inside her jacket in Napoleonic style, began a stirring recitation with a military flavour.

Altogether more straightforward were people like Lord Baltimore, who had vast estates in Ireland. He imported Nubian eunuchs into the servants' hall to keep watch on his harem. He usually travelled maharajah fashion with a complement of about eight women at any one time. Once as he swished into Vienna he was asked which one was Lady Baltimore. He huffily replied: 'A gentleman would never discuss his marriage with an outsider.'

Wives could be imprisoned in their own country houses. Lady Bellfield always vowed she was innocent, but her husband believed she was having an affair with his brother so locked her up, keeping her under house arrest for thirty years. Her children were not allowed to visit her and her luckless brother-in-law, ruined by the innuendo, died in a debtors' prison.

It is hard to imagine the opinion of the Nubians in an Irish servants' hall or of the hapless, imprisoned Lady Belvedere. The days of ancient bibulous butlers in Ireland are almost over, no more appearing in the dining room mellow from the careful decanting of several bottles of excellent claret, and breathing heavily in the hostess's ear suggesting marriage. 'Of course I accepted him,' Lady Caledon, Field-Marshal Alexander's mother, said and told him to continue serving. And it was all forgotten the next day.

Sadly today there is no longer that much good wine left in the cellar, and few of the whiskery maids and butlers who made life so amusing and unpredictable in Irish country houses – like the butler at Fota who sleekly followed with a decanter of whiskey on a silver salver as the Colonel rushed to help a hen being savaged by a red setter.

Nowadays the gardener has to change quickly at places like Glin, and a rosy complexion sits above the butler's white shirt as he serves Americans with egg mousse and handles the salmon as deftly as he might a rose with secateurs.

Owners loved their houses fiercely although they might describe them disparagingly as 'bucolic baroque'. Ecclesville became an old people's home eventually, and sadly, as happens so often in Ireland, Raymond Lecky-Browne-Lecky became an inmate in his own ancestral home, swishing in with an elegant wardrobe of tweeds and velvets. It is hard to know which was worse. Lord Massy moved with his wife into a chilly one-storey gate-lodge and watched the formal gardens go completely wild and trees sprout out of the conservatory roof.

Some stayed on in the old house and, with consummate dignity, would totter down avenues choked with weeds and brambles which grow at a triffidian rate in Ireland, to a servant's cottage pretending to inquire about the ancient groom's lumbago, but really wanting the warmth of a turf fire. Others simply took to their beds for the winter.

Transport was reduced to a pony and trap or infirm Renault 4 or Mini, all driven with a certain lack of regard for brake linings and clutch plates. Two years after an unceremonious ejection from Killyon Manor, County Meath, Lady Susan Carew has been living in a gate house near a car park minutes away from the ancestral home she shared with Sir Rivers Carew.

Eccentricity flourishes in impecunious isolation in these chilly houses. A few brandies late at night and oratory would flow: 'Why should we do anything for posterity?' Sir Boyle Roche asked the Speaker of the Irish House of Commons. 'What has posterity ever done for us?' But his best parliamentary sally was his belief that: 'No man could be in two places at once, barring he was a bird.'

His view of foreigners, particularly the French, was one of deep suspicion. 'If French principles take root in Ireland,' he very much feared, 'we will come down to breakfast one morning and find our severed heads on the table staring us in the face.'

What could be more natural or charming in Ireland than a belief in fairies? The elderly fifth Duchess de Stacpoole was in no doubt she had seen them on her Connemara doorstep.

The Stacpooles, a Norman French family who were staunch Catholics, came to Ireland in 1066 but, forced to give up their estates in Cromwellian times, fled back to France, Italy and Germany. The Duke of Stacpoole's title is papal, a reward from the Vatican to an ancestor in Italy in the eighteenth century.

The Duchess, widowed and in her eighties, found the fairies appealingly mischievous, moving inkwells on to the floor and lifting the first Duke of Stacpoole's portrait off the wall without ever harming it. A large grandfather clock fell face upwards. Irish houses all have that sweet melancholy sound of chiming grand-father clocks which spell Georgian silver teapots, cucumber sandwiches, white lace trolley cloths, chocolate cake and bone china.

The Duchess, who defied her mother by becoming a Roman Catholic, was charmed by two fairies. 'One was a little goat coming towards me, and I said to my niece Hilary: "I haven't seen a goat here for years" but Hilary did not see anything at all.' On another occasion it was a little blond boy. '. . . he had lovely corn-coloured hair, but when I put my hand out he wasn't there.'

'They don't frighten me at all,' she said, and talked about a 'most beloved fairy, you talk to him but he doesn't listen.'

The house, the Duchess said, has never known any sorrow or tragedy, and she continued: 'I live happily in a world of my own, absolutely.'

18

STEAMING INTO HAPPINESS

A happy path of bluebells, yellow flag iris, spotted wild orchids in the spring, imperious foxgloves and camelias as old as the century in summer leads the way to Shane's Castle, County Antrim. Raymond Clanaboy O'Neill, the fourth Earl, is at home.

A puckish figure in dungarees, he boards a beloved steam engine to go round the estate which sits prettily on the shores of Lough Neagh. He is fifty-six and was once one of the most eligible men in Britain and one of the band of Northern Ireland peers in love with Princess Alexandra. Attentive and humorous, a smile, however, is rarely allowed more than a hover.

His mother was the intriguing Anne Fleming, formerly Anne Charteris. Cousin of the Earl of Wemyss, she married three times, first his father Lord O'Neill in 1932, then Lord Rothermere, the newspaper proprietor, and finally she ran off with Ian Fleming, author of the James Bond novels.

The O'Neill train meanders through meadows and woodland of sycamore and willow. There is a flash of blue as a kingfisher skims by; swans compete for space on the water though it is the largest freshwater lake in the British Isles. 'Nearly as big,' the locals tell you proudly, 'as Lake Geneva.'

While Lord O'Neill is crazy about trains, his passion is not quite in the league of the train spotters in voluminous khaki shorts in

Above: Lady Mollie Cusack Smith, former Huntsman and Master of the Galway Blazers, relishes her image as an elegant shocker. Augustus John, admiring her youthful, pale skin and dark hair, christened her 'The Tulip of Tuam'.

Left: Lady Mollie in frilly lace disguising a tomboyish spirit; she seemed to prefer her leprechaun toy to the more conventional china doll. Her taste in stockings has not changed in six decades.

Opposite page: Lord Strathloch was a clergyman in Norfolk, England, when he suddenly discovered God was a woman. 'This, of course, changed everything.' His sister, Olivia Robertson, who had a mystic experience on a train to Bolton, and Lord Strathloch set up a temple to Isis at the family home, Clonegal Castle, in Enniscorthy, where they worship daily.

Left: Still game at 78, Mrs 'Melon' Daly appears to have no grey hair among her springy auburn curls. Amber beads set off an expensive tweed suit; red varnished nails rest on a beautiful past.

Below: Lord Dunsany – 'We go back to Noah' – and his wife Lady Dunsany are ready at a moment's notice to dash inside their fortified castle – the Irish climate has no surprises for them. 'I came home to die,' he says, 'but was a bit too early.

Inset: A door at Clonegal Castle which Miss Robertson believes 'opens the way to heaven'. On an ordinary day it leads onto the lawn.

Above: Cratloe, the seat of the Stafford O'Briens overlooking the Shannon, is a perfect example of the seventeenth-century Irish long house, unique in western Europe.

Left: Dunguaire is a place of enchantment on the west coast of Ireland, a restored fifteenth-century tower house, where there are harp recitals and readings from Yeats and James Joyce.

Right: Lord O'Neill, once one of Britain's most eligible young men and an escort of Princess Alexandra, is today an ardent steam enthusiast, and likes to take visitors to Shane's Castle in County Antrim in his favourite trains, 'Nancy' and 'Shane'.

Below: At 85, after the huge success of her latest book, *Loving and Giving*, Molly Keane was asked if she was working on another novel about the horse-mad Anglo-Irish; she replied, 'Oh no, child, I'm a barren old trout now.' A cult figure, she is happiest at home in Ardmore, County Waterford, with her dog Hero and admiring the deep pink hydrangeas.

Below: The astutely commercial Lord Altamont, heir to the 12th Marquess of Sligo, reads a bedtime story to his youngest daughter, Alannah, who realizes that 'Pinkie', the giant rabbit, may get more of her father's attention during the hours when Westport, the family home near Galway, is open to the public. He seems undisturbed by the presence of a crazed black bear.

Left: Lord Erne and h[is] Swedish wife, Anna, have learnt to live with intense security at the[ir] home, Crom Castle in County Fermanagh. The apparent tranquillity of the library is deceptive. Behind these rare leather-bound books, electronic devices are ready to bleep warnin[g] of a terrorist attack.

Above: Lord Dunleath copes stoically with dry rot but feels for the stags who look outraged by their removal from their rightful place high up on the walls of Ballywalter, County Down.

Lady Jennifer Bernard
takes a wry view of her
stately home, Castle
Bernard, County Cork,
burnt down during the
Troubles. 'I think,' she
suggests constructively,
'it is more fun imagining
how it must have been.'

Above: 'The Gay Mice' is how these three tiny, aristocratic, hospitable Blake sisters are known in the west of Ireland. The eldest, a widow, Mrs Leila McGarel Groves, enjoys smoking and visits to England; in the middle, the baby of the family, is Jane, an artist and unmarried; next to her, sister June and her husband Ian Bowring Spence. 'We love it here,' he says. 'Wouldn't live in England for all the world.'

Left: Grand times – a delicate trio: Norah and Leila Storr with their mother, the Hon Mrs Lycester Storr, who matched her daughters' petite charm when she presented them at Court in 1926.

India who at high moments of excitement open a can of vintage engine steam gathered on the line to Simla. 'A party of us did go to India to see the trains,' he admits cautiously. His enthusiasm dates back to an O-gauge clockwork railway set laid out on the drawing room floor for the infant Clanaboy. He graduated to an electric Trix-Twin railway with which he reluctantly parted aged sixteen.

When the old steam trains were being phased out on the Northern Ireland railway he was delighted to step in and save several. A great favourite and the largest locomotive is 'Nancy', another is 'Shane', a workhorse which 'did not like the flimsy tracks over Clonsast bog,' he says, giving them personality. The line from Belfast to Dublin has not lost all romance: the pink ticket gets punched with three little hearts by the collector.

Blackheaded gulls and sea swallows nest on an old concrete platform used in World War II for testing torpedoes. Now a skittish tufted duck makes the loudest noise in this dreamy stretch of water.

It may all look like Toytown, a Gothic Castle in an idyllic setting with a private railway line, platforms, signals and stations, a nature reserve in a lush part of County Antrim, but as soon as you get near the Castle, high security bars and checks speak for the tension in Ulster. These days even friends and relations hardly dare visit. 'We have had so many false dawns,' Lord O'Neill says, and like so many in the north, he too is disillusioned these days and far less hopeful.

His uncle Terence O'Neill was Prime Minister in the Government of Northern Ireland between 1963 and 1969 and seen as a 'charismatic' figure; but he became disillusioned and was made a Life Peer choosing the romantic title, Lord O'Neill of the Maine. Another uncle, Hugh O'Neill, was the first speaker at Stormont and became Lord Rathcarne, living to be a hundred years old. His grandson lives in Claggan, originally the family shooting lodge, and is a bouncy character responsible for the unexpectedly cheery atmosphere at Aldergrove airport in Belfast, which surprises. Airy and pleasant and apparently carefree, it reassures tense visitors. He is also a partner in trendy St Quentin's Brasserie in London.

In 1963, Raymond O'Neill married Georgina Montagu-Douglas-Scott, a relation of Princess Alice, Dowager Duchess of Gloucester and a niece of the Duchess of Buccleuch. They have three children: Shane, aged twenty-two, at Cirencester, Tyrone, twenty-one, at Salford Business Studies and Rory in Australia on a cotton plantation. 'My wife,' Lord O'Neill says, 'is a champion gardener. We are both fanatical. We garden away at our little house in Wiltshire.' Lady O'Neill was even trying to make flowers grow at Hillsborough for Tom King, Secretary of State for Northern Ireland, creating a little tranquillity in his garden at least.

Shane's Castle has been burnt down twice. The original O'Neill Castle down by Lough Neagh was destroyed by fire in 1816 just as Nash had finished work on the terrace and conservatory, bringing the elegance of his Carlton House Terrace triumph to this leafy part of Ulster.

Only in Ireland could a ghost be blamed for a fire. This one was believed to have been started by a resident Banshee, an Irish wailing woman ghost, who was outraged when the O'Neill family failed to leave a bedroom empty for her during a large house party.

'It was actually a jackdaw's nest at the top of a virtually unused chimney which set the fire off.' This is Lord O'Neill's sensible explanation, though not completely convincing. By 1865 Lanyon, another brilliant architect, had redesigned the castle, giving it a Gothic flavour impressive enough to host a ball for Prince Arthur, Duke of Connaught, on his eighteenth birthday in 1869.

But by 1922 Shane's Castle was in flames again. A group of Republican sympathisers had rowed across the lake in small boats, bullied a pantry boy into carrying petrol up to the Castle from the garage store and held estate workers at gunpoint.

'They were quite polite. My great-grandfather was eighty-two at the time and in a wheelchair; he decided to save the pictures rather than anything else.' O'Neill is not bitter but, almost worse than losing all the furniture was the loss of old family papers in the fire. It broke the old man's heart.

Slightly tongue in cheek, Lord O'Neill says: 'But we have a nice painting to show us how the house must have looked.' This is a rather naive painting of the old village Edenduffcarrick and the Castle done by someone sitting on the shores of the Lough.

The present estate office is in what was the servants hall of the second castle. In 1958, the large modern house where Lord O'Neill lives now was completed; he had used the butler's house in the grounds while the building was going on. He can still enjoy the eerie sight of the skeleton of the ruined original castle which looks dramatic and gaunt at sunset.

Sharing the philosophical attitude of his fellow Ulster peers, Lord O'Neill says, 'Security, well, if they are going to wait in a hedgerow to pick you off we are used to it. Anyone can be shot by a machine-gun or blown up in your car.' It is a burden, 'There can be tension.' He always has to be on his guard remembering not to walk in too exposed an area of Shane's three and a half thousand acres, wear bullet-proof vests, not something Cirencester Royal Agricultural College could have prepared this young aristocratic sprig for in the carefree days of 1955–6. But he farms seriously; it is lush grade II land and he concentrates on grass, milk and sheep.

Catholics and Protestants have always worked alongside each other at the castle, where there has been a long tradition of mixed tenantry. It is forgotten sometimes outside Ulster how much delicate harmony there can be between these religious groups.

Lord O'Neill had the fairly unrewarding task of being Chairman of the Northern Ireland Tourist Board, which he joined in 1975. He is shrewdly aware of ways of attracting tourists and every few years there is a worldwide Gathering of the Clan O'Neill at the Castle. The last, in June 1986, was a riotous success attended by a Portuguese O'Neill, the late Jorge O'Neill, who lived outside Lisbon and, watched by Ulster noblemen and Ian Moncrieff of that Ilk, was solemnly declared Head O'Neill of Clanaboy, though not entitled to Shane's Castle.

Hopeful letters flood in from round the world, especially from aspiring O'Neills longing for kinsmanship with this diffident earl who wears a sports jacket of elderly distinction with impeccably worn leather edging. They are sent a Clan newsletter with its sketch of the naughty O'Neill banshee on the cover.

'Clanaboy,' they say. 'Gee, sounds like thatta boy.' To Anna M. Creekman of Strunk, Kentucky and Mrs Lanette O'Neal who enclosed a photo showing a careworn grandmother, Lord O'Neill meticulously explains how 'the O'Neills are one of the oldest traceable families left in Europe, a branch of the ancient royal Irish

High Kings . . . We became Anglo-Irish and Protestant in 1600 during the Plantations and accepted British rule.' Most other Irishmen thought this monstrous. The family then split, dividing into the Clanaboys and Tyrone O'Neill's, the branch of the family who left Ulster in the Flight of the Earls. But the Clanaboys stayed put.

When he is not being an engine driver or under-water fishing, Lord O'Neill has other toys: a Mercedes SSK, one of the most glamorous sports cars in the world. 'Only nine have ever been made; it belonged to a Persian who had bought it on behalf of an Ayatollah.' Also in the O'Neill stable is an old bullnosed Morris Cowley, an Invicta and a Jaguar SS100. It is faintly ironic, he thinks, that in this uneasy province the BMW distributor in nearby Ballymena should be the most successful in the United Kingdom.

The dread amongst the superstitious at Shane's Castle is that one day the eerie rather sphinxlike black head in the tower near the lake will topple and with it the O'Neill family come to an end. It is rather hard to find this mask which is carved in profile near the top of one of the walls of the old castle.

Even the family coat of arms, the celebrated Red Hand, has about it a quirky Irishness. The legend tells how the captain of a Viking ship sailing towards Ulster told his crew that the first man who touched the shore with his right hand would be the owner of this scenic coastline.

Neil, one of the sailors, seeing he was losing the race, immediately sliced off his right hand and threw it from the coracle so it landed neatly on the shore well ahead of his rival. The bloody Red Hand of O'Neill would become the emblem for Ulster.

During the Plantations of Ulster, James I was rather taken with the Red Hand emblem and chose it as the insignia for the new northern baronets he was creating. Their titles were a snip at £1000 each, but the insignia has always been a trifle maladroit. A dopey herald transcribed a left hand instead of a right.

19

WHAT HERITAGE?

'Shall I bring you a cup of tea and a few auld scones?' A turf fire is burning in the Library and the glow throws a warm light on the William Ashford picture of Ascendancy visitors arriving for a picnic by boat at a castle in Lough Erne while liveried footmen carry hampers ashore. The house has all the flavour of a cherished Regency mansion and in two of the windows are Canova plaster casts given by the Pope to the Prince Regent who passed them on to Cork art connoisseurs.

Fota, its Norse-sounding name which literally means 'warm turf, warm sod', is a flamboyantly enlarged hunting lodge which once belonged to the Smith-Barry family. Philip de Barry arrived with Henry II and all the lush pasture land for miles around Fota where cattle graze like a scene in a Victorian painting was Barryland, home of one of the more distinguished Irish Anglo-Norman families.

Fota has the classic background of many important Irish houses. Built in the eighteenth century in English Regency style, 'Foaty' as it was affectionately known in the 1820s became a great place for carousing parties in the days of 'John the Magnificent' Barrymore, who had a special decanter which could hold nine bottles of wine. It was his son who created the Arboretum and a temple, a Fern garden and an Orangery, set up a place for wild animals, cheetahs, rare antelopes, monkeys, orange-crested parrots and flamingoes. When he visited Fota two years after the Famine the condition of the drive was so bad that his carriage had to be dragged by labourers up to the house.

In the next generation Arthur Hugh married the fourth Earl of Dunraven's sister Lady Mary. There was no finer place to bring home a Wyndham-Quin bride than to the luscious 27,828 acres which he owned in 1878. But, as so often happens in Irish stories, there is the malevolence of an offended woman, in this case an Irish wet-nurse.

When the Smith-Barry's first baby was born prematurely the longed for heir had to be put in the care of a local woman. But such was the fury of this local girl, who was dismissed when the English wet-nurse arrived, that she cursed the family. Her parting words on the doorstep were that there would never again be a direct male heir at Fota. And the baby died within a year.

But at the start of the nineteenth century, they had bred a wild and lascivious lot of heirs. They were not model landlords though at about this time they had some 79,000 acres spread over thirty parishes. Richard, who became Lord Barrymore, was nicknamed Hellgate by his great friend the Prince Regent, later George IV. His brother Henry was subtly named Cripplegate by the Prince for his clubfoot, while the youngest, Augustus, was less originally called Newgate.

These three often joined the Prince for Regency rompings when the Prince was lampooned by cartoonists as an obscene voluptuary. Eating gargantuan meals, with chamberpots overflowing, they smashed windows, misled frantic travellers, loved cockfights, boxing and gambling and were relentless in their search for nubile maidservants.

Augustus Smith-Barry rode his horse to the top of Mrs Herbert's house in Brighton – perhaps in the hope of terrifying her into submitting to his friend the florid Prince's attentions. The Catholic widow Maria Fitzherbert would insist on a form of marriage before agreeing to become the royal libertine's mistress. Not long afterwards he fell in love with Lady Jersey, a beautiful grandmother.

The Smith-Barrys were wealthy and contempt for the value of money was learnt early on by the orphaned boys; Richard was given £1000 pocket money at school. Their sister Caroline was hardly a shy, demure hostess for the Prince Regent. He called her Billingsgate because she had such a foul tongue.

Today Fota is comfortable, rich, with a pink stencilled ceiling in the drawing room which looks like a rose tapestry and walls ornate with gold; it sits on a lush island on the outer edge of Cork Harbour. A happily informal Robinsonian garden, a riot of pink and blue, rhododendrons and the Arboretum; its elegant, cantilevered staircase with brass banisters are inviting on a grey November afternoon.

The brass Greek key design glimmers; the butler's cupboard is rich mahogany; there is a smell of lavender on the highly polished Irish fetlock furniture. Everywhere you look you think perhaps a table is going to move away on its deer's feet. The original pale blue embossed wallpaper reaches to an ornate ceiling with a delicate rose and massive brass poles hold back tasselled drapes.

Stately homes being open to the public are still a rarity in Ireland and the old instincts of hospitality die hard. Instead of a crisp National Trust Sloane trusty – 'something to do now the children are in London' – in her trim Jaeger separates or one of the confident, articulate guides at Blenheim, the Duke of Marlborough's Palace at Woodstock, a cheery girl with red hair says: 'I am Teresa Boyce.' She tells you the scallop is the symbol of friendship and asks, 'Is your tea hot enough, too weak, too strong?'

During the tour, and the house is chiefly a gallery for a superb collection of paintings – Breughels, James Lathams, 'the Irish Van Dyck', but mainly idealized Irish landscapes – she chatters away artlessly. 'Walter Raleigh, now wasn't he the wan who brought cigarettes and the potato to Ireland?' and says the last visitor was a nun who had taught Eddie Gallagher, the IRA terrorist who raided the home of Sir Alfred and Lady Beit and held them at gunpoint. 'The nun said, "It was all that Rose Dugdale's fault" ' – she had a baby by him and now works for the underprivileged.

'In the dining room look out for the smiling lions – they are the Irish ones, the solemn ones are English.' Teresa's ingenuous babbling ends abruptly when a poised and knowledgeable Melanie Annesley takes over. Her parents own some of Ireland's finest gardens, lush with lily ponds, secret romantic paths and a scented walled garden of such old-fashioned prettiness. But typically in Ireland where things grow so wildly, shrubs become like giant rhubarb so you can hardly see the meandering River Awbeg.

Lord Barrymore and his neighbour Richard Grove Annesley were two of the dedicated handful of landowners who created beautiful gardens in Ireland. But amongst the few it was fiercely competitive. Somerville and Ross wrote of Lady Dysart gaining an advantage when she sniffily noticed, 'the weak battalions in his army of bedding plants, the failures in the ranks of his roses'.

However there were no failures at Annes Grove, where magnolias and rhododendrons leap to such bushy and extravagant heights the pretty eigthteenth-century house is almost hidden. Cork has an almost tropical climate so equatorial shrubs bask in the exuberant fertility of these havens for butterflies and bees. Cabbage Palm, Polynesian tree ferns and Philesia with coral pink bell-shaped flowers from Chile thrive happily in a familiar wet luxuriance.

Fota and Annes Grove are a tribute to those eighteenth-century botanist landowners. It was not easy then to get rare and exotic shrubs, but Annesley and Barrymore were generous in swopping rare ferns and other exotic finds. Today Richard Grove's grandson Patrick Annesley tries to keep the tradition going. He gave up a job in publishing in London to come back to Ireland though he and his wife Jane fear that the cost may be prohibitive and their daughters may never be able to share the heritage.

They are droll about the perils of opening the gardens to the public, who often come with spades. Nuns are a menace but are sometimes caught out by a torrential storm. From their primly carried umbrellas, when opened up, will tumble deutzias (flowering shrubs from China) and azaleas.

Patrick Annesley tries to keep an unobtrusive eye open and is more than happy to help with some horticultural query. On one occasion he was alarmed when he saw a large magnolia branch come crashing down and a flushed visitor quite shamelessly told him over her shoulder, 'I want to dig up dem pinky fellas.' All around people were helping themselves to flowers and 'one lady dropped cuttings from her knickers.'

He is dedicated and carrying on the old tradition, helping neighbours like Lady Bandon to replace every damaged shrub.

The gardens open from Easter to September, and the family drolly refer to the 'year of the sweet paper' or 'the year of the chamber pot'. Their younger daughter found a French boy peeing against the Regency front door.

Their daughter Melanie, filling in time before going to Durham University, gave a refreshingly off-beat, well-informed commentary on the pictures at Fota. She had just finished at St Columba's, where the Warden, instead of harshly forbidding smoking, put up an effective cutting from *Vogue* which warned the girls that 'smoking cigarettes can lead to the growing of a moustache'. Standing in front of a Richard Rothwell portrait of a knowing-looking flower seller in Dublin, Melanie wondered if, when the dark haired wanton opened up her hand, it might not reveal a small amount of crack.

There is something gloomy and oppressive about the great black gates at Fota with a castle and griffins, two seated wolves and the uncompromising motto 'Boutez en Avant' – 'kick your way through'. The slow decline set in a long time ago, though Fota was much loved by the Hon. Dorothy Bell, the last Lord Barrymore's daughter and her husband. After her death in 1975, as there was no male heir, 775 acres were sold to Cork University who put a solar energy plant on the farm; a wildlife park opened in 1983 and a bee farm was launched.

The interior would become the responsibility of an aesthetic dreamer, Richard Wood, as an act of philanthropy, and he filled the house with his personal collection of pictures. Then Fota opened with a fanfare to the public.

Cork University had begun to talk seriously about building time-share Swedish chalets in the grounds. 'As if the word Swedish makes it all acceptable,' Wood snorts, outraged. He has bankrupted himself to save Fota. 'It is our heritage,' cries this tall, balding young man whose brisk impressive walk has a touch of White Rabbit urgency. Abstemious, he ate a trout so meticulously that, if you had not seen the bone taken away, you would have been seriously worried.

Unmarried, this gentle man is not what you would expect in a family business which supplies slurry and sewerage pipes, calf and pig slats and concrete blocks to farmers, but also the money which made him an art connoisseur.

Born in 1945 into a liberal Protestant background, he was educated at St Columba's in Dublin, Ireland's main Protestant public school. A squat Gothic building, where paths drip with leaves, it sits in the shadow of the Dublin mountains but the gloom is only on the outside. In the days before the present enlightened Warden, David Gibb, 'Jews but not Catholics' were admitted. But today in chapel, which is compulsory, Catholics sit alongside large Nigerians in lacy surplices not quite long enough, singing lustily with 'wee frees' and Calvinists, baby Stacpooles and Fitzgeralds and Montgomerys and Annesleys the hymns everyone loves: 'Be thou my Vision' and 'Just as I am, Young Strong and Free'.

It is a school with old-fashioned standards and 'The children are basically nice,' the Warden says. 'They have a sort of innocence and perhaps they are not as intellectually trained or as competitive as they might be in England. But they are poised and articulate and develop a love of reading; the emphasis is on literature.' Politically the school is centre right.

A quirky custom at St Columba's is that cricket is played in the cloisters. 'It is not awfully good for their cricket,' says the Warden whose wife is a bubbly member of the Bernard family, sharing the same Ascendancy background as many of the pupils. She tends to dash away from solemn meetings with parents crying, 'I've lost my pussy' as she sets off in pursuit of a ghastly hairless Indian dog.

'We want children to be happy rather than rich,' Mr Gibb says in his study exotic with Shiva gods, fine rugs and books. He came back from India in 1964, was offered a job at Rugby but came to Ireland in 1972.

Richard Wood went on to read history and economics at Trinity, coming under the influence of the vigorous Ann Crookshank, Professor of Fine Arts, who spurred other young men into a dream of saving Ireland's heritage.

She liked him, thought him talented and he went on buying expeditions with her and learnt about hanging pictures. He adored his father who owned several Grand National winners.

In 1971 Richard felt confident enough about a picture he had seen to ask his father diffidently: 'Do you think you could ever lend me a couple of hundred. I've seen a picture in Dublin . . .' His father, who may not have been tutored by Professor Crookshank, said, 'Next time I am in Dublin, I'll come along.'

'I did not tell him about the one I really wanted which was 900 pounds.' However when his father arrived in Dublin they went to the gallery and prowled around. The old man, who 'had a good eye for a horse, a pig and a cow,' instinctively found his way to the best picture and, of course, the most expensive one, and, turning to his son, said decisively, 'That is the one.' This first picture hangs in Fota along with the rest of Richard Wood's collection, which began that day and is now thought to be the most important outside the National Gallery of Ireland.

Meanwhile the family business prospers – even today Richard Wood has a very fine herd of Gawsworth cattle, which he shows off from a muddy BMW. One of the oldest in the British Isles, it celebrated its Golden Jubilee in 1987. Richard, who would inherit John A. Wood, wisely did an agricultural course in 1963. 'I wanted to know how the world economics worked.' World perhaps but not domestic.

He walks round his home, a charming old country house high up over valleys around Cork, picks a peach from the wall in the kitchen garden and waves to his mother who is in a wheelchair. The house has the bleakness of a place from which all the good furniture and pictures have been moved to Fota and there are patches on the walls.

Richard Wood has lavished a great deal of personal money on Fota. He cheerfully admits he is broke and the answer is 'Yes' when people like Arabella Burton, wife of the Duke of Devonshire's agent, airily ask at a party, 'Are you really broke, Richard – how broke?' Yet Fota is his dream and, he thinks, 'epitomizes the age of reason and enlightenment'.

There is a tall grey daunting wall around Fota, but these days as the struggle goes on between the aesthetes led by Richard Wood and the commercially minded academics, children from Cork, as if knowing its elegance may be short lived, chase in and pull the peacocks' tail feathers – 'great gas'.

'What heritage?' asks a President of Cork University and Wood shrugs in disbelief. Happily, because it is Ireland, inertia, for once a blessing, gives Wood time to lecture and raise support. As a last resort he has vowed to send his pictures to the Ulster Museum rather than leave them at Fota. 'When the bulldozers go in, my paintings come out,' he has warned; a galling challenge for those Irish speaking academics.

As Richard Wood says, 'For the time being what is happening is that nothing is happening and I am delighted.' How Irish, how maddening, how lovable, how surreal.

20

NANNY

The very thought of parting with Crom Castle in County Fermanagh can make Lord Erne burst into tears. 'I have a passion for Crom. I love it like a person.' Crom, with its ancient oak trees, a lake dotted with ivory water lilies, is a place of enchantment. A small canopied boat drifts past high banks full of wild flowers; honeybees and rare purple butterflies dart round the yellow iris. This dream castle, in such a peaceful setting, is near one of the most volatile spots in Northern Ireland.

Lord Erne's grandfather once could boast that his land was so extensive, stretching from Donegal through Mayo, that he could almost be in Dublin without ever leaving his own acres. 'That all changed,' his grandson explains, 'with the Land Act at the end of the nineteenth century when everyone's estate was compulsorily reduced to a maximum of a thousand acres.' So it was with a great intake of breath that Lord Erne, who bravely flies the Lord Lieutenant's flag from the top of his castle, approached the National Trust in 1986 with a view to selling his much loved heritage.

In the grounds, it is believed there is a crock of gold being guarded by an Ulster branch of 'leprechauns', and while Lord Erne could do with the contents, family legend has it that the wee folk have stipulated that if the gold is ever found it could be the end of the Crichton family.

'I could have "rattled along" with 1000 acres in my lifetime, but my son would have been forced to change; things had been unchanged here since 1840. It is all a bit of a mild headache. I am a bit worried about the future, but never ever would I live anywhere else.'

The National Trust wanted the land, but not the Castle. Lord Erne is still proprietorial, but protests: 'I never went around saying "This is my Castle." I see myself as being a tenant for a lifetime.' Ever the affable Lord of the Manor, known to friends as Harry, and in the local dialect as 'Hurry', he likes to keep an eye on the lake. 'Good morning, good morning,' he says in a jolly patrician way to some birdwatchers admiring four nests of Canada geese. Full of enthusiasm and goodwill, he points out the oldest yew tree in Europe. The bird watchers smile, not quite sure who this amiable fellow might be, a man with a tendency to use old fashioned 'Holy Cow' slang.

Crom has a picturesque long winding avenue, where the roots of the handsome oaks stretch under mossy grass carpeted in the spring with coveted daffodils. On past estate cottages, stable yards and a large walled garden, suddenly the Castle appears, and Lord Erne is running down the steps, hand warmly outstretched. It is baffling, as there is no gatekeeper to telephone ahead.

The castle is filled with closed–circuit security television cameras, outlandish, raw and modern in the library, incongruous against rare leatherbound books and under old family portraits. Guests are spotted as soon as they cross the cattle grid.

Bravery marks these landowners in the north. As Lord Lieutenant, Lord Erne is vulnerable, he attends a lot of ceremonial occasions. 'Driving in spurs is rather difficult,' he says drolly; 'I open and shut a lot of things.' He missed the bomb at the Enniskillen Memorial service in November 1987 by two minutes. As Lord Lieutenant he is, he says sadly, attending 'rather a lot of funerals' these days.

These Northern Ireland peers give every appearance of normality, marking their social calendars with Henley, Ascot, a royal garden party or two and, of course, sittings at the House of Lords. The Duke of Abercorn is one of only two present dukes, the other being the Duke of Buccleuch, to have sat in the House of Commons. The fifth Duke of Abercorn, Northern Ireland's resident Duke, was Ulster Unionist MP for Fermanagh and South Tyrone from 1964 to 1970. The Abercorns have always been staunch supporters of Ulster Unionism. The ninth Duke of Buccleuch, who is fifty-six, does not think this unusual, and explains: 'He sat in the House of Commons before his father died in 1979.' The Duke of Buccleuch, as the Earl of Dalkeith, also sat in the Commons, from 1960 until 1973, so did the fifth Duke of Westminster, as Colonel Grosvenor.

A plane takes off leaving volatile trouble spots in the province, Bogside, the Shankill and the Falls, where even chimney pots look like weapons, and tension sparked by anger and murder can ricochet to sleepy, charming green estate villages.

These commuting peers have been warned never to do things on a regular basis; their windows are usually bullet proof. A sunny Northern Ireland peer may be settling down to a cream tea on the Midland shuttle to England, apparently relaxed. If not a proficient soldier, he is certainly trained to be exceptionally alert, subtly watchful of other passengers, with a military fitness and more than exceptional ability to handle a gun.

In a navy Aertex shirt and casual trousers, Lord Erne, who is now fifty-two, sits outside on the terrace at Crom on a bright morning. Lady Erne, graceful in seersucker skirt, white blouse and espadrilles, lies disconsolately on the grass. 'I feel so helpless,' her husband says; her brother had just drowned in a boating accident in Sweden.

His second wife Anna is Swedish, gentle and beautiful. Bells from the tiny church in the middle of the lake chimed romantically as they went by boat to his second wedding. There are no children by this second marriage. Lord Erne's first wife, Camilla Roberts, a wing-commander's daughter, became rather keen on UFOs, encouraged by landowner Desmond Leslie, a devout believer in these flying objects. They had five children, Damian twenty-eight, Viscount Crichton; three daughters, Cleone twenty-nine, Catherine twenty-six, Tara twenty-two, and another son John, now eighteen.

Lord Erne's first memories of Crom were school holidays from Eton when he came to see his grandfather, who had always gone by the autumn, saying it 'was indecent to be here after the leaves had left the trees'. He was three when his father was killed in the war in 1940. After Eton he did National Service in the Royal Navy and later joined the North Irish Horse, coming back as sixth Earl and taking over Crom in 1958.

Capital was poured into Crom: the land, overgrown and covered in rushes, was cleared, and electricity was installed on the estate. 'Now,' Lord Erne says wryly, 'they want central heating in the cottages.' He employs a staff of twenty-two, including a farm manager and a gamekeeper. He invested in 1000 pigs and built up the dairy herd.

This was before the Troubles accelerated in the north, when the Ernes could send their youngest to the local school. The only ripple and hint of things to come was when the Crom milking parlour was blown up. It was 'upsetting and inconvenient'. Otherwise it was a calm and happy time. But being at the local school, sitting at old-fashioned desks alongside the policeman's son and the game-keeper's children, created other problems. Lord Erne recalled being asked by his small son: 'Daddy what are you going to do today?' assuming he would say, 'I am going to work,' and puzzled by the reply: 'I am going to shoot snipe.' Asked 'Why?' – 'Because I'm me.' A sense of privilege is learnt early on.

Now the burden of running the estate at Crom has been lifted from Lord Erne's willing shoulders: 'I could not make it work.' Caught by inflation and 'the money we had to spend on modernization', he handed over to the National Trust. The lake is full of pike, perch and bream. It is easy enough to be seduced by Crom. It seems quite perfect, 1,350 rich, green acres in one of the prettiest parts of Northern Ireland, unspoilt land round Upper Lough Erne.

The hardest thing about handing over the estate was when Lady Erne asked the trust if they might still pick a few daffodils in the spring and were told: 'well, all right'.

There are only about fifty family estates left in the North. For the owners who stay on, it can be lonely. Fewer friends come from

England, scared by reports of isolated terrorist incidents. Yet if your car breaks down in Northern Ireland it is mended in minutes by a kindly passing motorist. On a dual carriageway into Belfast it seems a bit like Sicily: nice, new-looking cars seem abandoned on the verges. Everyone drives fast; lorries belt along tiny country roads.

Another dismaying sight is the desolate factories shut down; and saddest of all, the green sites with buttercups sprouting and big inviting I.D.B. signs: 'Won't you come and invest here?' and always the presence of silver grey armoured cars. Yet broken-down, boarded-up hotels still have a battered Georgian grace. You can be beguiled too by a beautifully deceptive stretch of tranquil blue water as you drop down into Belfast, only to be shocked by this town sealed off, at war, where a young girl in a wheelchair, dressed in jeans, propels herself at a furious rate to a theatre, where standards are exceptionally high.

If you leave your car unattended for a minute in a street in Antrim to run into a bank, you risk having it blown up by security forces. 'I've called the police, I'll have to put ye on a charge,' the warden says. Then the grim mouth turns up at the edges in a smile: 'If ye move fast, ye'll get away with it before they come.' There is always flexibility in Ireland, north or south, an impish conspiracy to bend the rules.

On the surface the Northern Ireland peers appear to lead lives as well-ordered as those of their squirearchical counterparts in Norfolk, Gloucestershire and Scotland, with estates equally well run.

Royal visits are a tonic which they love, and most Ulster peers seem half in love with Princess Alexandra. She is their ideal woman, a great favourite, her stately charm, that bitter sweet smile. But actually Princess Anne would be much better for them and their estates, and with her straight talking, no nonsense approach, she might even get north and south talking to each other sensibly.

'We are,' Lord Erne says, 'a close-knit lot. When there is a houseparty in the province, we tend to ring each other up, we are all friends, and say, "Who have you got?"'

The Ernes are selective in their socializing, and if people are . . . 'well,' he is too kind to say boring, uninteresting, 'we do not go.' They prefer to sit by huge log fires in winter, contained in the way of second marriages with time to enjoy each other's company.

'I hate people I don't like,' which is about the nastiest thing you will hear him say. Lord Erne is liked on both sides of the border, by the young soldiers on patrol, by the people in the village. 'Hurry Erne,' they will tell you, 'he's a nice fella.'

Lord Belmore, a neighbour, lives at Castlecoole, which is one of the most romantic houses in Northern Ireland and overlooks a lake full of greylag geese. A friend of Lord Erne's, they swop amusing experiences about the National Trust, each peer's attitude to this group of practical aesthetes being quite different.

Lord Belmore tends to see the Trust as an insensitive nanny, unlike Lord Erne, who sails above the tiny daffodil humiliations with ease and diplomacy.

Castlecoole with its serene Grecian grace and delicate façade of silvery Portland stone, once washed by men suspended in bosun's chairs, has an air of eternity, but is only a mile and a half south-east of Enniskillen, this northern flashpoint.

The trouble at Castlecoole started when the stonework began to look rather pockmarked after 200 years of persistent Irish damp, called locally 'soft rainfall', which meant it needed £3.2 million spent on a massive restoration programme.

Lord Belmore approached the National Trust, who bustled in full of good sense, saying Castlecoole would once again be as James Wyatt intended, with a little dismantling of the exterior cladding of the whole building. Lord Belmore agreed. But once 'nanny' started scrubbing the face she did not know where to stop. The Trust took on the interior, changing the creamy coffee of the north-facing oval Saloon to a cool grey.

When Lord Belmore noticed that the drawing room pictures had been removed he bit his lip, but when he saw the hall, where once the walls had been a gentle white harmonizing with the porphyr scagliola Doric columns he could no longer control himself, and blurted out naughtily: 'Germolene-pink', and thought: 'hate hate.' The trouble is he made his views known publicly. It has been an unhappy saga.

The present Earl's great-grandfather, the fifth Earl Armar Belmore, was a bachelor of jumbo proportions who fought hard to keep Castlecoole, egged on by his eight spinster siblings, the unusual Lowry-Corry sisters. He frequented a shop in Enniskillen where he would buy chocolates, and would rush to the railway station to award the prettiest and most deserving girl on the train a box of soft centres. In the end he was banned from the station. A Lowry-Corry great grand-aunt drowned in the lake and is believed to reappear from time to time disguised as a greylag goose.

It is an unusual family. A friend recalls how some of the present Lord Belmore's great-aunts were rather extraordinary creatures, always dressed in pre-war 1914 clothes in the 1940s, and speaking with guttural German accents, 'very . . . ach so, very Prince Albert . . .' Apparently they had a German governess.

Lord Dunleath in his Italian palazzo house over in County Down is lucky because he is wealthy enough not to need any help from the National Trust, even when a long-serving butler accidentally set the house on fire or, more recently, when faced with a bill for dry rot totalling £250,000.

Ascendancy houses and castles in Northern Ireland tend to be High Victorian Gothic or Scottish grey Baronial. Ballywalter Park has a quirky grandeur, a mixture of the Travellers' Club and the Reform in Pall Mall architecture has been successfully recreated in this sleepy, pretty corner of Ulster.

When Sir John Betjeman came to tea in 1961, the late Poet Laureate showed immediate 'signs of ecstasy', but as he was celebrated for mischievous humour the present Lord Dunleath was not sure whether or not to take him seriously, both men enjoying a subtle and understated humour.

Dunleath is a droll, slightly rubicund squire, with a passion for steam engines and organs. He likes to appear slightly harassed, speaking in low tones with some intensity, and has a certain Victorian formality for someone born in 1933. Shrewd, kindly, fortunately he took Betjeman seriously when he pleaded with him to save both the conservatory and the house, which the poet predicted would become a 'Mecca' for architectural enthusiasts.

Betjeman had helped to change his thinking; until that moment

'Everyone felt sorry for me, including my father before he died in 1956.' The feeling was that Dunleath was inheriting 'a Victorian monstrosity . . . a white elephant'. People suggested if only his ancestor Andrew Mulholland had not been so pretentious and had been happy with a modest classical house, there might have been a chance of survival.

The house has been in the family since 1846: 'when an illiterate Mulholland ancestor scraped together enough money to buy a couple of houses in Belfast.' Later Andrew Mulholland (1792–1866), who made money from a Belfast flax spinning mill, wanted to be a country gentlemen with a fine house and built Ballywalter. No simple, graceful Georgian-style would do; he wanted Italianate elegance.

In 1974 the house was badly damaged by the fire started accidentally by the butler; only very quick thinking by Lady Dunleath saved people's lives, paintings and some furniture. This butler is referred to meticulously by Lord Dunleath as Herbert M. Boyd. He was 'quite splendid' and came to Ballywalter in 1950 when Dunleath was seventeen. Boyd has now been retired, and is to be seen cycling dangerously about the countryside.

Lord Dunleath, who was an only child, likes to give the impression of a childhood dominated by tyrannical servants: 'seventy-five per cent of whose effort was expended in looking after themselves'. He complains of a diet, 'of Brussels sprouts, put on to boil at eleven for lunch at one' and a cook whose speciality was 'a leather omelette'. 'Those were the days before Interdens,' he explained, allowing a thin smile at the memory of an egg dish so tough it needed a toothpick.

There was a Cumberland nanny and a governess who was 'a dragon, like an NCO' and stomped around calling young Henry's ancestral seat 'an absolute dump'. After those early experiences, it was Eton from 1946–51, 'where there were a few good teachers,' and then predictably the army, joining the 11th Hussars in 1952. He read agriculture at Trinity College, Cambridge, and enjoyed the company of Jonathan Miller and Jocelyn Stevens. He inherited Ballywalter in 1956, took his seat in the House of Lords, 'so relaxing in comparison with Stormont', and married an attractive, able colonel's daughter, Dorinda Percival, in 1959. Lady Dunleath is an expert horse breeder, but her husband is not horsy – almost unthinkable in Ireland: 'I am very interested in horses,' he says. 'I keep out of their way.'

Ballywalter is well groomed, with rich bright green acres and mellow parkland dotted with shocking pink and white hybrid rhododendrons. The velvety green lawn outside the house is soothing; the eye is distracted from the dusty scaffolding inside where beams have been ripped out and the costly discovery of more dry rot goes on. In the billiard room stags' heads look balefully at one another, piled up under sheeting instead of in their rightful place high on the wall. Lord Dunleath takes out a large white handkerchief and blows the nose of one particularly doleful buck.

21

ROYAL PEDIGREE

Among those descendants of soldiers of fortune and pale aristocrats rewarded by grateful English kings, a fresh-faced young merchant banker, Pyers O'Conor-Nash, holds a royal pedigree. His family is the oldest in Europe. 'We go back,' he says simply, 'to Adam and Eve.'

Had things turned out differently, he might possibly be today's High King of Ireland. But he has inherited the house on his mother's side, without the title, so can never be known as the O'Conor Don. Nor can his wife Marguerite, a garage proprietor's daughter, ever be known as Madam O'Conor, though it would suit her well.

After such a distinguished start, directly descended from Milesius, first king of the Celts in the fifth century B.C., there was a hiccough in this family which produced eleven high kings of Ireland and twenty-six kings of Connaught. This genealogical swerve was not for the usual reasons of decadence, insanity or naughtiness, quite the opposite. In 1943 the heir Desmond O'Conor refused to become the O'Conor Don, renounced Clonalis, the family inheritance, and instead became a Jesuit.

This ascetic, unworldly man who taught at Clongowes, the Jesuit-run public school, took a great interest in his eldest sister's child Pyers, who says now: 'I was always very fond of my uncle, who taught me the facts of life, and how to ride and shoot.'

But this smiling, well-educated young man, shy, resilient and principled, was not prepared for the bombshell which hit him. He had a promising career in Dublin – 110 miles away – as a banker, was married to a pretty occupational therapist and had two children, Robert now six and Barbara three. When his uncle died, aged seventy-six, Clonalis, a house slap in the middle of Roscommon, was his, sans water, sans comfort.

The house was in a state of decay. It had been run by two of the cleric's spinster sisters and things were even more awry on the 1000 acres. It had been 'rather strange and difficult for maiden aunts to manage a farm', O'Conor-Nash suggests kindly. 'There had not been a man at Clonalis for fifty years.'

An expert called in to look at the contents of the house was not very encouraging. The house itself was not very important – a funny mixture of Victorian Italianate and Queen Anne – it could be a convent or institution, built as recently as 1878. But when a cupboard door was pulled open, out tumbled a glorious pile of old lace, Chantilly, Honiton, Brussels wedding dresses and eighteenth-century christening robes, wedding trains and satin slippers, making him very excited.

There was also a beautiful thirty-six-string eighteenth-century harp belonging to O'Carolan, one of the last and greatest Irish bards; a document signed by Louis XIV; an original facsimile of Charles I's death warrant and a most intriguing Penal Law chalice which ingeniously folded into three. This early piece of ingenuity could have saved a priest's life if caught on his way to say Mass in the secret chapel in Clonalis.

The tiny altar is something the O'Conors feel very privileged to own, more than any Louis Quinze furniture or Georgian silver. In his arms O'Conor-Nash holds his tiny daughter Laetitia, christened in the secret chapel in historic lace. He shows all the Irishman's diffidence about holding a baby, the first to be born in the cloistered stately home in 109 years.

It was not as if Pyers Nash grew up loving Clonalis. It was a place to be respected with its 25 B.C. Coronation stone where Kings of Connaught were crowned in Druidic times. Then it was filled with milk and the new king would place a foot in a step carved in the stone while a sub-king, usually a McDermott, would throw a golden slipper over his head as a token of good luck and submission.

These days it is filled with rainwater and usually the only thing flying overhead is an empty crisp packet. Clonalis is no longer in a wild and desolate part of Roscommon; opposite the main gates is a housing estate, and at dusk anyone who likes seems to be roaming through the grounds.

However Pyers O'Conor-Nash had a strange feeling that, no matter how hard the struggle, 'choirs of ancestors' would be 'caring' for him. He had one or two strange experiences on the staircase at Clonalis and is very much aware of a presence: 'In fact I saw a ghost.' So he decided he would get the Inheritance Act of 1976 changed so far as Clonalis was concerned. Otherwise this law would take about sixty per cent of the value of the property. It was curious, in a way, fighting for something he did not really want, and yet he knew if he let Clonalis go for twenty years – when he would be ready – it would be a ruin. This was in a climate where there is very little sympathy for the owners of big houses: 'We do not have any great appeal in Ireland.'

But there was an overwhelming sense 'of being put into Clonalis by destiny'. Madness, his friends told him, only the lawyers would prosper. O'Conor-Nash laughs at the premonition which made him become a barrister and a banker, so that he could grapple with the intricacies of an absurd law which stated that he should meet two charges of Inheritance Tax, on the estates of both his mother and his aunt.

When his Jesuit uncle died, Clonalis had been left to a young sister who died; then she left it to Pyers O'Conor's mother, Mrs Nash, who was in her seventies and died soon afterwards. For tax to be paid on these two deceased beneficiaries was, O'Conor-Nash says, 'in essence a nonsense'. After three years of agonizing and costly negotiation, the Finance Bill of 1984 was amended and Clonalis became something of a flagship of hope.

A charge was payable only 'on the death of my uncle, Father Charles. The circumstances were all so peculiar, but even with one

Left: Laetitia O'Conor-Nash has the distinction of being the first baby born in the cloistered calm of Clonalis, an Irish Catholic stately home, in 109 years. Her father, Pyers O'Conor-Nash, descendant of the High Kings of Ireland, reluctantly took up his inheritance aided by his capable wife Marguerite, who runs a shoot for French, Americans and Italians and cares singlehandedly for the family – Robert, aged six, Barbara, three, and the baby, who was christened in historic lace.

Right: Desmond Guinness, custodian of Ireland's heritage and darling of the Irish-American establishment, can raise an enormous number of dollars for a crumbling, Irish house by fund-raising in the United States and using his softly persuasive voice and Mitford blue eyes. His mother, Lady Mosley, widow of fascist leader Sir Oswald Mosley, and who lives in Paris, is the subject of the William Acton sketch hanging on Desmond Guinness's right at Leixlip Castle. The portrait by his left shoulder is of her sister, Unity Mitford, who took a great shine to Adolf Hitler.

Inset: The moment Irish stately home owners dread, when the auctioneer sets up his marquee and intones away the family possessions. Refusing to be 'trapped by pride', Lord Dunraven bravely coped with the indignity of saleroom bargaining and attended the auction of the contents of his home, Adare Manor, County Limerick.

Main picture: Adare Manor was bought by an American who has converted it into a hotel. Lord and Lady Dunraven have built themselves a Dallas-type modern house some miles away. In the best feudal tradition, villagers still have the right to walk through the grounds of the Manor.

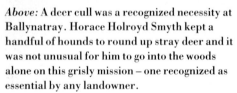

Above: A deer cull was a recognized necessity at Ballynatray. Horace Holroyd Smyth kept a handful of hounds to round up stray deer and it was not unusual for him to go into the woods alone on this grisly mission – one recognized as essential by any landowner.

Above right: Tessa Lefroy's idea of heaven was a cottage in Gloucestershire and working with the Tory Party. When her husband, Jeffry Lefroy, inherited a gloomy manor in Ireland's flatlands, she was admirable in her determination to turn the gothic revival house, Carrigglas, into the 'most prestigious loo stop in Ireland'.

Right: The West Waterford Hunt meet at Ballynatray on 25 March 1964. Catherine Fleming, striking in jodhpurs and hunting coat on the grey, always enjoyed a 'great, fast hunt', and the hounds worked very well for her – 'I had reared most of them from puppies'.

Right: A confident and relaxed Catherine Fleming flanked by the Duchess of Devonshire on her right, and on her left an amiable-looking Horace Holroyd Smyth. On the Duchess's right, Miss Clodagh Anson, one of the Waterford family. Colonel Smiley, in peaked cap, worked for the Duke and Duchess of Devonshire at Lismore Castle, County Waterford.

Above: All Lady Jennifer Bernard has left to remind her of Castle Bernard's stately charm is this sepia photograph of one of the drawing rooms.

Left: Somerville and Ross, authors of *Some Experiences of an Irish R M*, on that tranquil stretch of water near their home in Castletownshend, County Cork. 'We met,' Edith Somerville said, recalling the instant bond with her cousin, Violet Ross, 'when … we were … not absolutely the earliest morning of life; say, about half-past ten o'clock, with breakfast (and all traces of bread and butter) cleared away.'

Right: What a hoot! 'The Gay Mice' recall that this vampish beauty was a man, 'a thorough man', a Captain Dodson who boxed for his Regiment but fooled everyone at an Isle of Wight fancy dress dance.

Below: Butlers, ladies' maids, valets, cooks, footmen – just some of the staff at Stanhope Lodge, Cowes, home of the Blake sisters' maternal great-grandfather, the Earl of Harrington.

Above: Curraghmore, inspired by Vanbrugh's Blenheim and home of the polo-playing Marquess of Waterford, is one of the last well maintained, impressive houses left in Southern Ireland.

Below left: For the Gore-Booths a lasting memento of the rebel in the family, Constance ('Con') the Red Countess, who married a Polish count, Casimir Markievicz, who executed these unusual and strangely compelling wall paintings of some of the staff at Lissadell in County Sligo. The sisters Constance and Eva, in rose-sprigged hats, appear in the Sarah Purser portrait between the startling figures on either side of the marble fireplace.

Above: In a small top room of this elegant house, the 4th Lord Doneraile died of rabies, fulfilling an old woman's curse that he would die barking like a dog – revenge for his enthusiastic practice of the 'droit de Seigneur' principle with comely young girls in the village of Doneraile in County Cork.

charge that ran into hundreds of thousands of pounds and I had to sell off two-thirds of the estate.'

He now had to give up living in Dublin and, with his wife and two children, come back to Clonalis and open it to the public. When you ask the O'Conor-Nashes if it is a happy house, he immediately says 'yes' but she is not sure: 'It is a demanding house.' It is very still and like a church. They live in a small part of a rumpus room with a tiny modern kitchen.

This blue-suited man became used to being stared at by Sunday visitors. 'Ye'll be the royal family of Ireland – here Mary, take a squint at His Nibs.' Others clamber up the bookshelves in what is one of the best private libraries in all Ireland. Apart from first editions of Trollope and Gladstone it holds a collection of some 100,000 manuscripts, 5000 volumes collected over half a century by a scholarly, saintly family and the last recorded verdict in Brehon law on vellum: a decision given on a land dispute in what had been the Irish legal system until Elizabeth I stamped it out.

'There was a fellow on the bookshelves,' O'Conor-Nash explained, slightly embarrassed by the need to put up trellis for fear other visitors might try a similar simian leap. He was eager to see better the exquisite family poetry inscribed on vellum in Belgium by a seventeenth-century Irish monk.

In the drawing room Meissen porcelain sits comfortably and undisturbed on a gilt rococo consul table and a summery Italian landscape over the baby grand piano is warming as the landscape outside darkens and glowers.

Every year he is swooped on by some of the half million O'Conors from all around the world, but mainly America. 'It is extraordinary for we are in a vacuum – quite off the beaten track.' The response from America has been 'almost overwhelming'.

They arrive hungry for more O'Conor history; how Thomas O'Conor emigrated first in 1801 and tried farming in New York State but not very happily and lost everything, but his grandson became an impressive attorney – and another founded Tucson, Arizona. And in Wisconsin, call Janet and Gareth Dunleavy, who will tell you all you need to know about the O'Conors, whether it is about Rory of the Yellow Hound, Teige of the White Steed or Art the Solitary.

A celebrated Charles O'Conor was a Democratic candidate in the American Presidential election of 1872. The first Catholic to stand, he was defeated by General Ulysses S. Grant.

It is not that Clonalis is not working, but O'Conor-Nash has gone back to merchant banking in Dublin. His wife, bright and capable in her stand-up Sloane collars, runs a shoot for French, Americans and Italians, and the fifteen bedrooms, six with dressing rooms, are comfortable and warm. 'People have come to realize that we are not an Anglo-Irish house. Clonalis is rather unique as it is Irish. Irish and full of Catholic history.'

22

NOT TRAPPED BY PRIDE

The saleroom porters in green gold-trimmed aprons carry out more Victorian satinwood tables, held upside down, the legs carved like flanks and with cloven hooves of deer tilted up to the sun. Others struggled impassively with Lely and Kneller family portraits, Wyndham-Quin ancestors on their way, unceremoniously bobbing up and down in gilded frames, to Tennessee, Washington, San Francisco, Milan.

The whole atmosphere was of a summer garden party, Adare Manor *en fête*, grounds graciously open to the public as people picnic in the shade of immaculately kept rose gardens and savour whiffs of lavender.

A stir as the owner, the seventh Earl of Dunraven, arrives. Thady Wyndham-Quin has been in a wheelchair since he was sixteen, a marvellous handsome head, a body shrivelled by polio. He moves about and rewards the gawpers. Yet the big blue eyes restrain them too, his is a rare presence. A couple of housewives push their catalogues at him, and this gentle man, a descendant of Lord Mayo, signs his name.

The contents of his home, Adare Manor, which has been in the family for 300 years, are up for sale today. Soon all that will be left will be the indestructible shamrock-girt Kilkenny marble and the Gothic doorcases.

'We had to sell. You can be trapped by pride.' Dunraven succeeded to the title in 1965 and is a realist, philosophical too with all the dignity and gritty reasonableness of a last heir to this distinguished title. 'Hanging on, paying heating bills at ten pounds a day, maintenance £300,000 a year and insurance another £10,000 was too much.'

But Lady Dunraven takes it very badly. When they married in 1969, Ascendancy friends of the family wondered about this girl called Geraldine, 'daughter of an Air Commodore McAleer from Tyrone and Sheila Byrne of Ailesbury Road, Dublin' marrying their 'Thady', an earl's son who had been educated at le Rosey in Switzerland. However they would grow to admire her for her energy and devotion to him and were delighted when a daughter, Ana – the Russian version of the name – was born in 1972.

Cool and professional, the auctioneer Charles Allsopp boards the rostrum. In the huge marquee he looks quite pink standing in front of vases brimming with lilies, lupins and delphiniums, a nice touch, as if arranged by a thoughtful housekeeper preparing for weekend guests.

The sale hums on through the day; it has a fashionable buzz, and those who have driven from Dublin for this day out with 'the County' enjoy rubbing shoulders with commercial aesthetes, sharp eyed 'privates', academics, librarians and fine art dealers from Italy, Paris and New York. Others get a tiny vicarious thrill and link themselves with the Dunraven family, women in silk dresses are overheard saying to each other: 'Oh no, I don't think so, mahogany doesn't grow in Ireland' as they admire some rare Irish mahogany chairs; others sink gratefully into squashy old sofas or sit on button-back chairs and slip off their unsuitable high-heeled shoes.

Geraldine Dunraven's hazel eyes still mist over at the mention of Adare Manor and she seems to grieve more than her husband over the old house as if it had been hers all her life: 'It's still my home, my daughter feels the same, she is very emotional like me.'

Hardly noticed, she had slipped into the sale, keeping her head down rather a lot, doing her tapestry with a fierce concentration, every so often stopping only to scoop up her fair hair.

Hungry bargain hunters pick over empty tiara cases and nudge each other, laugh at the crested silver meat covers and thumb embossed leather-bound books.

The sale has been masterminded by the engaging Knight of Glin who represents Christie's in Ireland. There are those who call him the 'Shite of Glin' because of his shrewd eye and ability to outwit even the gypsies, but on this traumatic day he is protecting his Dunraven cousin's interests. The Knight says: 'If I am going to be the undertaker, I'd like to do it in the glossiest hat possible.'

As always, certain important valuable things have been spirited away ahead, wrapped in green cloth and put up in fine art sales for the cognoscenti in London and Geneva. An important Georgian silver teapot made in Dublin by Archdall in 1717 once held gracefully in unrivalled hospitality at tennis and croquet parties, pale pink of Albertine rose petals reflected in the polished silver, '£27,500 going, going'. It has gone.

There is no gloating today; the Dunravens never attracted unkindness. Any landed gentry or Ascendancy label is resented for they claim to have arrived in Ireland in 607 long before Cromwell. The Wyndhams made money, farmed in Wales and, through marriage, changed their name to Wyndham-Quin, taking their title from a Glamorganshire castle owned by Thomas Wyndham.

Adare village was created around the seventeenth century with a benevolent stipulation that the villagers could walk through the estate and clamber round the ruins of the Franciscan Abbey and Desmond Castle whenever they desired – a right of way that would prove just a slight deterrent to potential buyers.

Lord Dunraven, the present Earl's grandfather, was slightly unusual in being a member of the Free State Senate that was headed, under the new Constitution of 1922, by a Governor-General rather than a Viceroy. During the Republican campaign to burn down the homes of 'Senators and Imperialists', Adare Manor somehow escaped, perhaps because it had been a model village with a good landlord and Catholicism had been important in the family.

The droning voice of the auctioneer lulls even the most curious. Paintings fetch £17,000 each and a George III Langlois marquetry bureau, a precious family wedding present, goes for £5,000. Now the crowd has grown tired of staring at the Dunravens and the house is stripped bare. Guns, sabres, swords and armour are next; women lose interest; then a final flurry of excitement: tapestries and rugs, until the swallows fly low over the river Maigue and people begin to slink away.

Now the rumbling carrier vans roll out into the model village with its pretty thatched cottages with cheery gardens, tiny white windows peeking out from under eyelashes of honeysuckle and roses. Its almshouses could be based on models from a Gloucestershire village in P. F. Robinson's *Village Architecture*. Then on they go to the boring road to Dublin, where the great container ships wait for this exquisite cargo.

For the rest of the family perhaps the sale has not been so traumatic. Lord Dunraven's sister is married to the Marquis of Waterford; their widowed mother remains at Kilgobbin, a yellow Georgian house where she has always lived since her marriage to the flamboyant Sixth Earl of Dunraven who inherited the title in 1939.

Nancy Yuille was a Southern belle, the daughter of a millionaire tobacco tycoon in Carolina, when she met her future husband. He was twenty years older, but owned a spectacular yacht, a stable of thoroughbreds; an aristocratic sybarite he was considered suitable by her father, Thomas B. Yuille.

When asked by his wife-to-be, as they buried their toes in silver sand on a beach in Florida one cloudless day: 'Dickie, what is the weather like in Ireland?' Dunraven replied airily: 'Oh, it's like this,' telling a small white lie.

Guests at the Palm Beach Dunraven-Yuille wedding included the Astors, the Vanderbilts and the Pulitzers. Dunraven then whisked his bride home to County Limerick, one of the duller counties in Ireland best known for producing a huge number of priests and nuns. But Nancy Dunraven fell in love with Ireland from the moment she was driven up 'the avenue' at Kilgobbin with its approving sentinels: fifty handsome eighteenth-century oak trees planted by the original owner, the third earl. She even enjoyed neverending days of Irish mist.

The newlyweds would never live at Adare Manor so lovingly built by Caroline Countess of Dunraven and Wyndham, which was started in 1829 but would not be finished for another thirty years.

Instead they settled at the dower house, which would always symbolize 'happy times'. It was a perfect place to grow lilies, poppies and French roses. The restful lawns were studded with box hedges looking like embroidery and modelled on French châteaux seen by Nancy Dunraven in their travels. 'The avenue' would be softened by hundreds of lilac and pink cyclamen, a natural easy charm.

American flair and an artistic eye gave Kilgobbin a chintzy flamboyance. It is comfortable with lots of paintings, some by Sorine, a Russian artist; and brilliant coloured rugs from Mexico are draped across armchairs.

When her husband died in 1965, Nancy Dunraven stayed on at Kilgobbin. She travels a great deal, loves the Riviera and Florida's Hobe Sound but always homes back to County Limerick.

Adare Manor has been bought by an American who, sitting in his office one day in New York, thought: 'Hell, why not; this place is going for a song.' It opened as an hotel in 1988.

A much happier and youthful looking Geraldine Dunraven cheerfully springs out of a car drawing a horsebox. This is not the downcast spectator at the Adare sale two years ago. Instead she is brightly pretty in a flowery pink shirt, pink overshirt and flowery sprigged trousers, hair held back with glittery gold slides, and she is wearing her husband's signet ring.

Gentle, hospitable, in vivid golfing sweater, he propels himself through the hall of their newly built Georgian style house. He has the look of someone cherished; everyone says his wife is marvellous even if she is at times too protective – fluffing his hair, always solicitous; she was his nurse at one time.

Known as 'Sadey' by his family and friends, his full name is Thady Wyndham Thomas, which is a mouthful. The affectionate nickname is an abbreviation of Thaddeus. He is very much the host, though feeling a little fragile after a wedding celebration the day before when he had driven his invalid car too speedily and along a bumpy road. 'Geraldine does not drink – ' She chips in: 'I only like champagne,' and, he explained, 'She gets her revenge next morning.'

From the outside their modern house slightly resembles a Dallas oil tycoon's dream in its size and views of great unspoilt paddocks ribboning to a misty blue horizon. But there the comparison ends. Inside, a riot of bright traditional Georgian colours are a backdrop of distinction for the best of the family paintings: 'this Lawrence, for instance,' Lord Dunraven says, propelling himself towards a decorative Wyndham-Quin ancestor looking out from above a fur-trimmed brocade cloak. The furniture is opulent, ornate and antique. They kept the best. 'We are survivors,' he says; 'if I did not sell I'd be paying the highest taxes in the world.'

Lady Dunraven, who slots into the mechanics of helping her husband eat, attentively feeds him spring onions with his Irish cheese though he insists on calling them by their Irish name – scallions. Dunraven is proud of the family's Irish origins though their money came from Wales. 'Adare,' he says 'is the loveliest place in the world; it nearly killed us having to sell.'

It was a courageous decision. All over Ireland there are crumbling Ascendancy houses, in decline because of inflation and the 1974 wealth tax, but Dunraven feels other owners 'are too proud to sell.'

The irony is not lost on the Dunravens that their loss is the tenants' advantage – 'Sadey knew them all by their Christian names: there was a party for them once a year' – who have now been able to buy their houses on the estate for as little as £400. Some come to him and ask his advice: 'What shall we do? We have just been offered £11,000 for the house.' Suddenly they are in the middle of a property boom. A shrug. 'Everything has happened too late,' her husband says. 'If I'd had a son . . .' But the birth of Ana, now studying at Kylemore, a Benedictine Abbey, was a gift enough from the gods.

His mother has adjusted to a life without many servants. There are still cucumber sandwiches and scones made by her cook for afternoon tea but the dowager is pleased she is no longer quite so dependent. 'You see,' she says triumphantly; 'I have just discovered the teabag; I've finally found something I can cook.'

On a visit to France, when staying with friends, Lady Dunraven thought the fire irons were rather handsome and 'terribly like' the ones at Adare Manor. Absolutely right. Her French friends had bought them from a dealer. 'What a relief,' her son smiled; 'we had been awfully worried that things would go to the wrong people.'

23

SECRETIVE, WILD AND CANNY

The Guinnesses, secretive, wild and canny, divided into two main branches, the Iveaghs and the Moynes, continue to have great riches and some misfortune. They marry often, and have been tinged with the same glamour in Ireland as the Kennedys once had in America; they have the wealth of the Grosvenors in England, these two families still owning great amounts of land in places like Vancouver, Canada. The family has at times been ill-fated, though they all dismiss the notion of a curse.

In a recent decade, no powerful financial empire could have prevented an awesome string of tragedies: Tara Browne was killed in a car crash in Chelsea; Lady Henrietta Guinness, sister of the present Earl, rich and generous, ran off with an Italian waiter of whom the family disapproved, then threw herself from a bridge in Italy leaving a baby daughter. More recently, in 1987, the founders of Guinness would have been appalled by the scandal of the family empire being analysed, and the behaviour of its then chairman Ernest Saunders publicly scrutinized. In the same year Olivia Channon, daughter of Paul Channon, Minister of Transport, whose father was 'Chips Channon', a descendant of the Iveaghs, died from a drug overdose at Oxford. Everyone was struck by the bravery of Jennifer Guinness when she was kidnapped by the IRA. It is hard to imagine that the curse was not working its deadly rites when it claimed her husband, the good-looking sailing man and banker John Guinness, who fell to his death from the top of Mount Snowdon.

This exotic family had a modest beginning in 1759 when Arthur Guinness, who owned a small brewery, came up with a magic black brew and put it on barges steaming up the Liffey; it became famous all over the world. The Irish say it is not just hops, barley and yeast, but something to do with holy water, the brewery in Dublin being nicely placed by St James's spring. Old Arthur Guinness was not daft.

The first Lord Iveagh was another Arthur Guinness, a dashing figure who was given a title by Edward VII whom he had entertained in some style at Elveden, his home in Suffolk. His descendants, now rich titled Guinness girls, would make good, if not always happy, marriages. Lord Iveagh's three granddaughters, Aileen, Oonagh and Maureen, even as children were mysterious: like the Three Graces, unworldly, languid beauties with long dark hair. Their father Ernest Guinness, who died in 1949, left one million pounds to each of them, an income for life, yet not much instinct for self-preservation.

There is a cynical view that Guinness women, though much married, will always keep the name of the husband with the best title, like Lady Oranmore and Browne, and Maureen, Marchioness of Dufferin and Ava who married her cousin, Basil, the fourth Marquess, in 1930. Her husband was much loved, a delightful companion, but James Lees Milne would record sadly that his undoing had been at Oxford where he had been taught to drink by Lord Birkenhead, and the good mind – 'He had the best brain of my generation – ' was damaged by alcohol. Restless, questing, he was often melancholy, not unlike Sebastian Flyte in *Brideshead Revisited*. By the age of thirty, he was no longer terribly interested in life.

In the early buoyant days of their marriage, Lady Dufferin, a celebrated hostess and prankster, brought new life to the family house at Clandeboye in County Down, now a troubled part of Northern Ireland. Dressing up as a 'half-witted maid was the greatest fun,' and serving the wrong drinks to her guests had the men 'exploding with rage,' being given gin when they wanted whiskey, what 'a scream'. Never once was she recognized by her guests, 'such a hoot'.

Her mother-in-law, Brenda, Marchioness of Dufferin and Ava, was appealingly fey, claiming to be in constant touch with the fairies. She 'would sometimes get very excited, believing that they had chosen her as their queen.' She lived in terror of her servants, and would never send anything back or ask them to do something about the soggy strings from the ceilings, directing leaks from the roof into jam jars herself. Her world was with The Little Folk, and she worried that her son was a changeling left by bad fairies. Sometimes when he was trying to have 'meaning of life' discussions with Oxford friends, the elderly Marchioness would suddenly glide into the room, bare-footed and wearing a silver shawl, and would rush up to him hugging him frantically.

The first Marquess had been Viceroy in India from 1884–8, and chose the haunting name Ava in his title after the old capital of Burma, near Mandalay. All the Avas had charm. Lord Curzon described the Viceroy as 'Prince and paragon of diplomats . . . with that suave insinuating manner, that languid glance of the glassy eye, and that alluring smile which are his alone. But . . . he chattered on . . . called me "My dear fellow." ' Lord Curzon was critical too of the Viceroy's indifference to minor matters, 'careless about detail'. He would bring back to the family house in Northern Ireland strange carved figures, 'wooden ladies' he had found lying around the magical jungles near Mandalay.

The Irish believe in good and bad fairies. In Burma those spirits of the forests called nats were reported to be not at all pleased by the annexing of the Upper part of their country by the British, and blamed the Viceroy. The family began to believe that some of the exotic trophies were cursed, and that the Burmese gods were taking their revenge. Ireland is a place where superstitions flourish; and even the most cynical would find it hard to explain the sudden and unhappy end of this family.

Few Dufferin heirs reached old age. The Viceroy's eldest son, the Earl of Ava, was killed in the Boer War in 1900; his second son became the second Marquess but died aged fifty; the next son Basil had been killed at the Western Front in 1917, so the title went to

Frederick, the youngest, who suffered severe head wounds in South Africa, and was killed in a plane crash in 1930.

In 1945, the fourth Marquess, always called Ava by his wife Maureen, was with the Royal Horse Guards in Burma when he disappeared. By a strange chance it was somewhere near Ava. Their son Sheridan, aged seven, became the fifth Marquess. There were also two daughters: Perdita and her sister, Lady Caroline Blackwood, the distinguished novelist who uses part of the family name, Hamilton-Temple-Blackwood. In her book *Great Granny Webster* she introduces a barely disguised Clandeboye, the ancestral home, as 'Dunmartin Hall', reeking of fried potato cakes, paraffin for the heaters and homely cow dung.

Maureen, Marchioness of Dufferin and Ava, who later married a soldier, Major Desmond Buchanan, and then a judge, Justice Maude, who died in an old people's home, pinned all her hopes on her only son, Sheridan. This diffident, much loved aesthetic figure steeped in the avant-garde world was a friend of David Hockney and helped to establish him. He was not too drawn to the ancestral home with its Viceregal trophies, animals' heads and armour in the entrance hall, but was more at home in Chelsea than County Down during the liberating sixties.

In 1964 he married a Guinness relation, Lindy, dark, thin, energetic and aesthetically knowledgeable. There were no children to inherit; the title would die with the Marquess. Together they would make Clandeboye a sympathetic and fashionable haunt for artists.

The death of Sheridan, the fifth Marquess of Dufferin and Ava, of Aids in May 1987 shocked his friends. They had always admired his strong sense of irony and strange fatalism, but it seemed a particularly cruel blow that he should die from this killer virus at only forty-nine, though he bore the wasting indignity of the disease with extraordinary courage. The art world was shattered: he had been an engaging, delightful and effective patron, a trustee of the National Gallery and of the Wallace Collection, and co-owner of the Kasmin Gallery in Bond Street. He had an unselfish eye to the future, and one of his last acts was setting up a Dufferin Trust to help Clandeboye.

The wooden gods from Mandalay have gone from Clandeboye now; the family got rid of them, but a little too late. The funeral of the fifth and last Marquess of Dufferin and Ava was '. . . inspiring and far from gloomy;' the gods have been appeased with the death of this last special Dufferin, laid to rest protected by a circle of trees known as the Campo Santo in the woods at Clandeboyne.

A summer's afternoon at Leixlip Castle, a young couple on the grass lie sinuously entwined, he with a tee shirt pulled over his face. The Hon. Desmond Guinness sits sprawled on a back step in pale blue shirt and trendy baggy pocketed trousers. His wife races up from the garden excitedly brushing past bushy white roses: 'We've been given a huge bag of mussels,' but the ascetic nose wrinkles: 'I hate mussels; they are so messy to eat.'

'Don't go in there,' a local had warned at the gates of Leixlip Castle, just a short forty-five-minute run from Dublin on the N.4. 'They've got fierce Alsatians.'

'We need protection,' the Hon. Desmond Guinness, with his amazing ice blue Mitford eyes and low confidential voice says as he smiles indulgently at the flock of fat white geese pecking in front of the castle. 'They are the best security, a formula dating back to Roman times.'

Desmond Guinness, aged fifty-eight, is the second of the poetic Lord Moyne's children by a first marriage to an outstandingly beautiful Mitford. His mother, Lady Diana Mosley, would run off with the Fascist leader Sir Oswald Mosley, but he seems to have had little influence on his stepson. Desmond Guinness and his brother Jonathan, children of this first marriage, echo their mother's distinction. Now widowed and living in Paris, Lady Mosley says: 'We loved Ireland and the Irish. The people are charming and so clever at saying what one likes to hear. We were sad to leave . . . all the romance of Galway and the beauty of Cork and Waterford.'

Desmond Guinness's first wife, a spirited German princess Marie-Gabrielle Württemberg, whom he called Mariga, would show guests around Leixlip Castle, with its spriggy wallpaper, and ask them to 'excuse Desmond's awful Laura Ashley taste.' Irish houses tend not to be appealing as you approach, rather gaunt and grey, but inside, Leixlip is full of pretty touches, even a pink kitchen, lots of dimity walls with sketches and paintings of glorious clutches of Mitfords including Nancy, Jessica and Diana.

In the days before Leixlip Castle, Desmond Guinness and the flamboyant princess were shocked when, as newlyweds in 1954, they searched for somewhere to live and saw the wanton destruction of old houses in Ireland. They formed the Irish Georgian Society. That was thirty years ago.

They would attract artistic, caring people. The atmosphere at Leixlip was compared to that of the aesthete Harold Acton's court in Florence in its attraction for composers and writers. It was a tremendously vital relationship, but then the 'Divine Desmond' fell in love with a tiny creature called Penny Cuthbertson, a friend of Francis Bacon's, and there was a difficult parting from his first wife. There were two children, a son Patrick and a daughter Marina.

They were both always great party givers, and just because they were estranged the princess saw no reason to stop entertaining at Leixlip. Often when Desmond Guinness was away she would, much to the housekeeper's disgust, invite her friends to the Castle where they would be surreptitiously entertained, but could suddenly find themselves having to climb out from the battlements and shin down as the Hon. D. returned unexpectedly; all very comical were it not so miserable for the princess. Until her death in May 1989 she lived in a cottage on the Birr estate lent to her by the sympathetic Rosses, a somewhat lonely and distracted creature.

The atmosphere these days is less of a glossy magazine *Tatler* glitterati house. There is a staff of four at Leixlip and the Guinnesses spend more time in London, absorbed in each other.

Head of the Georgian Society, darling of the Irish Establishment, a crusader dedicated to saving what is left of Ireland's heritage, Desmond Guinness's noble face stares out from coffee table books about Irish houses and castles, bibles for those who care. At the moment Doneraile in County Cork, once the home of the predatory fourth Viscount, heads the list of properties to be saved.

Money gets the socially aspiring to his fund-raising parties. 'Were you at Desmond's?' they ask each other, and it is 'Desmond this' and 'Desmond that', though they may only have shaken his hand briefly, barely been introduced. But their cheques have been warmly received, and this entitles them to use his Christian name. You feel this diffident, slightly feline man must hate such glad handing.

Irish exiles in America are a useful source. The wealthy John Tomey Akrin in Ohio, chairman of the biggest trucking company in America, really cares about Georgian Ireland and wants to help. 'Like many Americans,' Desmond Guinness explains, 'he has been very generous and we have an endowment fund which produces about £20,000 a year.' Through this they managed to get just the right shade of green silk for the drawing room at Castletown and there was a successful outcome to an intense search for an expensive fillet, the gold trim. There was an elegant celebration party for the re-opening of this Palladian house in County Kildare once the home of the Speaker in the Irish Parliament, Mr William Connolly, and where Queen Victoria once stayed in the Chinese Chippendale bedroom. Visiting with Prince Albert, she was very taken by the Irish jigs danced for her on the lawn, and enjoyed being taken out in her host the Duke of Leinster's jaunting car.

People come to Desmond Guinness all the time, desperate owners, hanging on, trying to win his sympathy and interest. He listens, hunched in an attitude of patient attentiveness, almost like a confessional, guarded, charming and relaxed, but the blue eyes can be awfully cold. He himself has not known too much privation, the burden of a family house close to being shut and left to crumble into another mournful pile of stone like a chipped, unfilled wisdom tooth. Even if there can be no help from the Georgian Society, visitors are propelled in a masterly way to the castle shop. A boy is painting the Castle railings in a desultory way, and looks reproach- fully at the Honourable Desmond: 'Ah yes,' he remembers, 'there is a cheque up at the house,' smiles gently. He is not averse to making a sale in the shop, it is all part of survival. It is done appealingly, but that air of relaxation is masking a formidable dedication and professionalism.

Another Guinness relative is Garech Browne, the epitome of Celtic aristocratic feyness. Hair neatly in a pigtail, rather like the Marquis of Bath's son, he is one of the Iveagh Guinnesses while

Desmond Guinness belongs to the lower profiled Lord Moyne side.

The Hon. Garech Browne has a wistful charm, sitting cross-legged on a bar stool in a pub in County Wicklow. Grey-bearded, he is thinking about a visit to his lonely and neglected inheritance, Luggala. He likes to wear Aran sweaters, lilac or rich blue, and Connemara tweed trousers. He has the air of a hunter, like so many Irish boy-men in search of the chat, the crack. Precise, discerning, he exudes a rarified air.

A bit of a chameleon, one minute rather Irish and being very 'de Brun', insisting on the Gaelic spelling of his name as befits the founder of Claddagh Records. He is knowledgeable about music, and was the inspiration for the group called the Chieftains, though rebuked by an Irish politician: 'Why are you trying to damage the image of Ireland by making records of old people wailing by hearth sides, when what we want to show is an image of twentieth-century Ireland, with chimneys and factory smoke?' Garech Browne had unearthed folk tunes which he first heard on a boat going to Aran, laments played on a flute. Soon airs once played by the blind eighteenth-century harper O'Carolan were being heard again on a metal-strung Irish harp, distributed around the world by Claddagh Records. Browne is Chairman purely to keep an eye on the continuing integrity of the music, not on the bottom line.

A chameleon, his mood may be eastern; he is married to an Indian Princess, Purna of Morvi, and once had a Chinese girlfriend called Ting a Ling. He spends six months a year in India, where he much enjoyed overhearing a servant telling a visitor: 'Her Highness is on the pot.' When the Maharajah of Benares asked him what he did for a living, Browne replied: 'Nothing,' shocking the saintly prince.

There is about him a certain ambiguity. His life seems a pleasant balancing act, in Bombay one minute Belgravia the next. A British subject, the Hon. Garech Browne moves in a cultivated, highly social group which has included Iris Tree, Lucien Freud and once Cyril Connolly and Somerset Maugham.

He was born in 1939, Establishment style at a house called Glenmaroon so grand that one corridor stretched across the road. But now like so many of the old Irish houses it is a place for the mentally handicapped. Much of his childhood was spent at Castle

MacGarrett in Mayo in one of the old family feudal possessions, with a staff of 150. At school in Switzerland at le Rosey, he engineered a telegram from his mother saying, 'Due to unforeseen circumstances come home immediately.' It worked, and he was able to leave in the middle of the term. Boarding school was one of the few unhappy experiences in this charmed life. 'It was not a training for life,' he suggests, 'as nothing can ever be even remotely so unpleasant again.'

For financial reasons, he can only spend two months a year in Ireland. Luggala is let, so this visit by the son of the house is full of mystery and rather furtive. The Hon. Garech inherited Luggala from his mother, one of the celebrated 'Guinness girls', the sociable Oonagh, who married Lord Oranmore and Browne, whom Garech still calls 'my daddy'. Oonagh was given Luggala as a present by her father Ernest Guinness on her marriage in 1936. Divorced in 1950, Lady Oranmore and Browne now lives simply in Guernsey.

It was at one time a great place for parties. Bacchanalian romps could go on for days. Luggala has a tendency to get snowed in often and unexpectedly, throwing a strange selection of people together in this wedding cake house tucked into a valley in a wild and savage part of Wicklow. Cars which whisked out from Dublin along twenty-five miles of dry road, on reaching the stone gate posts would begin a slithery precipitous two-mile drop into an icy valley through moorland and forest and past a huge lake, normally brooding black reflecting the shaley hillsides, now diamond white.

The welcoming Regency shooting lodge, a castellated folly twinkling with lights, the flames of great log fires softly focusing on the Francis Bacon paintings, one of Garech Browne, and inside a whizz of people would be having a non-stop party. As the party daily grew and grew, it all became slightly surreal. Oonagh, Lady Oranmore and Browne, a clever hostess, found her skilfully orchestrated social alchemy could go completely awry. All good hostesses occasionally entertain their enemies to be *au courant*, but they were now thrown together, like the characters in a Sartre play about hell, some positively disliking each other, but locked together until the thaw.

John Huston, an American film director who enjoyed being a country squire in Ireland, was often at Luggala and snowed in. Unable to get on with shooting great films like *The African Queen*, instead he would be sitting meditatively on the floor in front of a dying log fire at 5.30 in the morning, in green velvet tuxedo and slippers embroidered with foxes in masks of gold. When asked solicitously whether he was coping all right, Huston shook his head. 'I feel sort of lost. Oldy losty.'

Sunk in a valley in County Wicklow there could be no better place for a little Chekhovian introspection, Joyce's agenbite of inwit . . . Hinds appear and mate on the weedy lawn. Sika deer are a speciality.

As the owner swings in through the gates a group of bewildered Germans and Danes who had been enjoying the granity view have returned to their gleaming car – one of those aggressive Swedish estate cars which always has sidelights on, even in the daytime – to find it had been vandalized, and in such a desolate place on the side of a small mountain.

They look hopefully at Garech Browne, but he drives through the gates along a forest of beech and lime trees below the lake, beckoning with a sinister stillness.

He jumps out and, moodily and sadly, tries to undo a crude tiny stone dam put up by the estate workers. It could hardly repel a raindrop let alone Hurricane Charlie. Appalled by the roughness of work, though only temporary, its ugliness upsets him and he crouches on the ground trying to tear up the stones. A young gamekeeper has spotted him and comes hurrying up behind: 'It is ugly; that will not do.'

The gamekeeper, who has worked on the estates at Birr for Lord Snowdon's half brother Lord Rosse and for the Dutch royal family, is the son of a Dutch farmer. He speaks perfect English and chronicles the loss of even more pheasants; Browne, his mood preoccupied and detached, listens and explains. 'The pheasants caught pneumonia and died at the time of the hurricane; we lost between three and four thousand . . .' not good news. And they are expecting the Saudi Royal family for a shoot.

In the house rooms are dark but when opened up they are full of strong dark Irish furniture, gilt candelabra and extraordinary paintings: one of Garech as a little boy, others by Lucien Freud and a Francis Bacon, of trousers dropping stage by stage.

He pulls back shutters; there is dust on the antique Waterford glass, on the Gothic mirrors, on the piano used by Fedorova, Weber and Handel and on the heavy marble tables, the Gothic bookcase; in a corner there is a gold harpsichord, and an Irish clock which plays God Save the Queen.

Garech Browne has a clarity; he can talk for two hours on the telephone entertainingly, ringing at 8.30 in the morning because he suddenly wants to tell you about John Field who invented the nocturne and went to Russia; how Chopin went to his concert and 'didn't enjoy it very much;' Glinka was a pupil . . . and how the obituaries reverently said 'Born in Dublin, dead in Moscow.'

Cynical about how things happen when you are not around, he has an elderly cousin keeping an eye on Luggala; but this custodian 'spitefully sits in a spot where he definitely cannot hear the telephone'. He had lunched with his father, and was in a mood for celebration, having just won £1,000 'in a libel', and was going to restore a memorial to his brother Tara by putting a ball on top of some pillars.

Neat, abstracted, entertaining, there is a certain meticulous apartness; he sits down. A huge portrait of him by Edward Maguire overwhelms even the splendid gloomy pieces of Irish furniture. His agent John Mitchell pops his head round the door; he is in the mould of all good agents – brisk, courteous, clean shaven. He appeals to Browne to 'come and see some of the things we are doing.' The small, pigtailed figure shakes his head and languidly picks up a book on Irish carriages, remarking coolly: 'I collect them, though I did lose one.' For a moment he is a maharajah, mercurial, languid and impenetrable.

24

DOVES AND SHAMROCKS

A wet summer's day and Catherine Fleming, a bonny, childlike woman dressed in green, is vigorously pulling out weeds in her garden high up over the valley of the Blackwater. Gardening can be therapeutic.

The white, Gothic Protestant rectory, emerging from dripping rhododendrons and huge shrubs, seems an unlikely setting for this cheerful gardener. In spite of the heartbreak and the loneliness, there is an ingenuous appeal about Catherine Fleming and the wrapping of a chocolate box prettiness which defies gloom. Even the local children who come to tease her at the gate, go away disarmed.

'Come in, come in.' In the sitting room with its good traditional furniture, she always sits in a button-back chair covered in pink and purple silk made from one of her favourite old evening dresses. From a gold oval frame a Fleming ancestor glares boldly down on Ballynatray, an Ascendancy house of classical pale grandeur. It is high on a sloping lawn, on what was once one of the finest estates in southern Ireland.

It snuggled deeply into the woods on the edge of the dark secretive Blackwater valley, a river more beautiful than the Danube, they used to say. It was always an exclusive stretch of water, attracting the Duke of Devonshire and the glamorous

Villiers-Stuart family. The Elizabethan poet Edmund Spenser thought it one of the loveliest parts of Ireland.

Ballynatray had been in the Holroyd Smyth family since the seventeenth century. Sir Richard Smyth, an English soldier who arrived in Ireland with Sir Walter Raleigh, had been given the estate as a reward for his part in the Elizabethan wars and the house was built near the sacred ruins of St Molanfide, an Augustinian monastery dating from the year 501.

For nearly three centuries, the family enjoyed a silken lifestyle. They owned the oldest private pack of foxhounds in Ireland, dating back to 1700; gave parties on the Smyth state barge gliding along the Blackwater on summer evenings and had their own orchestra. One of the last family barges, in 1900, had belonged to the captain of a wrecked Napoleonic man of war. In Youghal, they said, If you married a Holroyd Smyth, 'Wouldn't it be like marrying into royalty?'

Early in the evening, the deer would come through the amber bracken and be silhouetted at twilight as they delicately wandered across the richly wooded hillside in front of Ballynatray. The deerpark also dated back to 1700 and occasionally there had to be deer culls. Nothing else disturbed the peace except perhaps the splash of a bewildered porpoise or a surprised seal carried up river by a boisterous sea at Youghal Harbour.

For as long as she could remember, Catherine ('Kitty') Fleming's life was inextricably bound up in Ballynatray. One of a family of eight, this comely Catholic girl with a nice manner had grown up in this dreamy wooded corner of Ireland, and was irresistibly drawn back to the life of the Big House. The family loved her; she blended in so easily at Ballynatray with the five children, four sons and a daughter, and they all called her Kitty.

Their father, Captain Holroyd Smyth, gave her her first hunter which she called 'Yvonne'. 'The Captain' she would remember as a 'very elderly man, very kind'. Kitty rode well and soon was hunting with the West Waterford, strikingly slim in jodhpurs and hunting coat.

Apart from a happy personality, she was also practical. Whether it was preparing venison, doing the accounts or cheerfully fishing the Sprat Weir, a sly design of wattles to trap sea fish, she would be indispensable. They always said she knew almost more about the history of Ballynatray than the family; how the weir down by the Abbey's lopsided ruins, with stone archways whiskery with ivy where she waded through rushes for sprats, was the only one left in Ireland and in a specially holy place; how a Smyth widow had put up an urn to Raymond le Gros who came to Ireland with Strongbow and built a haven for the Knights Templar at Rhincrew.

The heir to Ballynatray, the eldest Holroyd son, John, was killed in the war. 'The mother,' Kitty recalled, 'was a sad woman. She never recovered from his death. She was a lovely person too.' Oliver, the youngest, married late, moved away and there were no children. A sister, Mary, despite the family's long tradition of Protestantism, became a Roman Catholic. 'She was,' Catherine recalled, 'always kind to me.' Another son, Brian, who had never married, also died.

So Horace Holroyd Smyth came home in 1944 to run the family estate. Almost a stranger in Ireland after years in Chile where he had worked as an engineer, he would rely on Kitty, this capable girl with her reddish blond feathery curls and round cheeks. Able and sunny, she mucked out the hounds, fished and earned the admiration of the Ascendancy, she hunted so brilliantly.

Holroyd Smyth, charming, kind, well connected, wealthy, highly regarded – his cousin was a Queen's messenger – was considered most eligible. 'A lot of women wanted Horace to marry their daughters. He was very tall and good looking, and the aristos round here all liked him; he was a tremendous catch.' But he had grown very fond of Kitty Fleming. Here were all the ingredients of an old-fashioned romance.

Before settling herself warmly to 'tell a tale' she gives a little laugh. 'The moral is that the colonel,' and drawing herself up, hands folded in the lap of her dress, she continued, 'must always marry the colonel's daughter.' With the instincts of a hospitable countrywoman, she presides over a genteel tea, milk in last in pretty bone china cups, forks for the apple tart. 'Down there,' and she nodded ruefully, 'I'd have had silver pastry forks,' and shrugged. An old man's fancy, they said, but she was never acquisitive.

It was Molly Keane, that sensitive chronicler of Ascendancy sexual antics, who, living not far from Ballynatray, would put out a hand of comfort to this guileless young woman swept into a fading Anglo-Irish society so rigid even in its twilight days; it was better to die than marry someone who was Roman Catholic or not the 'right type'.

As Holroyd Smyth relied more on Catherine Fleming, there were those at Ballynatray who watched with jaundiced eye. The housekeeper with that exaggerated below stairs awareness of propriety once tried to have her sacked, but gravely she was reminded: 'Oh no, you can't do that, I am one of the family.'

Gradually she and Horace Holroyd Smyth slipped into a pleasant way of life together. There was a small staff, a butler and a cook, no electricity. 'It was all Tilley lamps at those Christmas parties.' Kitty Fleming, who almost lived in hunting clothes, virtually ran the estate. 'You could be at a cocktail party every night, but I never smoked nor drank. I loved opera and ballet. I made no demands; it was a great relationship, we always had great fun.'

A simple quiet, hardworking life, so different from the days of *fêtes champêtres*, house parties and dancing on the lawn. 'If we'd bought a bit of farm machinery, we'd have supper in Cork.'

There were delicate moments and there had to be a certain tact over invitations. 'Horace,' a local landowner recalled, 'was well liked, but he never expected to bring her to our houses.' Sometimes in Youghal or Cork when the couple met Ascendancy neighbours, the awkwardness would be eased by Kitty herself: 'If we stopped for a chat she would just walk on.' When Holroyd Smyth caught up with a smiling Kitty pretending to look in a shop window, he would say apologetically: 'Now if we lived in America, this would never happen. Nobody would take any notice.'

'He liked America,' she recalled, 'had a lot of friends there.' But this was Ireland. It was perfect so long as Kitty appeared to be just helping out.

Trying to explain their relationship, she recalled how her family called him 'Uncle Harry'. 'He treated me like a niece . . . He was always very gentlemanly,' The innocence of this relationship gives it a special poignancy. 'Frankly it would have been like an uncle suddenly leaping on you, why it never entered our heads . . . We went swimming together, lying in the sun. All English people think about is sex all the time.' The liberation of the excitable sixties had evidently not yet touched these reaches of the Blackwater.

'But I was the one full of the bubble.' Kitty Fleming seems still to have those sweet nunlike high spirits. 'I'd be the humorous one, he'd be serious. We had a happy life. I had everything.'

'Kitty saw Horace as a sugar daddy, no doubt,' a local hunting woman put the popular view.

When the wedding was announced there were raised eyebrows and Kitty seemed to be seeing a lot more turned tweedy shoulders, but she managed to ignore the coolness. 'In Cork they kept saying to me "He'll never marry you," ' as they looked at her pretty engagement ring of diamonds and emeralds. The wedding cake decorated with doves and shamrocks was ready and the invitations had been sent. 'We were so happy, the music, the flowers . . . everything was all set.' Her voice trailed off. 'Horace and I hoped for a child for the estate when we married,' but she was outraged when it was spitefully suggested 'Horace Holroyd Smyth . . . he is too much of a gentleman for you to have a family with.' 'Excuse me,' Kitty Fleming replied. 'I am just as much of a lady; we are an old Norman family.'

Just before the wedding, Holroyd Smyth went to London to see his brother Oliver.

If there is any bitterness in Kitty Fleming it is when she speaks of this visit and the traumatic consequences.

This surviving brother, Oliver Holroyd Smyth, his body twisted by illness, is a widower living alone in one of those eminently respectable but rather cheerless red-brick buildings opposite Brompton Oratory in Knightsbridge. He has nothing to say about Kitty Fleming; he is crotchety and nostalgic, and longs only, he says, to hear a Percy French recording to remind him of carefree days at Ballynatray.

Kitty Fleming believes he warned his brother Horace: 'By marrying this woman, you are breaking tradition; ours is a Protestant house,' and advised him to 'think again.'

Unorthodox marriages had not been unknown in their family, with its power and majesty motto 'Cum Plena Magis' and bull crest. There were bulls' heads everywhere at Ballynatray, on the Gothic fireplaces and ceiling friezes. In 1835 a beautiful Smyth girl called Penelope fell in love with the Prince of Capua, younger brother of King Ferdinand II of the Two Sicilies. They ran off and were married at Gretna Green. The King, better known as 'Bomba' in Bourbon circles, was furious and there was a huge scandal. But in this case it was a Smyth who was not worthy.

'So you see,' Kitty concluded in a sad little voice. 'What chance was there for humble me?'

Until this moment she had been animated, reliving those days in 1964, the build-up to wedding; now her face was puffy and pink with emotion. 'When Horace came back from London all he kept saying was, "It was awful . . . awful" and he was upset and disturbed.'

A few days before the wedding, there was a deer cull at Ballynatray. Countrywomen do not wince at the need to keep down the deer population. 'They were routine . . . too many bucks,' Kitty Fleming explained in a matter-of-fact way, 'and you'd have venison to give to the neighbours.'

It was nearly dusk on that fateful evening, the light becoming too grey for shooting, but still Holroyd Smyth had not returned. Kitty Fleming went out in the Land-Rover to meet him coming back along the wooded avenue, as she often did: 'Same as normal, you see, we were devoted to each other, so happy . . .' Horace used to say, 'It is too good to last.'

Putting an unjewelled hand to her breast, she told how she had found his body in the darkening woods as the curlews flew low across the river with their lonely call. 'Horace was lying beside a dead stag.' 'Oh, the shock, he had shot the deer and then himself. I still get a lump here . . . in my heart.'

There was the eerie familiar sound of crackling bracken being crushed underfoot as deer who had escaped the cull were stepping tentatively back to life from the shadows.

'I was thirty-four at the time.' She looked flustered. 'I used to be so slim,' but she would never recover her slimness and is apologetic about her weight.

Comfortable, motherly, Catherine Fleming hardly looks a *femme fatale*, and as the words come tumbling out, the rain seems to beat weepily and unrelentingly against the rectory windows. But now she collected herself.

'Some say Horace walked out,' but Kitty Fleming knows better. 'He made sure I was comfortable.' Her home gives her pleasure; she dusts her collection of china 'Bambi' fawns. For a while she was an enthusiastic and star Irish folk dancer, with its curious ritual reaching a frenzy as the dancer with head thrown back, mouth taut in a grimace, pounds the floor with the heels of black patent buckled shoes in increasing vibrato to the wild fiddle music.

Living in such an entrenched Ascendancy stronghold – it remains a privileged corner of Waterford – she would never be accepted. But her church has helped this instinctively sweet nature which might otherwise have been corroded by a gossipy malevolent hypocrisy when Holroyd Smyth committed suicide.

Looking back, the local people make her smile. She mimics their solicitude: 'Ah isn't it a shame and you so happy, sure we were all looking forward to the weddin', wouldn't it have been grand, so?'

'It was jealousy,' she concludes, 'that did for us in the end, all that begrudgery in Ireland.'

Ballynatray was handed over in 1969 to Holroyd Smyth cousins, the Ponsonby family from Kilcooley Abbey, Co. Tipperary. 'Isn't it funny, do you know after all the commotion, he, too, married a Catholic.'

Her good spirits and natural buoyancy are back. Kitty Fleming smiles and says it has always struck her how many poor families in Ireland felt it an honour in the old days if the squire took a fancy to their daughter. This has nothing to do with her own chaste romance, and you are left in no doubt that she comes from a good family.

But the antics of the wicked old Earl of Mountcashell amuse. He was married to Sir Richard Smyth's daughter Charlotte.

'Old Lord Mountcashell had plenty of fling. I remember a daughter of a washerwoman who'd say, "That's my father" as he went by and they'd say "Sssh". What chance did pretty girls have going up to bedrooms with jugs of water?'

But sometimes it was the daughter at the Big House who fell in love with a village boy, and this is what happened long ago in the Fleming and Holroyd Smyth families.

Kitty Fleming's great uncle Patrick – 'he was a good looking lad and he and Lady Harriette Smyth, Horace's grandmother, she was a great beauty, eloped together in 1867.

'Horace's grandmother was brought back by the ear and she later married a Colonel Holroyd who took the name Smyth and Patrick Fleming sailed to America.

'One of my sisters bears a remarkable resemblance to a Holroyd,' Catherine Fleming remarked with satisfaction.

The damp dusk had crept into the sitting room unnoticed, darkening the creamy chintz; a shot sounded uncannily from the valley.

'You never get over it,' she said softly, and turned on a lamp to show her engagement ring and the old, yellowing wedding invitation with its silver lettering.

25

SAILING AWAY

'Egg', as the owner of Bantry House is best known, Egerton Shelswell-White, looks like a character from *Rose Marie* on ice, a smart hussar in black trousers with red stripe. In between answering the door to visitors, he rushes off to a quiet corner to play his trombone. He is due to give a solo at the Bantry Bay regatta but keeps being interrupted.

The sound of Tommy Dorsey's forties band playing 'In the Mood' has visitors bemused; in this eighteenth-century house they had rather expected to hear chamber music, something on a harpsichord at least. The older ones smile and begin to bop as they fish out their entrance money or look around the main hall with its mosaic panels casually picked up by the second Earl of Bantry when he went to Pompeii in 1828. He was a great traveller, bringing back Russian icons, a mosque lamp from Damascus, sixteenth-century camel bags, a charming Japanese scarlet lacquered table decorated with flowering trees and pheasants.

'Egg' appears to be doing everything; he is doorman, guide, cashier and programme seller. There is a great preamble, unlocking the door for each arrival at one of the loveliest houses in Ireland for all the world like a pretty French château on the shores of Bantry Bay.

From the tall windows in the Gobelins drawing room, with its eighteenth-century Savonnerie carpet, there is the best view. The Bay looks like an exclusive private lake dotted with wooded islands called Rabbit, Horse, Hog and Lousy Castle, and beyond the purply blues and greens of the Caha Mountains on a sunshiny day.

There are too many precious things in Bantry House to be casual about visitors; there is not the money for attendants, but nothing is roped off. In the Rose Drawing Room there are royal Aubusson French tapestries made for Marie Antoinette's marriage to the Dauphin, and rich romantic extravagant *fêtes champêtres* by Boucher. The furniture is elegant Buhl and Irish Chippendale. In the dining room amongst the coloured marble columns with gilded capitals, there is a portrait of George III and Queen Charlotte by Allan Ramsay, the Court artist, a gift to an early White from the King. In 1796 Richard White had helped suppress an invasion by a French fleet led by the Irish Protestant barrister Wolfe Tone, who was coming to support a rebel band called the United Irishmen, determined to see an end to British rule.

The King could not be more grateful, smarting under a reputation as the monarch who had appointed Lord Frederick North as Prime Minister and known forever more as 'the man who lost America'. Richard White was created first Baron Bantry.

Outside the drawing room window facing the Bay, there is a plaque to a young airman put up by the Warplane Research Group of Ireland. Flight Sergeant Newlove's body lay in this building prior to burial at Abbey cemetery, Bantry Bay, on 28 May 1942. During the last war Shelswell-White's mother lived virtually alone at Bantry House except for an Irish Army Battalion which included the 2nd Cyclist Squadron, who rode round the countryside on motorbikes helping to defend the coastline. Whenever a plane hit the mountains, this battalion would try to rescue the survivors and would bring back the bodies to Bantry House where whatever their nationality – it could be American, British or German – they would lie in state.

The money is taken. Mr Shelswell-White is courteous but distant, defensively warding off intrusive questions about the family history. The music changes to 'I Wonder Who's Kissing Her Now'.

The family stress that their White ancestor had not deliberately driven away the French, who were Ireland's friends, and that he originally sent out a friendly pinnace to meet the approaching ships, but it was never seen again. Alarmed, he alerted the British navy. In these sensitive times, much is made of Irish ingenuity in foiling this French invasion.

A simple looking peasant was allowed to board one of the French ships in the Bay, offering fresh food for sale, irresistible to any Frenchman. They questioned the simple soul, who, wide-eyed, told them the British Fleet was only round the corner and waiting on the shore 20,000 'fierce armed soldiers'. This immediately sent the French scampering back to Brest, not knowing that all they might have to contend with was a raggedy band of 400 ashore.

On a clear, crisp morning warm enough to sit outside, Shelswell-White is lying back in one of the old-fashioned quality brown wood deckchairs, the sort found on prestigious liners. 'Rather good, don't you think?' Shelswell-White says, looking down towards the Italianate formal gardens, lawns dotted with classical nymphs, Egyptian marble statues, fountains and silvery white beaked herons with crested collars, and imitates an American visitor, 'Yes, as they say, "heah in ma own back yard".'

Rosy, crisp mottled, with clipped hair, he spent part of his life as a soldier in Berlin, and finally training groups in Armagh in 1953, but also some time in Alabama where he taught history for five years. 'I loved it there, that is where I met my first wife. My two eldest children, Edward, who is twenty-five and heir to the estate, and Jane, who is twenty-two, grew up there, but I knew I would come back here one day.'

As a child, Shelswell-White, who is fifty-four, says he remembers how he used to pretend the house was a boat and was sailing away. He smiles, and is too smart to need a psychoanalyst to explain this make believe, but he loves Bantry.

Boats have always been important. His mother, who was heiress to Bantry, romantically met his father Geoffrey Shelswell on board ship near Zanzibar and, though engaged to someone else, she married him. His father was a professional soldier, and assumed the name White. After her husband's death in 1962, his widow

Clodagh Shelswell-White lived on alone in the house for the next fourteen years. Her son says: 'She loved it, was never frightened, and was looked after by Con, a treasured retainer.'

In the hall there is a photograph of Con with a Shelswell-White aunt taken in 1967 during the celebration for the 170th anniversary of the French invasion attempt. He is gamely holding the tattered Bantry Cavalry Flag and underneath it says: 'Con, over 60 years with the family, a trusted servant'.

Bantry was the first house in Ireland to be opened to the public. 'It was my mother's decision, a hobby really.'

Her only son took over Bantry in 1978 when his mother died. He is full of nostalgia for the old days when there was no electricity or telephone at Bantry; these innovations did not arrive until 1940. 'How romantic it was before electricity, all those concerts and dinner parties by candlelight.'

He had parted from his first wife, Jill Dumersque, and remarried a glamorous picture restorer, who had been living in Canada, called Birgitta. 'We had almost made up our minds to get rid of Bantry House, then Birgitta and I thought we'd keep it.' How Irish. 'She loves it.' It is frequently the women who keep the family homes going in Ireland with flair, dedication and often very little money.

Part of it has been redecorated for bed-and-breakfast guests who stay in rooms prettily done in trendy yellows with chests of drawers harmoniously stencilled and marbled by Birgitta Shelswell-White. In the wainscotting a creak, maybe a mouse, that old Irish country house familiar sound as you nod off. The breakfast room is a charming old country kitchen with gingham curtains and table cloths, and on the big dressers religious pamphlets.

'It is the bed and breakfast side which keeps us going,' Shelswell-White says; but it can hardly bring in enough money for the restoration work. Parts of the upstairs are distinctly rickety, sealed off with bits of sacking, a plastic Pluto, a Disney goofy dog, lies on its side, and the old baize door, once the boundary for Shelswell-White and his sisters, now has a hole in it.

'It is tough enough, and sometimes in the winter we wonder if we can carry on.' There is little income from the tenants on the estate: 'We were never wicked landlords,' he smiles. Today the tenants can buy the freehold. Money is short, arrears of rent are laughable, some tenants pay 50p a year.

Outside, two small Shelswell-White blond children, Sophie six and Sammy three – baby Anna aged six months is in her pram – romp around the grounds chasing their kittens who disappear under visitors' cars. It is nice for Shelswell-White's sister, too, Oonagh Vane-Yarrow, who also used to dream the house was a yacht. She lives in the estate yard. A woman of seemingly indeterminate age with the eyes of a girl, she is fifty-seven. Their other sister, Delia, he explains gently, has been in a mental institution since she was twelve.

The visitors' book on one of the heavy Kilkenny marble-topped tables opens at a page with a message from 'John and Karen Murphy from Texas', saying 'It's Brideshead revisited.'

When Shelswell-White finds he is getting too gloomy or introspective about his house, he plays the air from Tchaikovsky's Symphony No. 6, the 'Pathétique', on his trombone: 'I love it.' The best antidote is the Bay. He looked wistfully at a super yacht gliding out and, getting up from his deckchair, remarked: 'Mmmh, see, I am still on my yacht.'

26

A SINGLE LIFE IS AIRY

There is still a charm about Castletownshend, with its nest of surviving landed gentry families, the Somervilles, the Coghills and the Townshends in their old stone houses, with mullioned windows and high walls. It could be Gloucestershire by the water instead of West Cork, Carbery hunting country.

Nightingales sang at Drishane, the Georgian house in this Ascendancy stronghold where Somerville and Ross wrote *Experiences of an Irish RM* and created flinty, 'hard man' characters like Flurry Knox.

In summer the old-fashioned garden was filled with peonies, hollyhocks and tall ice-blue delphiniums, but they were writing *The Real Charlotte* in the summerhouse on the wooded cliffside and would squint at the Atlantic below. Now a glimpse of a white sail or a patch of blue through the green leaves and above their heads the call of the curlews. Edith Somerville, the older of the maiden cousins, would spot the *Titanic* on her doomed voyage sailing blithely off the Castletownshend coast 'into the glow of a fierce winter sunset'.

On a November afternoon in 1987 a moist grey film of mist lends a shimmer to the weather-slated roof of the eighteenth-century house; but the sound is not lyrically of nightingales but of crashing wood as more dry rot comes tumbling down.

'You can tell when you have got dry rot,' Christopher Somerville explains as he stops digging the gloomy wastes; 'it is when something pokes out like orange elephant ears from behind the furniture.' It came as rather a shock to him that the house must be preserved: 'Great-aunt Edith lived here for eighty years.'

This diffident, bespectacled academic, Edith Somerville's grand-nephew, who has inherited a rickety Drishane, does not strike you as immensely practical. He had spent much of his life abroad running the Literature and Arts Division of the British Council. His wife, small and brisk, is harassed by the army of workmen tramping through the house, which is dark enough without the dust of dry rot, with its black mahogany doors installed by one-eyed Tom, the Merchant Somerville, who built the house in 1792. The eldest son of a clergyman of Scottish settler stock, he exported butter to the West Indies and in return brought rum and rare black mahogany from his travels.

A little crowd has gathered on the hilly main street for the formal opening of a new sweet shop, where once Edith Somerville danced an elegant, long-step mazurka down the hill at dawn to join a waiting boat party. That was when she was a young girl before she became old and cross.

Born in Corfu in 1858, Edith Somerville grew up at Drishane and, though it is an enchanting place for adults, often complained of being bored. Her mother despaired of her appearance, complaining she looked like 'a grave digger,' and once on a train burst out: 'Your hair looks like a collection of filthy little furze bushes.'

But this 'lightfooted girl' had admirers and would dance till six in the morning. She wore decorative clothes and jewellery, studying Art seriously in Paris and London. Edith was gay, and rode well in waisted hunting costume with a long skirt. There were parties at the Castle which nestles down by the water's edge and a regatta each summer called Calves, a miniature of Cowes.

Now there are hardly any of the traditional little brown varnished mackerel boats, or competing schooners, sailing ships or delicate boats like the *Nadine* or *Miri Chin*, given to Edith Somerville by an admirer Herbert Greene.

Greene is believed to be the model for the long-suffering

Resident Magistrate captured so well by the actor Peter Bowles in the television series 'An Irish RM'. Greene, an academic, was considered a nice, decent, uncomplicated man. He had fallen in love with Edith Somerville before he went up to Balliol, bombarding her with proposals of marriage and poems from Oxford, where he became a Classics Don. Eventually he gave up hope; the Somervilles were sad, he was so eminently suitable. But by 1880 Edith had decided she would be an 'ould maid'. 'A single life is airy,' the twenty-three-year-old suggested to comfort her mother.

Edith was thirty-seven and her cousin Violet Florence Martin, known as Ross after her home in Galway, was thirty-three when Violet visited Drishane in 1886. Getting on so well, they could do that most difficult of things, write together, and had almost instant success with their novel *The Real Charlotte* about Ascendancy life, the snobbery, the cruelty, the hunting and the fun. But their mothers, who were first cousins, were shocked and unhappy when their daughters rejected roles as wives and mothers, what Margaret Mead describes as that 'retreat into fecundity'.

'When we first met each other we were, as we then thought, well stricken in years,' Edith would say '. . . not absolutely the earliest morning of life; say, about half-past ten o'clock with breakfast (and all traces of bread and butter) cleared away.'

Martin Ross would live at Castletownshend but would grieve terribly at finding rabbits on the steps of the family home in Galway, neglected after her father's death in 1872. She too came from a solid Anglo–Norman background. One of her most celebrated relatives was 'Humanity Dick Martin', an Irish MP who founded the Royal Society for the Prevention of Cruelty to Animals in 1824.

He owned more than one-third of County Galway; one chunk of Connemara alone consisted of 200,000 dark peaty acres sixty miles wide, with twenty coastal harbours and twenty-five very blue inland lakes. He converted a tumbledown castle into a private prison. If he found anyone being cruel to an animal he conducted their trial himself, and if they could not pay the fine, would escort them to Ballinahinch Lake and personally row them out for a few days' detention in his homemade prison.

Whenever he went to Westminster – he was the Member for County Galway – English MPs laughed at his Irish accent.

It has been suggested that Edith was a man-hater and incapable of normal sexual love. But Ross, who had thick spectacles and always wore soft grey handwoven tweeds and a man's tie, was never a warm person, and could not cope with even the slightest romantic sexual innuendo in any of their books. This would be left to Edith, older and more worldly, who would always be the practical one, the farmer with a pedigree herd of Friesian cattle, encouraging her sister Hildegarde to start a violet farm and raising money for kennels for the West Carbery hounds.

Their bantering style: Martin is called 'a lazy slut' and a 'Queen of Pigs feet', is hardly the language of Sapphic besottedness, rather more the talk of elderly schoolgirls, tomboys at heart. If they had arguments it was over the pronunciation of Mrs Cadogan and how it should be 'Kaydagawn'. They had a marvellous ear for dialogue.

Somerville and Ross were liked, if not quite understood, by servants and villagers. Speaking admiringly of Edith after a visit to Violet's home, one of the servants, Matt Kenealy, was impressed by her agility: 'Didn't I see her put her hand to thim palings and lep over them! Faith I thought no ladies could be as souple until I seen her.' 'I seen' and 'I done' are still popular vernacular in rural Ireland where Castle Matrix became Castle Mattress.

But he was disappointed and there was a little rebuke: 'But indeed the botho'yee proved very bad that yee didn't get marri'd and all the places yee were in.'

Edith's studio was in a stable in the courtyard at Drishane where she used to go and talk to Mike Herlihy and listen to his stories over the fire and sniff the soap and saddles. Now rats gnaw away at the panelling. It is not to be compared with the love lavished on Kipling's house, Bateman's in Sussex, where it looks as if he has just left his desk to mull over the possibility of another poem, 'Because' a sequel to 'If'.

The Irish RM, published in 1894, had people rocking with laughter round the world, especially outside Ireland. Those caricatured were not always so amused. Some of the villagers say 'Ah, they made great fun of us in West Cork.' But nobody was safe: the two joked about everyone.

The authors were criticized for their 'supercilious Ascendancy view', but later Edith Somerville would complain about 'Some . . . English people whose honesty and innocence would be endearing, if they were a little less overlaid by condescension.'

Often what appeared to the Irish as patronizing was in part due to shyness and courtesy in a land as foreign as Ibadan or Amritsar in the Punjab. This earnest diffidence was mocked wickedly by a contemporary writer, Honor Tracy, who a few years ago was tending her cottage garden in the Aran Islands when a car drew up, and out tripped some English visitors.

The man pointed to Miss Tracy with her fine head and silvery hair, and said: 'Here you have a typical peasant woman; the menfolk have all gone to America, driven to emigrate . . .' and, raising his hat bowed: 'Good day to you.' Immediately Honor Tracy, of impeccable Anglo-Irish descent, assumed a burring vernacular and, when he asked where the little road would lead, smiled up at him: 'Sure sir, it'll take ye wherever ye want to go.' Completely charmed, he turned to the others: 'Y'see, isn't that marvellous?' and pressed a half crown into the distinguished author's hand.

Captain Paul Chavasse, at seventy-nine, says that as far as he knows he is the only surviving member of the West Carbery to have hunted when Edith Somerville was Master. He is a jolly, welcoming figure in this contained village where his stone house is right by the water's edge. A log fire crackling, he pours from a cut glass decanter of sherry. He and his second wife, Patricia Chavasse, treat like gold the so far unpublished Somerville and Ross's *Red Riding Hood in Kerry*. The title alone is inviting.

He has vivid memories of seeing Edith Somerville hacking home in the evening. 'Even as a small boy it was important to make your mark with her. I sorted out her terriers in a dog fight,' and acquitted himself nicely.

'The real "Flurry", in *The Irish RM* was Aylmer Somerville, Edith's brother, and "my father-in-law". He was five-foot eleven-inches tall, cruelly known as the "Half-Sir".' 'His shoulders are those of a bull,' his sister told Violet Martin, hoping she would like this jolly brother who alone in the Somerville family had a strong brogue. Although an expert on Rossetti, a publisher of dictionaries and knowledgeable about the languages of the Solomon Islands, he could be rather hoorayish, shoving chewed grapeskins down the backs of two women guests, who squealed . . . 'It was delicious . . .' Elsewhere an energetic partner retrieved his false teeth from his companion's bosom during a hunt ball, remarking: 'Not the first time down that avenue this evening.'

'He was passionately keen on fox hunting, and like his sister Edith Master of the West Carbery Hounds. He was heartbroken when rabies got into the pack and it had to be destroyed. It nearly killed him.' In the last ten years the West Carbery has reassembled after years in the doldrums and is now fully recognized again by the Association of Irish Masters of Foxhounds. Slipper, Chavasse recalls, was 'that dreadful reprobate modelled on a flamboyant local character called "Pack", who lived in Skibereen.' But 'Pack' was eventually trampled to death by a temperamental stallion in the village street.

In 1984 Patricia Chavasse tried to organize a Somerville and Ross exhibition which was opened by Molly Keane. The task was almost impossible as there seemed to be so little memorabilia, so she ingeniously draped a scarlet cloak round a dummy, swept a wig into a hair net, put a palette in her hand and on top Edith's ancient straw hat, one she wore until her death in 1944, hoping she had created a likeness.

Now there is dry rot in the Hall at Drishane where Edith Somerville always had tea at 5 P.M. 'Everyone sat around in great discomfort in front of a dismal stove eating bread and jam and Sally Lunn, a hot sponge cake,' another relative remembered. She was abstemious and vegetarian and never liked being called Miss, preferring Doctor. To the inner circle she was 'D'.

Edith Somerville was without vanity although she disliked the sulky and imperious mouth she had been given in a portrait and ordered the artist to redo it, changing to a curly one instead.

Christopher Somerville smiles. 'I remember Edith wearing a stuffed seagull on her head. It was clearly a favourite because she wore it again and again, to weddings, to gallery openings and literary lunches. Sometimes the bird seemed to be sitting on a green sea made from layers of chiffon.'

He points to a few personal treasures in a glass case in the drawing room at Drishane, a crumbly box which holds a touchingly tiny pair of her kid gloves and a blue-green Parker pen which helped create characters like Mrs Cadogan and Slipper. Even the fairy's shoe which was found in a bog in Kerry is now locked away in a bank. In the past, people paid to see this tiny slipper and believe in its magic.

Violet Martin died on Tuesday, 20 December 1915. After her death, Edith would continue to write, was awarded an honorary doctorate in literature and a Gregory medal; she played the organ and the violin and was interested politically. In her early days with Violet Ross they went campaigning as Unionists in East Anglia against the British Liberal party, who stood for Home Rule, and the two were referred to as 'Irish locusts'. But Edith was at heart a Nationalist; she used to sing 'The Wearing of the Green' while Violet always remained a staunch Unionist.

Her beloved brother, Admiral Boyle Somerville, was assassinated on 24 March 1936 on his own doorstep and his wife watched him die. The IRA left a card explaining the murder: they believed Boyle was a British recruiting agent. His death was based on flimsy intelligence that he was writing references for boys wanting to leave a strife-torn West Cork to join the Royal Navy.

Edith was very taken with spiritualism and automatic writing after Violet Martin's death. The twin blows, the death of two of the people who were closest to her in the world, led her towards seances. Outsiders often found the house eerie; the atmosphere is not light even now. She was psychic and reported how once a small table had followed her across a room. On another occasion: 'Aunt Flo's basket trunk has suddenly, 11.30 P.M., become possessed of an evil spirit and has waved its lid about of its own accord.'

Towards the end of her days, Edith's sister, Lady Coghill, now a widow, ran Drishane. Edith had become a horse dealer and sold to America; but she always poured the tea.

She could strike terror in the village. Her dog, usually a smooth-haired terrier, went everywhere with her. Once in church a rector sent her a note asking if she would remove her howling terrier; both she and the terrier were sitting in the organ loft. She swept out of the church, complaining that 'The . . . sermon was eminently adapted to infant negroes.'

When she was eighty-eight she reluctantly left Drishane and moved into the village into a house aptly called Tally Ho. 'I feel,' she would say, 'like an old horse out to grass.' Her brother Aylmer's son Desmond Somerville inherited.

Mrs Rose Marie Salther Townshend, whose father was Edith Somerville's second cousin, lives in the Castle by the water's edge, where shells in the family coat of arms show that they went to the Crusades. 'This is where Dean Swift stayed with my great-grandfather,' she says. 'He put the h in Townshend. The h is silent,' and his great-granddaughter puts teatowels on the backs of chairs as antimacassars. The setting, the harbour and woodland, is so lush and idyllic, it makes up for the spartan interiors of the East and West Towers.

A cousin by marriage of George Bernard Shaw, Rose Marie, thin and astute, explains: 'There were two leading Ascendancy families in Castletownshend, the Somervilles and the Townshends. The village grew up around Drishane – the coachman married the lady's maid – and to people in the rest of Ireland we are an enigma. There was a time when they played God Save the King in local pubs followed by the Irish National Anthem. Edith would arrive at the Castle and say, "I am Taspy," meaning in high spirits.'

'She had two things in common with Edna O'Brien,' Mrs Townshend suggests. It certainly was not a dress sense, Dr Somerville in tweeds and brogues and Miss O'Brien, with her feminine love of high, lacy, romantic clothes. But both, according to Mrs Townshend, 'always carried a notebook, and never went anywhere without it. They jotted down every single little remark, so you get genuine dialogue in their book, a typical example would be, "How can I be dirty? I wash my face every Saturday night." '

The little church of stone from Horse Island on a hill overlooking the Atlantic holds most secrets. You climb through the churchyard to a grave where there are white azaleas, 'My beloved has gone down to gather lilies' – Joscelyn Somerville, a brother of Edith's who died aged two. There are charming stones to 'justly beloved wives' and to husbands, fathers, sons called Milborne-Swinnerton and Pilkington; there are not too many Murphys or Flahertys among these graves of Somervilles, Boyles, Chavasses: admirals, generals and loyal servants of the Empire.

American friends and admirers contributed to an Edith Somerville plaque, and with delicacy pay tribute to both women: 'To her name is joined as she would have wished that of her beloved cousin and collaborator Violet Florence Martin 1862–1915.'

There is a superb stained glass window by Harry Clarke, a celebrated glass craftsman who died in 1931. He and Edith had argued; she was irritated because he put in brown cattle and she wanted him to feature her black and white pedigree Friesians. But the floor mosaic is hers, based on Celtic symbols including the fish.

An oar from a *Lusitania* lifeboat rests over the teak door of the church where Edith Somerville played the organ for seventy years. This simple piece of wood 'in memory of the twenty-seven victims whose bodies were brought ashore in Castletownshend' is more eloquent than seeing the wrecked hulk of the ship torpedoed by a German submarine off the Old Head of Kinsale.

Edith Somerville's funeral was not uneventful. There was a slightly comic incident when it was discovered that her chosen place beside Violet Martin was solid rock. Not until they had sent for dynamite from the Gardai and blasted the quiet hillside could she be lowered into the ground where today she lies alongside her friend, the grave marked by a rough country stone on a small hillside; and when there are no leaves on the trees you can just see Tally Ho.

27

NOTHING TO DECLARE

'My dear come with me on the Ho Chi Min trail.' Desmond Leslie's estate, originally a gift from Charles II, straddles the border in Monaghan. He loves to whizz visitors to Castle Leslie up and down border country, zig-zagging along the lanes now in Ulster, now in the Republic, always skirting the official checkpoint. Finally, laughing so much at his own game, he stops and, looking like Rodin's Thinker, sits perched on a crumbling wall explaining that this derelict spot on his land overgrown with cow parsley is where he can put one foot in the north and the other in the south.

A massive figure with a busy walk, Desmond Leslie in white polo neck and blazer, exudes a smiling benevolence, an authority as he peers through tortoiseshell glasses for friendly faces. An irrepressible boyish spirit, he swathes through officialdom whether at the airport in Belfast or the border: 'But dears, we have nothing to declare,' to a nonplussed young soldier.

The border is famous for black marketeering. It attracts terrorist fugitives on the run looking out for a little green lamp in the window of a 'safe house', and there is a great deal of smuggling of old lorries and cars from Belfast, where there is no shortage of wrecks, into the impoverished south.

Two of Britain's finest writers, Iris Murdoch and her husband Professor John Bayley, were held up for hours at this border.

Desmond Leslie in mocking admiration describe a typical couple owning a 'safe house' nearby: 'They will have made so much money, their bungalow is filled with jacuzzis and saunas; there are televisions everywhere all on the blink; they drink all day, until they have a row, when one of them will jump in the Mercedes and that finely tuned German miracle of engineering will be driven into a boggy ditch and the keys thrown away.'

A soldier on the telephone gives the nod; we can go. 'You see he is very bored, talking all day to headquarters, saying, "Hector bravo, sewer chi chi, Suzy out."'

'Now we are crossing Checkpoint Charlie; we are leaving the fascist hyena occupied zone,' and you are in no doubt that you are entering what Desmond Leslie calls 'the glorious people's bankrupt republic' as the car bumps over some cavernous potholes. The roads may be awful but the people are smiling.

As if in celebration, the Mountains of Mourne suddenly appear. It is a rare treat to see their heathery blue tips as they are usually covered in the proverbial Irish mist. 'It is a soft day, thank God,' the Irish say, smiling in torrential rain.

Leslie has just returned to Belfast from London. 'I have just had my aura brushed and dusted at the White Eagle temple in Kensington. Oh, it was wonderful dear.' He has found being one of the White Brotherhood, sometimes known as the Alchemists or the Martinists, a most satisfying mystic belief, and was touched when a white pigeon rested near him in the South of France, an encouraging symbol apparently.

The temple is in a quiet, residential Kensington cul-de-sac. On a snowy March evening, a young priestess in a blue caftan, Jenny Dent, the granddaughter of the founder (a medium called Mrs Grace Cook), urged a bedraggled band of men and women to listen to the wise words of White Eagle and learn about affirmations. Above a small altar, a white painted eagle is suspended from the ceiling.

Mrs Dent, a slim pretty redhead who smiles a lot, tells the weary looking group that an 'I am beautiful and slim' affirmation has worked for her. 'I was a fat child and always thought myself ugly, though my husband told me I was beautiful.' One morning in a private swimming-pool near her home in Hampshire she had been able to get rid of feelings of aggression about a particular person by lying on her back and pushing her legs out; she had felt a rose bloom, and patted her middle encouragingly. Downstairs, an elderly woman was fielding calls about 'healing' times and coping with distressed members of the White Brotherhood, asking a colleague: 'Have you managed to help that poor man who was having inexplicable things happening to him . . . awful, wasn't it?' White Eagle helps on everything.

Visits to London are not just for spiritual refreshment. Desmond had just been to a 'tremendous party' at the Cavalry Club given by a friend who, at fifty, advanced his 100th birthday celebrations. At other times, it can be to 'sell a little something' at Sotheby's.

Now nearing Glaslough, so green and unspoilt it seems a million miles from the guns and barbed wire at the border, intrepidly the little car bumps into a forest of romance and mystery. On the edge of the Leslie estate, it is full of trees planted by generations of Leslies, California redwoods and Douglas firs, and there is a smell of wild garlic and the innocence of bluebells. Desmond Leslie smiles at some pretty girl going by on horseback. 'It was in these woods,' he confides, 'that I had my first sensual experience on a fairy cycle' and gives a delighted shiver. 'Nanny said no more reading.' The yellow iris billow left and right, heads waving in gay mockery. They say on quiet, still nights mysterious bumping rustling sounds are heard around the dense tree trunks in this lovingly named Old Wood.

The eye is drawn down to the edge of the 'green lake', across the overgrown Italianate steps where Desmond Leslie's sister the novelist Anita Leslie is buried between two tall trees 'to keep an eye on her naughty brother', the family say; and on the island on the lake a charming signpost says '398 miles to London' put up by Leslie children decades ago. On summer solstice nights, when Wagner is played in the abandoned old pine library, the drum beat echoes down across the water and the brass from 'Hagen's watch on the Rhine' from Act I of Wagner's *Götterdämmerung* carries magnificently into northern Ireland.

At first glimpse of Castle Leslie, it really is a wonderful sham castle. Ireland has always had a fancy for calling large houses castles, but never downgrades 'castles' into houses. Originally a medieval fortress, this castle had a dungeon and a moat, but it has been rebuilt over the centuries. Today in its grey 'black Protestant' Dungannon stone, the iron making it so forbiddingly dark, it looks a cross between a religious institution and a French château. It has also been compared to the Queen Mother's home Glamis but there the resemblance ends as many of the windows at Castle Leslie have no glass and huge sheets of polythene rustle in their enormous task of keeping out the wintry north wind.

The door, leading into a hall meant to inspire a feeling of Italian Renaissance but conveying one of unadulterated Gothic gloom, is opened by the old retainer Brigid Curry – the family call her 'Mrs Danvers' – who has been with them for thirty-six years. She peers up shrewdly at Desmond Leslie towering above her as he bustles importantly past the Ionic columns and into the conservatory.

Brigid Curry barely remembers when Glaslough was mellow and cherished, attracting poets and artists just at the end of Sir Shane Leslie's time.

Always a flamboyant unpredictable figure, he learnt the Irish language and, proud of his Scots ancestry, liked to wear a saffron kilt. The Leslies had been great supporters of the Stuarts and defied Cromwell. One of them, a clergyman John Leslie, galloped from Chester to London in twenty-four hours at the age of ninety to celebrate the Restoration of Charles II.

Sir Shane wrote ghost stories, fiction and poetry, and is credited with a much-loved apocryphal Irish story. He claims that when he was at a railway station, a porter was seen shovelling an Ascendancy figure into the train rather the worse for wear. The station master turned to Sir Shane, observing out of the corner of his mouth: 'Will ye look at that, there's Lord Massereene and Ferrard and the both of them drunk.'

While at the station, Sir Shane took the opportunity to ask the station master why the two clocks on the platform always told different times with twenty minutes between them. The official scratched his head and, with faultless logic, replied: 'Sure if they didn't both tell a different time, what would be the use of having two clocks?'

When he died in 1951, his heir, the present fourth Baronet, Sir John Leslie who is seventy-two, had no intention of returning to Glaslough. A captain in the Irish Guards who had been wounded and taken prisoner during World War Two, he remained in Rome and the Italians made him a 'Knight of Honour and Devotion' which, Desmond Leslie irreverently swears, makes his bachelor brother a 'Knight of Chastity and Perpetual Poverty'.

Glaslough was then to be shared between Desmond Leslie and his nephew Tarka Leslie-King, his sister Anita's son. But neither she nor her husband Bill King, a forceful, ebullient character and a round-the-world yachtsman, could cope with the estate's demands. They moved to the west of Ireland to a twelfth-century castle at Oranmore where he hunted with the Galway Blazers and his wife wrote *Edwardians in Love*, about her American great-grandfather Leonard Jerome and his stunning daughters.

One, Jennie Jerome, married Randolph Churchill and became Sir Winston Churchill's mother, and her sister Leonie married a Leslie to be the amusing and perceptive chatelaine at Glaslough. Young Winston loved the Castle but was briefly out of favour with his aunt and her husband because of his support for Home Rule, unthinkable in a family boasting three successive generations of Leslies at Westminster. But Shane, their unconventional son, would stand for the Nationalist Party in the City of Londonderry, contesting the seat against the future Duke of Abercorn.

'The Abercorns thought they owned the seat,' Desmond Leslie explains. 'My father missed by only sixty votes; but the Abercorns never quite forgave him; they were outraged by a turncoat nationalist in their midst.' His conversion to Catholicism, influenced by the Oxford Group, particularly 'Ronnie' Knox and Baron Corvo, would be almost more of a dreadful shock to this Orange Unionist Protestant family and other great landowning families in the north.

Leonard Jerome was 'an amazing man'. His great-grandson, wistful about the four fortunes made by his American ancestor, chuckled. 'He was richer than Vanderbilt.' He would say 'I've had a rotten day,' admitting, in downcast mood: 'I only made thirty thousand dollars today.'

Desmond Leslie, who has an exotic sallow hint to his skin, says the beauty of the American Jerome sisters stemmed partly from their grandmother, who was a 'lovely Red Indian princess'. His mother, Lady Marjorie Leslie, was the daughter of Henry Clay Ide of Vermont, a Governor of the Philippines, and his godfather was Queen Victoria's youngest son the Duke of Connaught.

In the end, Castle Leslie would pass to the dreamy Desmond, now sixty-seven, who with his leonine head, shoulders straight, walking like an Earl, may look the very model of a quirky Irish landowner but talks and thinks like a poet. Not in the least practical, he has the old-fashioned bushy charm of habitués of the old Chelsea Arts Club who received free drinks in return for the brilliance of their conversation.

His early life, as a student at Trinity, where he was 'peripatetic about lectures', then as a pilot and later a musician discovering the synthesizer, was hardly preparation on how best to run a good estate. Glaslough, however, was no longer unwieldy; it had been broken up amongst the tenants; 'a most enlightened view,' Desmond Leslie says gratefully; 'if the Russians did that, it would have saved a bloody revolution.'

He compares Glaslough to an old ship. 'You can't crew it anymore but as long as you keep the hull watertight it is not going to come to much harm.' The family motto is Grip Fast and that is the prayer for the roof.

Inside the Stygian house, the conservatory overgrown with white jasmine as thick as a weeping willow where a cherubic terracotta bust has rolled over on the dusty floor is an oasis of light. Everyone is careful not to smoke near the study; the scion of Glaslough gets nasty asthma attacks.

A languid smile, he listens to an answering machine. Desmond Leslie pretends to be puzzled by technology, hates Filofaxes but loves his word processor, which he tucks under a brocaded dressing gowned arm and takes to his four-poster bed reciting 'a jug of wine, a Japanese word processor' and, depending on who is around, '. . . and thou.'

On floppy disc at present, his latest novel. He chortles as he describes his characters, singing: 'Palestrina's great motet

"Filofax in terra" in the Fitzwilliam, all in their pretty velvets and things, at the installation of the new master at Terminal College Cambridge; then the Anthrax professor of Greek recites . . .' (Here the author sings quaveringly.) ' "Odol, odol, colonis in vinyl, eucryl eucryl, pepsodent euthymol," whereupon he collapses and is carried away.' Always entertaining, though friends find his brilliance ephemeral and get bored with 'Have you read my book *The Jesus File*?' But with a natural shrewdness and sense of survival, he can manipulate most people. Locals happily succumb.

His desk is covered with photographs of a 'Junoesque' blonde, his second wife Helen, a colonel's daughter of impeccable Stewart Scottish ancestry. His first wife was a Hungarian actress Agnes Bernelle. 'She used to outza Zsa Zsa Gabor,' her former husband says. His own best theatrical experience was bopping Bernard Levin on the head for giving his wife a bad review when they were appearing together on 'That Was The Week That Was', a satirical show on television.

They had two sons and a daughter. Mark is an architect in London and Sean is at Glaslough, and rather preoccupied by a golden light he saw when in London recovering from a poisoned foot. Both father and son spend quiet contemplative hours in the temple in the Castle, a White Eagle branch in a little peaceful whitewashed room.

Deathly pale, Sean is urged by Brigid Curry to eat some cake but it is unlikely that a crumb will get past those pale full lips. He sometimes ventures out to the local pub in the estate village of Glaslough dressed as a woman, and appears to fool the hard eyes of teenage girls kicking their feet in angry boredom by the Castle gates.

His wife Charlotte – he wears a Russian wedding ring – another recent buxom addition to the family collection, is in Italy trying to sell her body shop in Venice. 'The Venetians do not wash or use soap,' according to her father-in-law.

In the drawing-room with its white and blue Della Robbia chimneypiece there are more photographs of Churchill and Leslie children on the piano, one of Desmond Leslie's daughter, the 'gorgeous and irrepressible' Antonia, in Princess Alice the

Dowager Duchess of Gloucester's Coronation dress, giving it a wild sensuality as she danced with head thrown back and a mane of uncontrollable hair.

Her father dotes on her. 'She is a very naughty girl; everything with 'Anita' is bounce bounce bounce,' he says of this daughter so unlike his horsey and academic 'Sammy and Milly', children by his second wife. Samantha is an excellent horsewoman who trained at Sievewrights at Siddington in Gloucestershire. She is involved locally and runs the Castle's not inconsiderable Equestrian Centre. Camilla is trying to get into Oxford.

A deliberately spooky atmosphere is cultivated at Glaslough and there is a serious interest in the occult. Red Indians have been known to appear during seances. Indeed Desmond Leslie's whole world is one of fantasy. 'We are,' he is convinced, 'being watched with great interest by benign creatures who visit us but do not want to upset us at this explosive time in our history.' He also believes that 'This planet may be on a motorway,' and is very keen on UFOs, particularly on showing these 'swinging orange lights' to attractive women such as Lord Erne's first wife.

The house is open to the public. When some nubile schoolgirls were visiting, the owner hid behind a curtain in the cellars and made eerie creaking noises and a teacher fainted while the 'ghost' enjoyed a fiendish but full-blooded laugh.

But 'nothing,' he says, 'is so much fun anymore.' So many people have gone – 'friends like Glenavy, dear Paddy Campbell; Lord Rossmore too, and no money dears to entertain in the old way.'

'And now my heart,' he says, 'has done the dirty on me.' So he no longer hunts: 'If I do three fences I stop breathing.' A sigh. 'I wish we could be more like the Romans. If life became intolerable, and you were fed up, you would invite all your friends to a very good dinner, get into a warm scented bath, have champagne cocktails or bloody Marys and then a surgeon would come and cut your wrists; as the water became tinted you just floated away. It was all perfectly proper as you came back with a new body, so why wait and hang on to this one, my pet?'

28

THE INHERITANCE

'The inheritance!' Lady Jennifer Bernard, a stocky figure in denim, chuckles hoarsely and shakes her head as she looks towards a dramatically beautiful ivy-covered shell. This is Castle Bernard, burnt by the IRA in 1921.

She locks the bungalow door, makes sure the guest caravan is secure, a small boy runs ahead. 'Can we see the murder hole where they used to pour boiling oil on people?' His aunt smiles, her nephew Philip Carter will inherit what is left of the folly, one of the best in County Cork. She carries a torch.

They tramp purposefully through fields to the castle, stopping by a chestnut tree which covers half the demesne. Jennifer Bernard has a surrealist view of the Castle. 'I think it is more fun,' she remarks, imagining how it must have been, 'a mixture of Regency and Victorian crenellated'.

It is dripping with stalactites; ravens and barn owls are nesting in what was once the drawing room, and there are kestrels in the billiard room. The gabled ramparts are covered in creeper and the huge Gothic window is letting in the last of the evening sun.

Down by the lake the corn was being gathered in, giving the castle an air of normality, the reassuring, slow comforting turning of the seasons.

'Daddy was delighted it had happened. It was a huge, unheated barracks and the ceiling was so leaky, he remembered umbrellas over the beds.' Her father, the fifth Earl, was an Air Chief Marshal with the Royal Air Force, preoccupied with flying and not at all enchanted by the Castle, which he inherited in 1924 when he was twenty from 'Uncle Bandon and Aunty Doty'. He had two daughters so the title died with him in 1979.

The Castle remained a ruin. Three cottages were strung together rather charmingly to make one pretty house except, as Lady Jennifer recalls, 'You had to go outside to get to the next bedroom.' One had been the gardener's cottage where a desolate Lady Bandon hid when her husband was led away by the IRA and the castle was burnt down.

The fourth Lord Bandon had married in 1876 and it was a highly fashionable wedding. He gave his wife 'Doty', a daughter of Lord Carbery, a gold and diamond locket with a coronet of pearls and, as a joke, 'two tiny spitting kittens'. They were an immensely hospitable showy couple and known socially as the King and Queen. Lord Bandon was a great practical joker who at their rollicking houseparties would sometimes substitute a live cockerel for a chamberpot in a mahogany bedside table. Bandon Castle was known as one of the 'cheeriest houses'. The end of this charmed junketing was rather sudden.

The castle, rather more a castellated mansion, was burnt down early on a fine June morning in 1921. Some fifteen country houses around Bandon had been set on fire the previous week.

Lord Bandon, as Lord Lieutenant, had been a marked man for some time. The IRA had been on the lookout for him, but Lady Jennifer explained that even this had a humorous side. They planned to abduct him on a certain evening but were disappointed when there was no sign of him on his usual route. 'Your Lordship, we thought you had an accident, sir.' But eventually they were successful and kidnapped him when they came to burn the Castle down.

Very little could be saved, some books and a few portraits. During the fire, the lawn was covered with empty chairs and occasional tables as if for a firework party which had gone slightly wrong and all the guests had vanished leaving smoke swirling round the front of the house.

The ruin of the castle was 'absolute' and all one could do was wander across the masses of debris in those precious rooms 'of that best beloved house'. Lord Bandon never really recovered from his ordeal at the hands of the IRA; all the fun and swashbuckling spirit vanished despite his claim that he was given 'Napoleon brandy every night' during his captivity. But 'it broke him; his hair went completely white when he came out; he was over seventy.' He and Lady Bandon left almost immediately for England. But what really angered him was the sight of the empty wine bottles on which the IRA had binged in his cellar; the empties are still in the ruin. 'Those bastards were drunk in my cellar,' he told his son-in-law.

All Jennifer Bernard and her sister have left is a beautifully bound book listing paintings which were burnt: Rubens, da Vinci, Kneller, Titian, a tremendous collection of Old Masters had all been destroyed.

Her parents are dead. Lady Jennifer Bernard took a series of jobs in London which included 'carting foreigners round and showing them England, I also worked for John Lewis as an assistant registrar. If someone had difficulty with money, I was a sort of troubleshooter in personnel.' Before returning to settle at the Castle, she did a bit of 'kerbside cleaning. I called myself KKK, kerbside car cleaning. I operated in Wellington Square, Chelsea, had a sponge; there were very smart cars there in those days; the chauffeurs showed me how it should be done.'

Now she gamely tries to farm the land. She has leased the bogland and lets out 135 acres. She drives a little tractor to pick up sugar beet. A woman farming in Ireland is not taken seriously, the view is of someone mildly potty asking the way. The local Gardai smirk, 'Oh she's not a farmer, she's a landowner.' Friends like Patrick Annesley, owner of the luscious gardens at Annes Grove, help and encourage by lovingly replacing every plant in her garden which has not survived.

Hearty, plump, with big eyes full of compassion, she agrees with friends who suggest it is a hard life. In her jolly hockey sticks way she explains that a woman in Ireland is supposed to be a second-class citizen, but that there are advantages. 'As just a weak woman I have all the fun; the men do the hard work.' There is no bitterness about the past, and as with many of the Ascendancy used to possessions, almost a sense of relief that none are left to worry about. Yet her home, a modern single-storey house, is built around a glorious chest of porcelain, virtually 'all that was saved from the fire', and looks out across her land to dark woods where the River Bandon flows, keeping its secrets.

29

I ACHE FOR TULIRA

Even the name Tulira has a romantic ring. It once belonged to Edward Martyn, a literary Galway landowner, one of the country's rare Catholic landed families. He was a friend of Yeats, Lady Gregory, Synge and George Moore; the cultivated cobweb spread wide from the castle at Ardrahan in County Galway, over those hunting reaches in the west of Ireland.

In a drawing room heavy with leather wallpaper, Yeats and Martyn enjoyed arguing until late into the night, sitting by a fireplace with the four seasons carved into the stone pillars. Eventually the poet would carry a candle up the stone steps, tall and imposingly silhouetted against the red Victorian walls while his host played the organ in the Gothic hallway.

Edward Martyn's mother, who had always dominated him, insisted he must have the finest house in Ireland, so Tulira became part castle, part church and heavily Gothic. But eventually Edward Martyn became too old and gouty to clamber up the steps. He died in 1923 and at his own request his body was used for dissection by medical students and then put in a pauper's grave. The house passed to a nephew, Lord Hemphill, who had to absorb the name Martyn before he could inherit.

Known affectionately as the Edge of Empire, that part of Ireland in the far west has always had a robust distinction. Even the

Anglo-Irish attracted to that remote, beautiful part of Ireland seem different from the more respectable breed drawn to the east and south.

Galway, perched on the absolutely outermost edge of Christendom, has always been European, a city with a French or Italian flavour. An Italian cardinal visiting in the sixteenth century preached in Latin and was surprised to find these 'semibarbarous' Gaelic people understood him perfectly.

In the west they went native early on; foxhunting was not a sport but a passion. In time, with all its distinction, its Oratory and wonderful library, Tulira would be taken over by the hunting crowd when Peter Patrick, as the present and fifth Lord Hemphill is known, and his wife Anne moved to Tulira in the early fifties shortly after their marriage in 1952. He succeeded to the title in 1957 and had already assumed the name Martyn. Now a different sort of brush would be celebrated, not the kind in the hands of artists capturing the elusive brightness of a spring day in Galway Bay, a sky of fleetingly fresh Impressionist blues dotted with blobby white clouds as if angels were suddenly throwing buckets of meringue.

Horse mad, Lady Hemphill was a Whipper-in with the Galway Blazers. 'Nobody paints in our house,' she would say cheerfully, 'but we hunt and shoot and we sail.' As a couple, they were hardly steeped in the Irish literary renaissance, though her mother was a grand-niece of Augusta Lady Gregory, at whose home Coole Park in County Galway the seeds of the Irish Literary Theatre movement were sown.

A good day's hunting with the Galway Blazers was stimulating enough for the Hemphills and, perhaps anticipating these earthy priorities, Edward Martyn would, infuriatingly, leave his library to a strict order of monks and his paintings to the municipal galleries in Dublin. 'Gosh,' Lady Hemphill, in her almost girlish honesty, would often wonder, 'What would Edward Martyn think about us?' Guests included people like the Irish Prime Minister, Charles Haughey, who was galloping over their land when he heard the news that President Kennedy had been assassinated. Here the film director John Huston and film stars enjoyed good-humoured bargaining over Connemara ponies, and people raced up and downstairs during hunt balls with not a thought about iambic pentameters or the delicacy of Greek and Irish mythology.

Lady Hemphill's husband, Peter Patrick Martyn-Hemphill, was educated at Downside, read law at Oxford and then worked in the City, but soon became restless in London. His mother left the fourth Lord Hemphill to marry Ion Villiers-Stuart in 1945. A descendant of the great earls of Desmond and also of Barbara Villiers, one of Charles II's mistresses, he had fallen in love with Lady Hemphill, an attractive American, formerly Emily Sears from Massachusetts. Her son by her first marriage, the present Lord Hemphill, was the same age as her Villiers-Stuart stepson James, both born in 1928; the two have always been close. Divorce from Lord Hemphill was impossible as theirs had been a Catholic marriage in 1927, so like young lovers Ion Villiers-Stuart and Lady Hemphill ran away to Reno to be married, shocking the county. Sadly Ion Villiers-Stuart died only three years after their romantic wedding. His widow, Emily, is a frail but mentally vigorous eighty-six-year-old living in London.

James Villiers-Stuart adored his spirited English mother Elspeth Richardson, a generous, wayward and spirited hostess. Elspeth Villiers-Stuart was 'always rather wild', Claud Cockburn's widow Patricia recalls. When she died in 1943 a dowager remarked disapprovingly: 'I see Elspeth Villiers-Stuart fell off her bicycle and broke her neck on her way to tea.'

During the luscious party days at Dromana there were butlers, maids, scullery maids, cooks and chauffeurs. There was a forty-eight-foot drawing room, and every window looked down on the River Blackwater. A darling of society, Elspeth was sometimes home only for three days in a year: the rest of the time was spent in Paris or the South of France. She was 'very gay' and friends thought she should perhaps have married Charles Cavendish, one of the wild Waterfords, instead of Ion Villiers-Stuart, who was rather solid but adored her.

The present Lady Hemphill, then Anne Ruttledge, had vowed originally that she would become a vegetable if she stayed in Ireland and had gone to live in London. Her father is a distinguished ornithologist, Robin Ruttledge, from an old Mayo family, and is proud of an ancestor who married Strongbow's sister.

Lady Hemphill grew up in the west but today her parents live in a small pretty house in Wicklow, but so chilly they wear their huskies in the sitting room. Hospitable and kind, they manage to be contemporary; laconic and fatalistic about change. Life is not easy for them. Like other Ascendancy families, the Ruttledges' family portraits and great embossed gold mirrors are a clue to the height of the Adam ceilings in the old ancestral home, but now sit uncomfortably in a smaller house.

They moved to Wicklow because of Mrs Ruttledge's arthritis, which has now much improved. But they feel isolated from their daughters, and find it a huge adventure to go west or to visit their other daughter in Suffolk, who is married to one of the Duke of Grafton's sons. Robin Ruttledge says sadly: 'All the old originals are gone.'

The Hemphills reluctantly gave up Tulira six years ago and now live in a stylishly decorated modern house. Lady Hemphill can hardly speak about Tulira without tears. 'I see the castle standing over me; it is something magnificent, peaceful and quiet and I was never lonely there.' She remembers life in Tulira constantly, how her neighbour John Huston would call unexpectedly and was in the library one afternoon when she arrived back from hunting, 'We couldn't shoot today,' he said, introducing a pleasant, fair-haired man.

'Oh dear, not good enough snipe and duck?' she commiserated. 'No,' the great film director explained; 'the light was not right.' So they had decided to come and buy a pony. Huston was joint Master of the Galway hounds. Lady Hemphill rustled up Patsy Whelan in the yard and brought all the ponies to the front of the house.

'We had a very pretty Dutch girl working with us, and I wanted to introduce her, so I said to the young man: "Oh gosh, I am sorry, what did you say your name was?" ' By now the au pair had nearly fallen over in a swoon, goggle eyed, 'because of course she had recognized him as Paul Newman.' He meant nothing to Lady Hemphill except he bought 'a lovely pony'.

The Hemphills vied with John Huston in party giving. 'I remember once calling Cary Grant Gregory Peck. He didn't like it.' Lady Hemphill smiled mischievously. He would have earned more recognition had he excelled on the hunting field. Lord Hemphill chuckled and remembered Ursula Andress: 'She came here with Jean-Paul Belmondo.' 'They were not married then,' His wife added swiftly, 'Ah, all the people we used to have fun with . . .'

The house could not have been more loved. Her first glimpse was on a dank wet dreadful evening but she 'absolutely fell in love with it'. As she went in by the castle door with her future husband her thoughts were: 'Is this a church or something?' The hall was so imposing but gloomy with a smouldering fire giving out precious little heat but smoke all over the house.

There was nobody in the castle except an old retainer: 'We ordered a big tea and we had it in the morning room shivering and shaking but still it was marvellous.' They crawled all over the house, then left to rejoin friends who were staying for the Galway Blazers hunt ball. The following year they were married, living in London but longing to be back in Ireland.

'We couldn't bear London and decided we would come back to Ireland even if my father-in-law wouldn't give us Tulira. Then my husband went out to dinner with him.' When asked if he would hand over the castle, 'By all means,' Lord Hemphill, who died in 1957, replied with alacrity, 'if you think you can do any good with it.' It had practically no roof, no electricity, a turf range and no light.

They set about restoring the house. Soon instead of bats flying in every direction and rats and mice and the disapproving air of Edward Martyn – 'he was a misogynist' – it would be filled with laughter. Their son was christened in the castle oratory by the Abbot of Downside in full vestments, the baby being carried down the grand stairs by his godmother followed by the Abbot 'in all his regalia'. The dowager Lady Hemphill, who used to walk in the garden to pinch a plum or a peach, used to complain about her grandson's extravagance over horses. 'So we always lied about the number going past; she was such a miser.'

There were fields full of ponies; occasionally you might see a fox strolling amongst them; birds singing; but always that rather gloomy sound of the rooks at dusk. But the rooks were part of Tulira, and when Lady Hemphill was young, first married and holidaying at the castle, her husband's grandmother used to sit in one of the alcoves in the drawing room and refuse to go to bed until the rooks had come back to Tulira.

'My husband would go off duck shooting at dusk and I would be left sitting with her; it would be quite difficult to think of something to say; she would keep jumping up and down to see if the rooks had returned. She died when she was ninety-four. That day she had lunch and her usual cigarette and went upstairs to do some mending. I was sitting in the library about half an hour later and heard her calling me. I ran into the hall and she was leaning over the banisters as white as a sheet, and died peacefully that night.'

Lord Hemphill is droll and philosophical about the literary inheritance going to the monks. 'Edward Martyn left all his papers to the Carmelites in Clarendon Street. We couldn't find the bequest anywhere. A few years ago a funny old man there said: 'We threw out some old stuff . . .we have a new library in the monastery now.' And Lord Hemphill shrugged off the monkish philistinism and the loss of the letters and papers which would have been a cherished part of Ireland's heritage.

Their present house is delightful. Hessian is mixed with chintz, squashy furniture, stripped pine shutters, walls lemon yellow or eau-de-nil, a dark red dining room. A foal tumbles in a meadow; a great Dane wanders across a Japanese bridge; the bell pull does not work.

'I have to do everything.' The days of parlourmaids, butlers are over. Lady Hemphill, with her bright, bird-like face and brilliant thirties' bright red lips, rushes off in navy cords and Guernsey, shoulders slightly hunched, cheerfully to watch some crême caramel which was burning and lamenting that any help she had were people 'mad as hatters' from the village. 'We had a darling girl, she was about seventeen, but my daughter-in-law in England nicked her.'

A painting on an easel in the dining room propped in a place of high honour is of a favourite dog. The caption reads: 'Portrait of a Remarkable Terrier'. It is the work of a local artist Jane Storr from Ardfry. Horses and dogs are featured everywhere. Lord Hemphill is a Senior Steward of the Turf Club, and they were given a shamrock by the Queen Mother when lunching in the royal box. He is guarded, a typical Establishment figure, and all he will say about leaving Tulira is: 'Everything is sad that doesn't work.' You feel he is embarrassed by his wife's emotion, but secretly may share her pining for the old house.

'I ache for Tulira,' Lady Hemphill says, and implies they are not happy in Rafford, their present house which many people would love. Her husband is much more reticent. 'He doesn't understand,' she whispers as he sits legs outstretched in front of a log fire with a hunting size cup of coffee.

When his step-brother James Villiers-Stuart had to give up Dromana, the wrench was traumatic.

The house had been lived in by the Villiers-Stuart family for 700 years, so James Villiers-Stuart thought it only fair to offer it round the family. A great-aunt came to the rescue; ' "Great-aunt Gertrude" bought it back and offered it to me again. This great-aunt had stipulated that whoever got Dromana must live in the house. But her nephew James replied: "No thank you", I did not want to end my days sitting on a rock worrying.' The house was then offered to a cousin who was just retiring from Kenya. 'This incumbent,' James Villiers-Stuart suggests with a little distaste, 'pulled down all the Georgian part of the house.' 'Come away, leave it,' Lord Hemphill said. 'Come and live in Galway, forget about Dromana.' James Villiers-Stuart and his wife Emily tried running an oyster farm in the west, but could never forget Dromana. They have moved back to Waterford, buying Ballynaparka in the shadow of the old albatross.

Almost all that is left now of this grand house is the Hindu-Gothic gateway, a surprise wedding present of dotty charm from Henry Villiers-Stuart's mother when he brought home his Viennese bride, formerly Fraulein Ott, to Dromana in 1826.

Now the urns are filled with weeds; Dromana looks ghastly: desolate, grey and windswept, and half of it has been stripped away. Emily Villiers-Stuart, a neat little bustling figure, jumps out of the red battered Toyota truck which she has driven from their home to Dromana with a dog curled around her neck; she has to knock at a side door in a howling wind. Their surly Dutch caretaker, who lives in gloom at the back of the house, glowers until he recognizes her. But yes, she may go into the shell of the house where, as a young bride, she hurled herself in one leap from the top of the stairs, shrieking into her husband's arms when, heavily pregnant, she had met the ghost of Dromana.

This was Edward Villiers-Stuart, who always makes an appearance on a corner of the staircase near the nursery. 'He appeared first as a white cloud –' and she paused by a charming painting of this restless ancestor of her husband's who had stabbed 'a little Moroccan to see how human blood ran'. Afterwards she regretted not waiting to see if he wanted to pass on a message. But the safety of her unborn child came first. They have two daughters, Caroline and Barbara, both living in Ireland.

Walking briskly along the empty corridors, Emily Villiers-Stuart is more relaxed and open now and able to speak about the old house.

At times her husband seems close to tears as he talks about leaving Dromana, the long Irish upper lip quivering. 'But thank God,' he says practically, 'everything to do with the house and estate, all the archives, is now on microfilm.' Like so many in declining grand houses in Ireland, they have been visited by bogus archivists who turn out not to have been genuine historians but dealers keener on taking away some papers or a bit of Ming and Dresden to see if it is genuine, and not returning them.

Dromana is a shell; once a gloriously extravagant handsome creation high above the deep flowing Blackwater River, famous for its parties, people arriving by launch or on their own yachts. Now the potholes are so vast, James Villiers-Stuart says bitterly that people have asked if they plan to let the fishing rights on the avenue.

Leggy, red skinned, painfully defensive, with a deep beautiful speaking voice, he is proud of his roots: 'Call us West Britons – Anglo-Irish, it is recognized that we speak with a different accent, but we are as Irish as they come, going madly back to Florence, madly back to Troy.'

He is sixty-one now but still harks back to his childhood: 'I grew rather wild,' and proudly admits: 'I was never really tamed. We had two or three housemaids – a head housekeeper, a scullery maid, footmen and butlers – my father always said you could not live at Dromana without at least seven servants. I remember in the housekeeper's hall seeing the butler sitting at one end of the table and the housekeeper at the other.' While the butler and housekeeper were dining formally, young James was happily living in muck carts and steam rollers: 'one cross word from a governess and I was away.' 'Dromana,' James recalls, 'was one great big working family. I think that is why I am not in the least bit conscious of class, which is a good thing in Ireland today.'

His mother whom he remembers as 'a gay and fiery personality', died suddenly when he was twelve; his toes almost turn in, and curl, when he talks about his childhood. His wife, supportive and watchful as a terrier, wears a tight teeshirt which says Rumps are Trumps and redoes her red lipstick frequently. He seems so vulnerable, still hurt, recalling how as a child: 'I used to watch the deer swimming across the water.'

Both pick fleas from the dogs abstractedly – there were clicks as they threw their finds into the marble fireplace.

Dromana goes on crumbling. When James Villiers-Stuart found it impossible to maintain the land was sold to the Land and Forestry Commission and the house is now looked after by a cousin, Patrick Villiers-Stuart. His address in a remote part of Kerry is the Shamrock Inn as he recovers from a massive thrombosis, complaining of a pain in his leg one day when he called on James and his wife, his car full of sheep and dogs. He now wonders about letting some Buddhists take over the house and in the last year has made several improvements, keen to let it to anyone who might appreciate this place of memories.

By many standards the house they live in now – Ballynaparka, near Cappoquin, Co. Waterford, a nineteenth-century house whose great windows extend to the ground – is elegant, though there are the ubiquitous damp patches on the old wallpaper. It is fine enough, but wearily Villiers-Stuart admits: 'We are bloody lazy. Solicitors and people are now the backbone, the ruling class in Ireland.'

'We are both in our sixties now,' Emily Villiers-Stuart explains, and is obviously glad not to be making the supreme effort of caring for a vast unrewarding house any more; her husband says he has time now to shoot and sail. He is a talented landscape artist.

In the gloomy dining room, the table is laid bleakly for two and an old whiskey bottle has orange juice in it, barely up to the quarter mark. Bending down over the table James Villiers-Stuart shows long wrists as he looks about distractedly for a scale map depicting the grandeur of old Dromana. Walking in the lonely grounds of his house, he says sadly: 'Oh for a place you could get your arms around . . . I find I am always a little late.'

He is a little cynical about Ireland today. 'The people are not interested in old houses; football is the thing.' Smiling thinly he suggested that the resilience of the Ascendancy was due to 'protein and education'; otherwise, 'They would have been knocked off their perches long ago.'

30

NO IRISH WOOLLY SHEEP

'Come out, come out . . . oh hairless one.' Jeffry Lefroy's wife appears in white blouse and billowy tweed skirt: 'Oh darling, I am dying for a drink.' Her husband continues his search for the dog. The last of the day's visitors are leaving and with them their small daughters, who have been cheerfully bouncing on the Carrigglas *chaise-longues* in Sunday best frilly white knickers.

'Mairead, will ye look at the one?' An adoring mother watched her plump three-year-old girl running round a tableful of dusty old Waterford glass and later leaving a damp patch on the green watered silk. The guide was far too diffident to give a governessy National Trust rebuke.

Flushed and triumphant – takings had been not all bad – Tessa Lefroy is about to go inside but turns her bright beam on a bespectacled, intense young man in black who is reluctant to leave.

The lingering visitor wants to know more about the family. 'Gosh' – another favourite word is 'hoot' – Tessa Lefroy breathlessly stresses how her husband's ancestors were 'really quite Irish'. Huguenot silk weavers, they fled Cambrai after the massacre of St Bartholomew's Night in 1572, no question of being Ascendancy bloodsuckers, and a quick look to see if this is striking the right note.

There are those who fear for Tessa Lefroy. This forty-six-year-old pleasant looking woman with reddish, fairish hair, lively, funny, if slightly high pitched, her conversation sprinkled with 'absolutelys', she could never really be absorbed into Ireland. To Irish country people just south of the border – Carrigglas is delicately placed on the road to Ulster – she may appear just a bit too like a friendly Mrs Thatcher, and a reminder of a British presence in the north.

'So you see, Colonel Anthony Lefroy was the first to come to Ireland in 1760; he settled and married here, loved the greenery and . . . absolutely,' babbling on about Lefroys marrying Irish girls. Her questioner nodded coolly. Silence.

'I don't know your face,' she said suddenly. As far as Mrs Lefroy was concerned this conversation had come to an end, politely, charmingly, but definitely over. Her hostile audience of one still did not move. When asked brightly, 'Where do you live?' he replied: 'I live on the road into the town.' 'Ah yes, that is a very well-lit part.' A tactful reply about an ugly stretch of bleak pebble-dash gaunt houses. Years canvassing in Gloucestershire have not been wasted.

Her face lights up as Snippy the dog scampers out from behind a velvet curtain and into the hall. Dogs and children ease many an awkward moment. The young man leaves.

At last the doors can be locked and Tessa Lefroy, who is being congratulated on her skill, confesses, 'In politics you learn the art, the awful art, of insinuation.' Her husband jokes about the days when 'Tessa was Ridleying'.

'I was enjoying life hugely, thank you very much,' working for the local Tory Party, 'selling poor old Nicholas Ridley to the public.' Nobody could do it better. The Minister for the Environment was at that time – 1973 to 1979 – 'out in the cold' and in need of marketing. All that was BC, before Carrigglas.

In the library, as his wife thankfully sinks into an armchair with Snippy and a gin, Jeffry Lefroy makes quite sure everyone has gone. He is quite keen on his walkie-talkie and security checks.

'You have tremendous liberty here; the other side of the coin is you have no protection. If somebody cuts your throat nobody bothers.' He shrugs. His wife asks: 'Darling, did you turn the horses' water off?' He nods, picking up a huge heavily bound book of family documents: 'She is always interrupting.' Horses are important. The Lefroys bred an Irish Olympic hope, Carin Hill, a recent winner at Tidworth and Tweedlesdown and the 1984 champion at the Dublin Horse Show, where they are often seen smartly dressed in horsey huddles.

Tessa and Jeffry Lefroy came to Carrigglas in 1976, to take over 'this rat infested Gothic pile' which they now love. The first time she had been to the house was soon after Jeffry Lefroy, a noted oarsman at Balliol and a professional soldier, had proposed and then said: 'We'll go and see the old cousins in Longford, cousin Phoebe, head of the family, her mother Kathleen, and cousin Constance, who looks like the carpenter in *Alice in Wonderland*. They'd better have a look at you.'

'Longford?' Tessa Lefroy wondered. Seventy-seven miles from Dublin, celebrated as Oliver Goldsmith's birthplace, holding Maria Edgeworth's family vault and the tomb of Oscar Wilde's sister Isola, who died when she was nine and for whom he wrote the poem 'Requiescat', Longford had some fine lakes, but little else, except of course, the cousins.

It was a forbidding introduction. Whatever the time of year at Carrigglas, mid-summer or mid-winter, 'The beds,' Tessa Lefroy recalled, 'were always wringing wet and water ran down the walls.'

The house had been horribly neglected, left empty for years. The 9th Lancers were billeted there during the First World War and had, the Lefroys recall sadly, 'an awful deer hunt; there have never been any deer in the park since.'

It was lived in again in 1922 by a brilliant but eccentric inventor, 'cousin Hugh' Lefroy, who ate iron filings because he believed they were good for you, filled the valleys of the roof with manure to grow potatoes there and pruned his trees by night with a miner's lamp because it would hurt them less than in daylight. A butler's pantry was his laboratory. Poisonous liquids would eat into the floor, and the ceiling below would collapse.

He and a friend and neighbour, Major Stuart Hales at Strokestown, decided they should split the atom. However Hugh Lefroy the more scientific of the two and an electrical pioneer, advised: 'Could be one hell of a bang.' 'I know, old boy,' the major nodded sagely; 'that is why I have a couple of fast horses tethered outside.'

Hugh Lefroy's wife Helen was a familiar evangelizing figure as she swept around Longford, trying to convert the locals to Protestantism. On one occasion when addressing a straggly band with nothing better to do, this dramatically dressed figure told them with fervour: 'Last night I lay in the arms of Jesus.' A voice came out of the crowd, shouting: 'How are ye fixed for tonight?' She joined the Salvation Army when her husband died in 1954, and the three cousins took over Carrigglas.

In spite of her first visit, when a chandelier crashed on to the dining table, a bulb landing neatly on Tessa Lefroy's plate to be skilfully retrieved by eighty-year-old 'cousin Kathleen', who used her walking stick with the brilliance of D'Artagnan, Tessa and Geoffrey Lefroy were married and settled to army life in England and Germany.

The next time Jeffry Lefroy was at Carrigglas was in 1971 for 'cousin' Kathleen's funeral. When he arrived on a whistling dark windy night and walked into the unlit hall he was rather surprised to bump straight into 'cousin Kathleen'. This normally phlegmatic soldier who affects the same doleful lugubrious air as the actor Peter Ustinov admitted, 'Gives you an awful jerk. There I was with a bag in each hand and Kathleen was in her coffin, open for viewing by the tenantry.'

Once over seedcake and sherry at a local funeral, he overheard his 'cousin Constance' say as she glanced contemptuously at a neighbour who was rather poorly: 'Really, common people have no idea how to be sick in a genteel way.'

'Quite unexpectedly,' Phoebe, an artist and graduate of Trinity, suggested quietly to Tessa when they were alone: 'What would you say if I told you I was thinking of giving Jeffry this place?' She gulped. 'Gloucestershire was the hub of my universe; we had a dream cottage, roses round the door and an apple tree in the garden . . . heaven.'

Jeffry Lefroy had grown up in Yorkshire, but his military father – who had a distinguished war in Italy but later on holidays would boom in tavernas about things being 'pericolosa' – had made sure his only son was born in Ireland so he could acquire Carrigglas.

For the move, one of the most traumatic events in their lives, Tessa Lefroy was on her own. 'I was quite alone. No, that is not quite right, I had mice and rats coming out from every corner, four hundred rats precisely,' she recalled. Her husband was abroad and, while he could not help personally with the move to Ireland, his assistance from a distance would be most effective.

'I am frightfully dynastic,' he smirked. 'A Lefroy had been the Entymologist Imperial – but he injected himself at Imperial College with an overdose of flykiller. However we invited the firm he founded [Rentokil] to come and do their stuff on the "*Mus musculus*" and "*Rattas norvegicus*".'

Tessa Lefroy then set about shaping this bishop's Jacobean manor, still a rather daunting grey Gothic Revival house, into what she hopes will be 'the most prestigious loo stop in Ireland. All those blue-rinsed ladies and prostate old gentlemen desperately need to stop half way through Ireland, what better place?'

In the seventeenth century this was the bishop's house and was known as The Little and Old House. In the first part of the century, when local Catholics rose up against the Protestants, Bishop Richardson moved out of Carrigglas to avoid being slaughtered by the mob and, as the house was in his gift, he left it to Trinity College. The University leased it for some time until it was bought by an admirer of Jane Austen, Thomas Lefroy.

In amongst the collapsed ceilings, and in cupboards, Tessa Lefroy found a great deal of old Huguenot lace, brought over by early Lefroys, but threw away the eerie bags full of hair combings. There is an air of Victorian propriety about the building. Dimity Laura Ashley wallpaper suits its solemnity; these inexpensive spriggy wallpapers lend the house the prettiness it craves. On the landings, lifesized dummies, a woman in a nineteenth-century long lilac taffeta silk dress and a little boy in 1740 pantaloons, are quite startling at night on the lonely staircase on the way to a turreted bedroom.

Carrigglas has a ghost. In spite of his achievements the dashing Thomas Lefroy, who became Lord Chief Justice of Ireland and had bought Carrigglas with its 3,500-acre estate from Trinity, was rather restless after death. He haunted his home fairly relentlessly in the 1930s and 1940s, following the estate carpenter's son every-where until the man, exasperated at another appearance, challenged the ghost by asking why he was so tall when he had the reputation for being a small man. To this the ghost gave an inimitable Irish answer: 'When you are dead, it is the size of your personality that counts.'

Much is made of Jane Austen's delicate as lavender flirtation with 'the very gentlemanlike Thomas Lefroy, who was believed to be the model for Darcy in *Pride and Prejudice*. Jane Austen confided in her sister Cassandra, in what sounds at first the language of torrid innuendo: 'I am almost afraid to tell you how my Irish friend and I behaved . . . everything most profligate and shocking', but then, delightfully Jane Austenish, it was 'in the way of dancing, and sitting down together'.

'I can expose myself only once more,' she thought, as the relationship with this 'good-looking pleasant young man' was about to end 'because he leaves the country soon after next Friday on which day we are to have a dance.' Thomas Lefroy, who employed the Kilkenny architect Daniel Robertson to redesign the house in Tudor Gothic Revival in 1837, dismissed the flirtation as 'boyish love' and married someone else.

His great-great-great-grandson Jeffry Lefroy was once locked in the roof by a poltergeist, but as the best bath baritone in Ireland he hummed the dreary hours of spook imprisonment away.

All that is left of the original estate is 400 acres. The Lefroys are happy keeping half and leasing out the rest. Jeffry Lefroy is a keen forester, cherishing a bosky park full of healthy trees, 130 acres of hardwood and thirty-three for conifers.

The Lefroys are out, standing by the lake; more ducks are dead. 'Irish children have a passion for killing live ducks, so we have had to put in two decoys.' Turning to his wife he says: 'Darling, Emily says she can get us a duck tomorrow.'

His wife, looking dreamily at the water, wonders if it is a Chinese duck, 'the one I want, I mean a mandarin? Oh and someone must make me a Chinese junk or a pagoda, so it can be towed on a raft.' Jeffry Lefroy smiles at her optimism, and the unlikelihood of either duck or pagoda surviving.

Tessa Lefroy races off. Full of energy, there is just enough time before the house opens to do a bit of work on a biography she is writing of her uncle Sir Thomas Monington, president of the Royal Academy.

'If only my ancestors had been decent eggs,' Jeffry Lefroy says, 'and left it in a position where it was falling down. I could just have dynamited it with a clear conscience.'

His wife reappears. 'Our hope is that our sons will come back when everything is looking super.' Her husband suggests that it would be a very good thing if Randall, aged twenty-three, and Edmund twenty-one, married first and brought a pair of good healthy Sloane girls in wellington boots back to Ireland, and not, he stresses 'Mayfair dolly birds': using lovely dated sixties' jargon. They would be useless at Carrigglas.

'Dear sweet Mrs D', who does the accounts at Carrigglas – Tessa Lefroy's world is inhabited by 'sweet' people – is taking the first tour. Her husband, Tessa jokes, would happier, better suited, with a junior officer or a subaltern in the office rather than the indispensable Mrs Dennigan.

He teases his wife as the first lot of visitors arrive, saying he does much better tours. 'Oh darling, you intimidate them. Jeffry is a born actor, you used to frighten army brides – you were horrible.' Shrieks of laughter, 'absolutely horrible.'

Restoration work goes on. The Georgian stables designed by the distinguished, neo-classicist James Gandon in 1790, are really more elegant than the house. Graceful limestone archways have created, the experts say, 'an expressive combination of delicacy and power to the farmyard', which is certainly more than you can say for most Irish farmyards. The dairy will be restored and become a craft shop. 'But I am refusing,' Tessa Lefroy says firmly, 'to have any shamrocks or Irish woolly sheep.'

31

THE GAY MICE

'Go out to Oranmore,' they said in Galway, 'just zig-zag and you will find the Castle at Ardfry.' Nobody mentioned that the castle on the shores of Galway bay was just a shell, a complete ruin and carried a warning about the 'danger of entering'.

The owners, one of the fourteen distinguished tribes of Galway, are to be found living contentedly in an outhouse in the grounds, happy as long as the old inheritance is always in sight.

The Gay Mice, as these three tiny, hospitable Blake sisters are affectionately known in the west, are just settling down to an afternoon watching 'The Irish RM' on television, tippling something sweetish from a decanter and snuggling into a sofa for the antics of Somerville and Ross's roguish Flurry. A piece of curtain which looks not unlike sacking has been pulled across the window blotting out the ethereal light over the Bay and the blues of the mountains tinged with purple. Peals of laughter encourage the four dogs to jump into jodhpurred laps and share the fun of Flurry's struggles with a recalcitrant steeplechaser. On a rare and beautiful marble table a bit of elderly celery sprouts from a jar of water.

'Put your car on the grass where the crest is,' the colonel had suggested, and sure enough, lying unceremoniously on its side, was a chipped grey stone coat of arms 'Virtue Alone Ennobles'. Ian Bowring Spence, husband of June Storr, the practical sister, introduces himself. 'Isn't it grand here?' he says '. . . wouldn't live in England for all the world.' Striding out against the Galway elements this spruce figure in claret Guernsey and gleaming brown leather shoes is like a young World War I poet, heroic looking, chin up, all attentiveness and ease with the potential of a royal ADC.

'We have the most heavenly sunsets over Galway Bay. The Irish,' he confides, 'the locals, near us, are absolute pets,' and then an aside, 'most unreliable people of course, but I do love it here. Of course Irish villages are frightful; you can't beat an English village, Tudor buildings, cobbled streets, Petworth or Graffham.' Chest out challenging a mischievous Atlantic breeze, he sidesteps crotchety, squawking bantams and walks on with the assurance of a landowner inspecting his cherished Capability Brown estate.

In 1969, against all good advice from aristocratic cousins – the Earl of Harrington was one, 'Bill's father was Mummy's first cousin' – the diminutive trio, granddaughters of the fourth Lord Walscourt, came home to Galway abandoning a comfortable life in England. The title became extinct in 1922, when their mother's brother, the fifth Earl, died at the age of forty and only girls survived in the family. The second wife of the fourth Lord Walscourt had sold off the lead on the roof to try and pay off some of her huge gambling debts.

Back they came stirred by misty memories of childhood holidays at Ardfry: kitchen gardens of espaliered pears against sunny reddish brown walls, peaches and nectarines warm and furry against young mouths; maidservants in crisped frilly aprons; and three small cottages for the land agent, the head gardener and steward at the castle, now their home. 'We always loved the place.'

The castle had been burnt down not by rebels but by agreement when John Huston was making his film *The Mackintosh Man* with Paul Newman. It had been covered with ivy and the sisters asked that the two little trees planted when their mother and her sister were born should not be harmed. 'Whatever happened they must not damage those. They were very good.' Not much else was left at Ardfry, just the bell which once summoned the servants and the sisters like to give a tug occasionally. Bells could chime unexpectedly at Ardfry, as the third Lord Walscourt, a flamboyant fellow, liked to walk nude about the castle and had been prevailed on by his wife to carry a cowbell so that 'the maids could scuttle out of his way.'

Everyone worried about the sisters' survival. Funny and guileless, they were hardly robust, June Spence preoccupied with horses and dogs, Jane Storr unmarried and an artist, and the eldest, Leila Theodisia McGarel Groves, a widow and quite frail.

They had grown up on the Isle of Wight, in the rarefied royal atmosphere of Albert Cottage where Queen Victoria's daughter Princess Beatrice lived for a time.

'Albert Cottage had a huge ballroom with a real sprung floor, a lovely music room,' they chirrup. 'But of course it was small compared with Osborne House,' Queen Victoria's grand Italianate house which was handed over to the nation. The Prince of Wales, the future King George V, disappointed his father by turning it down and part of it was converted into a convalescent home for officers.

'Mummy' – and obviously the daughters adored this sprightly war widow: 'the darling, she wore high heels until she was eighty-nine' – was thrilled when she could buy Albert Cottage. Her husband had gone missing in the First World War but, convinced he would come back one day, 'She never dreamt of remarrying.' Her mother was the Lady Jane Stanhope married to the fourth Lord Walscourt. His second wife was an inveterate gambler. Her step-granddaughters tell bitterly how she gambled everything away at Monte Carlo, gambled on the horses, on the tables, had a great time, lost everything. 'Mummy saw very little of her.'

'In the end,' a helpless little giggle, 'because of hard times, grandfather had to sell a lot of the estate.' Ardfry was ransacked; the roof was taken off. Later there was the usual Ascendancy property wrangle but eventually, in 1950, it went to the 'Gay Mice' and their mother. These tiny women with delicate ankles managed to win back ownership of the Castle and thirty-three of the original 2,000 acres in a Land Commission court, seeing 'orf' a marauding nephew of a step-grandmother. Sadly for the Mice, the nephew had already chopped down a lot of trees and sold off the timber so there was little protection in their flimsy home at a lonely, windswept Ardfry.

They remember having 'absolutely nothing, just one or two chairs. We camped out for about eight to nine years with an Elsan and cooked on a primus stove.' What sustains this family is a gaiety, an innocence; to be with them is the fun of escaping from the real world. Besides at that time Ardfry was only for holidays; home was still the snugness of Albert Cottage on the Isle of Wight.

The colonel, a cousin of the celebrated architect Sir Basil Spence, not long out of the British army where he had served from 1936 to 1946, had settled in a pretty cottage on the Isle of Wight 'with beans and hollyhocks, that sort of thing'.

When asked where he met his wife, at a dance on the Isle of Wight perhaps, 'No,' he replies briskly 'at a bus stop,' an answer inviting a Lady Bracknell echo of astonishment. He too is filled with the same fey optimism as his wife and sisters-in-law.

Colonel Spence had spotted mother and daughter waiting for a bus and offered them a lift in his trusty Austin 12. His first impressions seem to have been more of his mother-in-law than his future wife. 'Ah, you should have seen their mother; she was like a Dresden doll, little lace-up boots, tiny ankles.'

The colonel was invited to tea at the 'cottage'. 'I went around and of course it was a vast mansion, lovely balustrades, lots of carvings, a great ballroom.' The romance was going well and he began to think about marriage.

Sitting back in an old Victorian button-back chair at Ardfry Bowring Spence explains how first he had to have a frank chat: 'I said to June, "I am extraordinary, I don't want children, I have nothing against them, but all I want is sex and companionship." Well, June liked horses and things so that was all right, in fact it was ideal' and, agreeing to this reckless proposal, June Elizabeth Storr and the colonel were married in 1957.

The colonel's eyes dance with pride as his wife takes up the story of how almost single-handedly she won back Ardfry. 'When Mummy died in 1967, Ian and I decided to come and live in Ireland. We knew this was where we wanted to be.' Her sisters would follow and all would leave the genteel cosiness of the Isle of Wight. Ardfry was in their blood.

The Spences sold their cottage. 'It was getting too built up around us; the Isle of Wight was changing. It was not very nice for the horses, fields were being taken over, so they did not have much of a life there.' The comfort of the horse is put fairly high in Anglo-Ireland; dogs are next, old houses a close third; husbands, lovers and children are in a different category altogether.

The sisters sold Albert. Two voices wail: 'Oh, it was hard to give it up; it was horrible but really it was too big for us.' Albert Cottage was sold for £11,000 and has now been divided into flats.

Friends and responsible members of the family were seriously worried about this move to Ireland. 'Sheer madness,' they said, 'you cannot live on scenery alone.' But that is where they were wrong.

It is a cause of great merriment to the sisters, that distinguished ancestors, in elaborate and ornate gold frames more suited to a graceful drawing room or Gothic staircase, have been cut down to fit in the low-ceilinged cluttered rooms at Ardfry. They look decidedly grumpy and uncomfortable with their hunched shoulders and feet rolled out of the picture.

'That is our great-grandmother; she used to be above the piano at the Castle.' They are not in the least concerned. 'All these paintings here are only copies, every year we are more hard up.' Gales of laughter. All the originals are in the eleventh Earl of Harrington's home at Greenmount Stud in Limerick. After Eton and Sandhurst and serving in World War II he became an Irish citizen. 'He is,' they say generously, 'entitled to them.'

Spence and his wife lived in a separate part of the three converted outhouses; they call them cottages. There is nothing around except a wild natural beauty.

Their house is comfortable, light and airy, filled with his sculpture and his wife's paintings, and far from disorganized. When they lived in the Isle of Wight, one of their great friends was Uffa Fox, and Jane Storr was commissioned to do some table mats for Prince Philip. In the bathroom, pausing by a mural of a full-bosomed mermaid by his unmarried sister-in-law, the colonel smiles: 'Makes me feel ten years younger.'

It gets so cold in the winter, he said he was often in bed by 6.30 with an electric blanket: 'Turf is so wickedly expensive,' and that was the only hint of a complaint. He is rather proud of making the *Sunday Express* newspaper last all week: 'Been reading it since 1932, have a few books as well.'

There is a television set at the end of his bed. 'I keep in touch with England, those Agatha Christie things on television with Joan Hickson as Miss Marple. I have nothing against England. I just can't afford to keep up; I really am very hard up.'

'We enjoy it here, we are very pro Margaret Thatcher. Now that girl Jill Gascoigne with the cat's eyes,' he asks about the actress, 'is she communist or labour or what? June and I can't bear people making fun of Prince Charles . . . that horrid "Spitting Image",' and for a minute he sounds more like Enraged Cheltenham than Relaxed Ardfry.

Like three little birds, at 6 o'clock the sisters fell on toast with savoury paste and tea poured from a Georgian silver tea pot, talking gaily about when 'we pop awf' and rummaging through photograph albums: 'Ah, days of glory' as they look at a picture of their sister Leila, a straightbacked debutante in a slinky twenties dress, very Charleston. 'Now we are broke to the wide,' they say cheerfully.

A little sigh as an old catalogue falls out showing exquisite antique family furniture (including a rare Regency rosewood chiffonier, an inlaid brass and tortoiseshell French Buhl dressing table) made pedestrian by being broken up into lots and numbered, the contents of Albert Cottage. 'It all went for about £2,000,' another sister chimed in at the dismayed silence. 'That was in the 1960s before there were high prices for antiques.' All agreed, they had no idea where it had all gone. But anyhow, 'You can't starve amongst all these antiques.' They still have some beautiful pieces of furniture meriting a visit from the Knight of Glin wearing his Christie's hat. 'He was pleasant.'

'Did you know we are connected to the Duchess of Semanita?' one asks. 'Oh I love ruins,' said Jane. They all talk together, June with a slightly nasal theatrical twang.

The sisters' gaiety, their Bohemian slightly ramshackle lifestyle, endeared them immediately to the west of Ireland. They were immensely popular and their fancy dress party on New Year's Eve was famous. 'They were great fun,' the Colonel reminisces; 'I was a sheikh once with a moustache and when I was young I was a chorus tarty girl with false lashes and things.'

It is all too expensive now to entertain on this scale, they are in their late sixties – 'Leila is nearly eighty' – and in any case were never as clever at makeup as 'Mummy' was.

'Do you remember,' June asked the others, 'how Mummy made up a man for a fancy dress party? He wasn't anything to look at, I am not sure he wasn't baldheaded.' Chiming in, another sister thought, if she remembered rightly, 'He was a boxer. We lived near the convalescent home for officers at Osborne; he had a wound on his arm, anyway Mummy covered it with feathers.'

It is unlikely in that remote part of Galway where you can almost see America on a clear day, that the sisters could have the same fun or success with the Irish farmer who is refusing to pay his grazing rates down by the gates. 'Bloody fellow,' one of the sisters mutters, but smiles when she is reminded of the boxer's success at the dance.

'Mummy had made him look so stunning, very vampish, at this dance, he flirted with the House Governor all evening.'

32

A TITLE IS SUCH HELL

Antrim, all the glories of its coastline are safe, where flowing-maned sheep are held from the sea by fine, inoffensive wiring, no ugly fencing binding the cliffs, and gorse sweeps down these greenest of hillsides giving them a sunny Indian yellow. Windy roads, white-washed cottages, Ireland as it once was, before it was haciendaed.

No money pours into Antrim; its beauty is safe because it is ignored. Tourists are frightened and the few Italian or American groups take a speedy run to the Giant's Causeway and then 'get the hell out of the north'.

On a crisp, tranquil Sunday morning, Lord Antrim is standing outside his grey castle with its pepperpot turrets and mullioned windows. This is Glenarm, which one Lord Antrim described as 'late Grotesque'. It is almost mediaeval in its wooded setting, nestling below a glen once full of stags and game. From the dining room windows you can see the lighthouse on Mull and from the porch, the mysterious glen. But the view the fourteenth earl is enjoying most is the sight of an old Lagonda which has just been driven on to the lawn. Vintage cars are one of his passions.

A diffident and contemporary man, dressed in cords and shirt, he says he has always found having a title – he is fifty-four – 'such hell', despising the 'snobbish wimpishness' it often attracts and prefers his earlier title Viscount Dunluce.

When his eldest son, the Hon Randal McDonnell, was about to go to public school, he put a notice in *The Times* saying in future the boy would prefer to be known as plain Randal McDonnell. The boy's grandmother, a daughter of Sir Mark Sykes, was 'very upset' and thought it unfair to her grandson who is now twenty-two. Recently a serious girlfriend has been Joely Richardson, Vanessa Redgrave's twenty-five-year-old actress daughter, who has been taken to Glenarm and loves it, though, she says, 'It always rains.'

Wayward and a bit contrary was the opinion in Northern Ireland, where the landed gentry tend to conform and value their aristocratic titles more than anywhere else in Europe, except perhaps those relics of the Austro-Hungarian empire.

You feel the present Earl is possibly happiest in the Tate Gallery, where he is head of Conservation, and being involved and excited by the new Tate of the North instead of Glenarm which has never really worked for him. Today it is like a beautiful woman living in reduced circumstances. Lord Antrim visits once a month, though home is really Hampshire; even the drawing room seems sparsely furnished but there are some fine 1760 Irish hunt tables, called mahogany coffins. The house is deserted and has a haunting stillness.

Once there were 100,000 acres, now there are 1,200 and everyone seems to have right of way, though there are no footpaths. The present earl has never enjoyed country squire pursuits. A very good little salmon river runs down the glen in 'little sparkling jumps'; but he says: 'I haven't the urge to kill anymore.'

Not to hunt would have been unthinkable a generation or so ago, especially to his celebrated great-grandfather, nicknamed the Buzzard by the children who loved him. He married the delectable Louisa Grey in 1875; she firmly believed that her family were descended from a Red Indian Princess Pocahontas.

When she became a lady-in-waiting to Queen Victoria and later Queen Alexandra, with whom she was a special favourite, the Buzzard grumbled: 'Why should my wife have to wait on anyone . . . like a damn servant.' He did not care for London, but quickly realized that his beloved Louisa, far from being a servant, was having a glamorous life; she would be in demand as a lady-in-waiting for twenty years. He was not jealous but lonely, missing his elegant wife, who had a pretty 'little straight nose' and was stately like Tennyson's 'Maud', who 'walked like a deer'.

Queen Alexandra, herself a great beauty, appreciated a lady-in-waiting who had a refreshing chic, not always dressed in drab clothes smelling of peat and dogs, or old tweeds run up by a woman on the estate. The Countess wore designer clothes, shopping at Paquin in Paris. Her sister Mary had married the Earl of Minto, a Governor-General of Canada who would become Viceroy of India. He rode in several Grand Nationals, hated wearing a top hat, and on his birthday always insisted on oxtail soup and tapioca pudding. The sisters, a high-spirited pair, were proud of their reputation as flighty 'wild and unruly' girls.

Once Court mourning for Queen Victoria was over, there was all the fun of preparing for the Coronation. Lady Antrim sent notes to husband 'Bill' at Glenarm about Edward VII's having to chivvy Queen Alexandra, who was notoriously unpunctual, even on the morning of the Coronation, 9 August 1904: 'My dear Alix, if you don't come immediately you won't be crowned Queen.'

Some antique gold embroidery which had been put away in 1812 at Glenarm was unearthed by Lady Antrim for the Coronation. She wore it on a gold and white dress, with a tiara borrowed from her eldest sister Sybil, Duchess of St Albans, and a family necklace, hoping this would help her to 'hold my own with the other ladies' in their 'gorgeous jewels': strawberry-leaf diamond tiaras, rubies, emeralds and sapphires. Lady Londonderry's coronet fell down the lavatory but was fished out with merry cries of 'forceps'. The Duchess of Devonshire tripped while pushing her way out of Westminster Abbey and 'fell over like a rabbit'.

Other little snippets about court life reached Glenarm, the postman cycling in through the barbican gate with the parchment royal crested envelopes. Sometimes the only glimpse the Buzzard got of his wife was when she had herself 'Kodacked' at a skating party at Sandringham; lunching with the Empress Eugénie; going backstage to meet the great actress 'the divine' Sarah Bernhardt in Paris or with Queen Victoria on the luxurious Train Special with its brass door handles and pale yellow, grey and blue upholstery, on their way to the South of France.

Exciting travel for the Buzzard was going to Scotland to buy cattle, bringing them back from Stranraer on a steamer, and then from Larne, driving them himself on foot along the eight miles of wonderful coast road to Glenarm.

Time together at Glenarm was precious for the Antrims: 'Bill very glad to get me home.' The Buzzard took up motoring in 1903, and was wildly enthusiastic about his crimson White's Steam Car which the family called the Fire-Engine. In spite of gout, he would drive over the rickety Antrim roads in his grey felt two-gallon hat, though his wife recorded how 'It shook and jolted horribly.' On one occasion he shot out of a side road and ran into the hearse being drawn by normally placid, experienced horses. Terrified, they reared up, whinnying so the coffin toppled into a ditch. The mourners grabbed their bicycles and hissed disapprovingly at the Buzzard and his offending steam car.

Lady Antrim was happiest at Glenarm, cycling, doing tapestry and flowery watercolours, being in her wild garden within sight of massed fuchsia hedges, or lying on a *chaise-longue* hearing her caged birds sing and reading exciting new novels with names like *The Typewriter Girl*.

The Buzzard never shared his wife's silken tact, and berated his daughter Sybil even as he took her up the aisle for her wedding at St Margaret's Westminster because she was marrying a man from the middle classes. He hissed right up to the moment they reached the altar: 'You might have married any of Louisa's stuck-up friends, and you go and choose one of these dull conventional Smiths.'

The hapless bridegroom, Vivian Smith, a banker, recalled that when he became engaged to Lord Antrim's daughter he was warned by his future father-in-law: 'You can do what you like here, as long as you don't have a woman within seven miles of the Castle.'

Had Lady Antrim not been away at the Palace, perhaps the hapless hot gospeller who called on Lord Antrim might have had a more civil reception. Instead he had the misfortune to ask the Buzzard, 'Are you saved, My Lord?' and, doubting the reply 'certainly', pressed further: 'Are you quite sure, My Lord?'

'Cock,' the Buzzard replied, and at this the evangelist persisted smarmily, 'My Lord, I see you dislike religion.' This was too much for the Earl, who replied: 'It isn't religion I dislike but your filthy fingernails,' not unlike the peer who had been having nervous depression and went to see a psychiatrist. After the first few minutes, when asked by the doctor: 'My Lord, what is in your head right now?' his aristocratic new patient replied: 'I was just thinking what a common little man you are.'

When Queen Victoria visited Ireland, the Buzzard refused to make an appearance. 'I am so afraid Buzz not coming to Dublin will make her think the family cranky,' the Countess worried.

On one occasion when the Buzzard had to leave Northern Ireland for the Houses of Parliament at a time when Fenianism was rife, he alarmed the police horribly when asked to show the contents of his Gladstone bag. 'Dynamite,' he barked, 'all lie down.' On another occasion he called a meeting ostensibly to talk about Home Rule. There was hardly an uninhibited flow of ideas as he began by placing a revolver on the table and boomed: 'Anyone mentioning Home Rule will be shot.'

He died in 1918 at Glenarm and left orders that he was to be buried standing up on top of Paddy's Hill looking out to sea. But the estate workers got exhausted carrying him up the hill, and in the end he was tipped in upside down and facing inland. His widow moved to Chelsea and remained sprightly almost to the time of her death in 1949, aged ninety-four.

The present Lord Antrim grew up at Glenarm, went to Downside and then read history at Oxford. He went to France and stayed with a family called Vilmorin, 'big seed people', believing they sounded like characters from Proust; there he would do soil analysis and study the genetics of dahlias. Paris was a fairly lonely time, but he started painting and going to exhibitions and recalls hearing 'Vittorio de Sica playing the piano frightfully badly.'

Keeper of Conservation at the Tate Gallery since 1975, he began work as a picture restorer and worked with Lucy, Sir John Rothenstein's daughter.

His father had promised that he would give everything over to his son if he came back to Glenarm, but things were not quite so straightforward and he went back to England and to the art world.

His first marriage to Sarah St John Harmsworth had broken up in 1974; as well as his heir Randal, there were two daughters, Flora aged twenty-four at Exeter and Alice, twenty-three, at Oxford. Losing Glenarm and distressed by the failure of his marriage, he felt his life had 'crashed'. But three years after the divorce he married Elizabeth Sacher and succeeded to Glenarm. By now, however, he was ambivalent about his heritage, and he moves in a world where talent counts and not a title.

He loves Glenarm, appreciates it with a connoisseur's eye and is proud of his artistic mother's witty and strange murals. But although he relies on a good and loyal staff, it is an impossible place for him to maintain.

One of his best friends when growing up in Antrim was the gardener's son, Jackie Wilson, who now runs a model radio and tiny aeroplane shop. They are still in touch and he may have influenced the future Earl in questioning his heritage: 'After all we went about in long boats, we were marauders. We were Catholic and then changed.' In the eighteenth century, the eldest son, an orphan, was sent to Mass, but much to everyone's surprise he came back a Protestant.

The present Earl of Antrim gets a quiet pleasure out of being addressed simply as A. Dunluce Esq: 'That is what I put on my bills.' The Buzzard might have quite approved of this unconventional great-grandson. A free, unpredictable spirit himself with little time for obsequiousness, he once told the villagers at Glenarm when they asked if they might put up a plaque to a respected vicar: 'Do what you like; dig him up, stuff him if you want.'

33

WHAT LARKS

It is the old ladies in Ireland who have the most precious memories. Miss Clodagh Anson, eighty-five, with her retroussé nose and flat girlish figure, has the gaiety and skittish innocence of a certain type of unmarried Anglo-Irishwoman. She lives in an old millhouse in the shadow of Lismore Castle, the Duke of Devonshire's Irish home.

You never laugh out loud but quite often feel creased inside at her droll and gently mocking view of society, shades of Evelyn Waugh and Nancy Mitford, whom she admired so much. She remains close to her sister, the comely 'Debo', the gardening Duchess of Devonshire. A delicate throat gives Miss Anson a wonderful way of saying 'what' like a startled bird and stories have an extra charm when told in a faintly conspiratorial whisper.

Tall and thin, a silver teapot in one hand perilously at an angle, she swoops with gladiatorial swings between kettle and pot, both snugly by the hearth of a crackling wood fire. A stray leaf of Earl Grey is pursued intently. The pot is rinsed and warmed for perfect tea, served with paste sandwiches and a barm brack, a peculiarly rich Irish cake filled with charms at Halloween. Fresh strawberry jam, bulging with plump red fruit the colour of the roses on the desk, is savoured with the excitement of a vintage wine, a special pressing: 'First of the season.'

Her mother, Lady Clodagh Beresford, was a sister of the sixth Marquess of Waterford. His grandson, the present Lord Waterford, a swashbuckling polo player, is said to be one of the rudest men in Ireland. A former admirer of Princess Margaret's and with a reputation for being tough on poachers, he is quite disarming to meet.

A family curse once predicted that the eldest son, nearly always called Tyrone, would die young; but the present Marquess, a robust fifty-six year old, has survived a life of strenuous polo round the world, in South America, and with Prince Philip at Windsor.

He is one of the few landowners in Ireland who really looks like a lord, even his way of wearing a scarf has a polo player's panache. He refused to be photographed in his ancient woolly hat outside Curraghmore, the handsome family house inspired by Vanbrugh's Blenheim, and redesigned in the eighteenth century by Sir Marcus Beresford when he married the heiress Catherine le Poer.

Lord Waterford's aunt, Lady Katharine Dawnay, 'aunt Katy', is another fineboned, autocratic figure. She is Miss Anson's first and second cousin through both sides of her family, cherishes rosy memories of an Edwardian childhood at Curraghmore, which seemed to her to be a miniature kingdom.

Life ever after, including a happy marriage to another first cousin, a distinguished soldier, may never have had the same lustre for her as that early 'peace and stability of Curraghmore fostered by the presence of an English nanny, butler and coachman and Scottish housekeeper . . . naturally we took everything for granted.'

In a pipingly clear voice, and in between spoonfuls of mush-rooms farcies, she read from a childhood diary: the fun of visiting great-grandmother Louisa, Duchess of Abercorn who, were she alive today, could boast over 200 descendants, among them the Princess of Wales and the Duchess of York, and how this spry ninety-two-year-old in a white lacy bonnet did 'an energetic little tap dance'.

It was a typical Edwardian childhood. Lady Katharine would be taken to the drawing room dressed in a white frock with a blue sash, to demurely play with a music box. But she was aware that when her mother gave birth to another baby, which arrived in quick succession to three others already in the Curraghmore nursery, that 'an heir had been secured. Poor little Tyrony; sometimes he was not too happy, his quaint loud boohoo.' The sixth Marquess sent his wife a grumpy message – he was in Central Africa at the time. 'Never no more babbies under any pretext,' he instructed.

The Waterfords, descended from Norman barons, are one of the most eminent as well as among the more outrageous of the Anglo-Irish aristocratic families. In the 1880s the legendary escapades of the wild Beresford boys, Lord Charles, Lord William and Lord Marcus, were the talk of London; they had more than a hundred horses stabled at Curraghmore; they dragged a horse up to their mother's bedroom, stole a whipping-block from Eton, and one rode a pig down Piccadilly. However, this was seen as high spirits and they were rather admired. What would bring this premier family into disrepute was the row between Lord Charles Beresford and the Prince of Wales, later Edward VII.

Commander in Chief of the Channel Fleet, Beresford was rather volatile, a characteristic shared by many Waterfords. He is reported to have struck the Prince of Wales during a furious row at Marlborough House about the affair they were both having with the lovely Lady Warwick.

'You see,' Miss Anson, who heard all about it from her mother, explained, spooning more jam on to a scone, 'they were sharing Daisy.'

The Prince of Wales was very fond of the Countess, writing to her as 'my own adored little Daisy wife' and signing himself 'for ever yours, your only Love', believing her totally his own. However the Prince's little darling made the fatal mistake of writing an indiscreet letter to her other admirer, Lord Charles Beresford, and in it she made lots of jokes about Edward VII's stomach and also Beresford's wife.

The letter was discovered by Lady Charles Beresford, who, bored one evening: 'She was on her own a lot, Charley was always going off to parties without her,' decided to while away a few hours searching through her husband's pockets. Her reward was the discovery of Lady Warwick's letter. In a fit of pique she immediately had the letter copied and 'sent it round to everyone in society to try and ruin Daisy.'

The outcome, as Miss Anson remarked sanguinely, was that it ruined Daisy, 'But it ruined Aunt Charley too.' Nobody spoke to Lady Charles Beresford anymore; she was ostracized in royal circles, banished from Court by the Prince of Wales and became a terrible embarrassment to the family. The Beresfords were re-united, but when, aged sixteen, Miss Anson was taken to see the infamous 'Aunt Charley', the girl was disappointed to find her lying in bed wearing a black nightdress. 'She was in mourning for Charley who had just died; she was terribly made up, and wearing three sets of black-pencilled false eyebrows.'

Then their daughter Katharine, at the age of forty, shocked the family when she 'upped and married a Turk.' Miss Anson repeats 'a French Turk' as if he had come from Trichinopoly; 'He was,' she remembered, 'a most ridiculous man, French bourgeois,' the sort the Waterford feared might easily tuck a napkin under his chin. He loved to shock her aunts, 'saying in pinky pooh: "I 'ave three mistresses." '

The reason the hapless girl was single until she was forty, Miss Anson claims, was because 'She had never been given any parties.' But this is a slightly contrary view as her own time as a debutante at Court was 'terribly boring', and 'my knees always cracked when I was curtsying.'

On one occasion at the Palace, an old family friend, Lady Beasley Carew, was commiserating with the Anson girl who was discon-solately eating sandwiches and drinking lemonade, when suddenly she said: 'Now I must go and talk to some of my dowdy old friends.' 'And there she was,' to Clodagh Anson's surprise, 'up on the dais with Queen Mary.'

Dinner parties could be excruciating too, sitting alongside 'a frightfully grand guardsman'. Miss Anson, who was quite shy, found they were often monosyllabic, but it never failed if she asked where they got their boots made. It was '. . . a hoot; it always worked; one immediately took me up to his room and showed me rows and rows of boots.'

For her, real fun times began when Charles Cavendish, the present Duke of Devonshire's uncle, and his wife Adèle, sister of the dancer Fred Astaire, took over Lismore Castle. 'Charley' was Miss Anson's 'naughty and wild' hero.

When he was in America, he was known as Lord Useless. Sacked by the industrialist Pierpont Morgan, he complained: 'I go to America and all I get is hiccoughs.'

He was keen on conviviality and Miss Anson recalled that she often had to play dominoes with his wife Adèle to keep her calm. 'She got very annoyed about people leading Charley astray and encouraging him to drink.' Miss Anson was not in the least surprised when she saw from the top of a bus in Piccadilly, billboards outside the Ritz announcing that Charles Cavendish had been arrested. 'Charley you see had been trying to rescue tarts, pulling them out of the police van.'

Not even a game of dominoes could soothe Adèle Astaire when she heard that her brother Fred, nearly eighty and still dancing, had married a young jockey.

'Adèle threw a dreadful tantrum . . .' Miss Anson looks puzzled. 'She was a very good jockey; he died in her arms.' Not long afterwards Adèle Astaire had a stroke and died herself. At her memorial service in Dublin in 1981, the choir sang the hymn of her choice, 'A Pretty Girl is Like a Melody'.

Today the Castle is lived in by an agent and his wife, Paul and Arabella Burton. The Duke of Devonshire rarely visits as over the last few years he has been under threat of assassination in Ireland.

In his house in Mayfair, over morning champagne, this elegant rangy man, his long legs wound round each other like the Pink Panther's, accepts that it would be foolhardy to go to Lismore for the moment. It makes him sad. Suddenly this Rhine maiden, fairyland castle in County Waterford seems as alien, foreign and remote as a villa in Chile.

Once he enjoyed fishing from the banks of the River Blackwater which runs through his land. Brimming with salmon, sea trout and brown trout, it turns a shade of navy blue on summer evenings. He even taught the Gardai, his special security men and constant companions, how to fish. 'They were awfully good, they acted as ghillies.' But with the mercurial climate in Ireland today, the Duke is too much of a security risk.

A gangly leap to the champagne, and he shrugs with unspoken sadness about Ireland. 'I love it; when I was in government I took boxes over, but never looked at them, and found a peace and relaxation there as nowhere else.' Lismore came into the family in 1748 when the fourth Duke of Devonshire married Lady Charlotte Boyle, a wealthy heiress and daughter of the fourth Earl of Cork, though the present Duke jokes that it was 'through the murder of an ancestor'.

The Duke and Duchess are both 'mad keen gardeners'. The only difference between well-ordered Chatsworth, the Cavendish ancestral home in Derbyshire, and Lismore is the impossibility of getting a clear answer from the gardeners. 'The trouble in Ireland is that they tell you what they think you want to hear, so if you ask them how something is doing they'll say "It'll be grand so." ' Even so things flourish at Lismore. It will, the Duke vows, be the last of his houses to go.

34

NOT FOR LIVING

Farmer, adventurer, Labour peer, writer, ecologist and pilot, Lord Kilbracken, lean with a peerish elegance, has that shriven, dry spare look of a man who has been to hell and back; in his case, it was the Kurdish mountains where he lived as a tribesman wearing voluminous trousers, a sabred belt and a winding turban over high cheekbones. 'Our Man in Afghanistan', smuggled in by the Kurds, would be the first to tell the world about the invasion of Iraq: the country's leader left the war room to tell him. John Kilbracken has also been instrumental in negotiating the release of twelve hostages kidnapped by Kurdish guerrillas in Iraq. In Ireland they call him the Good Lord.

These days he is sixty-eight, but he finds the House of Lords – 'I love the place, it is the guardian of our democracy' – as exciting as his glamorous 'Lord Copper' style adventures: a foreign correspondent striding into newspaper offices: 'Just off' to the Hindu Kush, the Yemen or China; round the world on five guineas a week, a princely retainer thirty years ago.

One of his main achievements in the House of Lords, he teases, and achieved with the help of Lord Gormanston and some successful lobbying, is that the bar now stocks Jameson's Irish whiskey. Whenever there is an important Bill, these Irish peers are over like a shot, their flights paid for by the taxpayer.

Lady Falkender, formerly Harold Wilson's secretary, looks blooming in a white polo neck and grey skirt, not unlike another Mrs Thatcher. She is being embraced by peers who seem to be getting younger. 'This is a boring bill,' says Kilbracken, giving the television monitor a perfunctory look, but the Duke of Marlborough, driven by Churchillian conscience, heads for the corridor to add his voice to the Contents or Not Contents.

The Earl of Longford stops by for a chat. In the same House of Lords bar, he chivvied Lord Brookeborough about his grandfather, Sir Basil Brooke, for being an 'old bigot' sacking Catholic workers on his estate in Fermanagh.

Today it is his turn to be teased by Kilbracken in Establishment red and white pinstriped shirt. 'The Pakenhams,' he says 'are pure Ascendancy,' and, even more wounding: 'The English aristocracy, they come and they go.' Not fair to Thomas Pakenham, Lord Longford's fifty-six-year-old heir, who has tried so hard to make a go of Tullynally Castle, the family estate in Ireland. Pakenham admits with regret, 'I have had to retreat,' using the military language you would expect of the author of *The Boer War*. It has been a valiant fight ever since he took over Tullynally in 1961.

Tullynally was the home of the present Lord Longford's eldest brother Edward Pakenham who succeeded at the age of thirteen when their father was killed at Gallipoli. Not only did he inherit land which had been in the family since the seventeenth century, a gift, their friend John Betjeman says, 'from that brute Cromwell', but also the town of Longford and half of Dún Laoghaire.

Betjeman and Evelyn Waugh stayed regularly at Tullynally, all a little bit in love, as were many of their Oxford contemporaries, with Elizabeth Harman who married their host's brother Frank Pakenham, becoming a literary wife and spawning a brilliant writing family of which Antonia Fraser is only one.

Betjeman, in a constant naughty search for 'dim Irish peers', instead found nothing at Tullynally but hilarity, erudite conversation and theatrical appreciation. He was only slightly rewarded when he discovered Lord Farnham's two daughters in Cavan were called Verbena and Verbosa, and they were quite pretty. The poet much enjoyed visiting Lord Longford's tweed shops in Dublin where the manager confided that some tweed suits were held over a turf fire to give them, 'an authentic Irish smell' for visitors.

Far from being a sought after 'dim' peer, Edward Longford, a playwright himself, had backed the Gate Theatre with its celebrated thespian duo, Hilton Edwards and Michael MacLiammoir who played Oscar Wilde so brilliantly, a couple irreverently known in Dublin as 'Arsenic and Old Lace'. They created an atmosphere that made the Gate a beacon in Dublin's theatre world, its stimulating bill a mixture of plays including *She Stoops to Conquer* and Greek tragedies, unlike the Abbey which concentrated on Irish themes. The two theatres were nicknamed 'Sodom and Begorrah'.

At first nights, MacLiammoir would recall, his 'hugely fat' patron would arrive with a party, 'striding into the theatre with his sudden infectious cackle of laughter, wearing an orchid on the gingerbread homespun,' so unlike the aesthetic, tortured Yeats. Theatregoers looked for the poetic head thrown back with its mane of silver white hair, rapt attention, an arm stretched along the back of Lady Gregory's seat, a huge signet ring on an elegant hand.

Edward Longford, who died in 1961, was extremely wealthy and could indulge aesthetic tastes. He and his wife Christine collected valuable oriental porcelain and had a handsome library at Tullynally which included several Jane Austen first editions.

'There were four gardeners and a maid was employed solely to clean the footmen's boots. It was a rich man's estate.' Thomas Pakenham, who has never used the title Lord Silchester, says regretfully: 'It should have been a goldmine,' but fifty-seven per cent went in death duties.

When Thomas Pakenham, always a slight figure and frugal, took his young wife Valerie to the ancestral home in Ireland he knew that as a writer she would savour all the lovely literary associations with the novelist Maria Edgeworth. Even though Betjeman suggested they were not exactly neighbours since there was 'a vast Serbonian bog' between Tullynally and Edgeworthstown with its lilac and peonies and, sometimes, snow on the roses in June.

Tullynally was a 'wonderful old house'. Outside there was a lake with white swans and 'merrymaids', the Irish word for mermaids and the local description of the eighteenth-century stone sphinxes in a 'dreamlike park'. But inside all was decay. The bright reds inspired by Lady Ottoline Morrell at Garsington looked extremely depressing. 'It was like the ruins of Pompeii with miles of old and deserted servants' rooms with unpainted walls and old pots in cupboards.' But together they restored it, and Thomas Pakenham would run the farm with a team of advisers.

'Oh Mummie, do tell about the first time you went to Tullynally.' A young daughter with her mother's blossomy potential is studiously reading a Kingsley Amis novel but keeps chirruping from the back of a large sofa.

'We were astonished,' Valerie Pakenham says. This couple who could happily live on a good Stilton found that between them, in that first year of marriage at Tullynally, they appeared to have eaten 'eighteen bullocks, fifty-two sheep and thirty-six pigs'. 'The accounts were still being kept in Dublin by a Dickensian agent; nothing had changed for centuries,' Valerie Pakenham excuses any ineptitude.

Even with that much nourishment, 'Tom' Pakenham could not succeed with these 'boggy acres' deep in the flat turflands where you get the best of Ireland's broken light.

He manages to be humorous about those unrewarding six years trying to be a successful farmer. He even anticipated the Irish habit of saying what they think you want to hear and would ask his farm managers: 'How many sheep lost?' 'How much foot and mouth?' in the hope of getting near the truth. He began to have nightmares; the most disturbing was when he dreamt that a cow picked up a concrete block in her mouth and threw it at him.

He feels badly about not being a farmer anymore, a victim of galloping inflation in 1973 and the wealth tax in '74. 'I thought I would be able to make it work, but I started running into debt on the farm,' and shrugged smiling at his wife sitting in a rocking chair. 'It is Valerie now who is making it work.'

His wife seems more in love with Tullynally than her husband and can be there alone, still finding it novel and romantic. 'I could live there all the time,' she says, but her husband disagrees and says quickly: 'I couldn't.' Why not? And he replies: 'Because I am a professional writer.' But surely that quiet land would be perfect? 'The atmosphere,' his face clouds, 'is not conducive to writing.' No London Library for research. Besides he prefers to be in their large Bohemian house in Notting Hill where the talk is of books and books about to be written.

Always the meticulous historian, he traces the Ascendancy decline in Ireland, peering at a large book spread out on the round pine table in a vast kitchen; the detailed map shows about thirteen big houses left intact in the south.

The Pakenhams find that in Ireland today whereas they once had forty or fifty 'like-minded friends within an easy ride, now they are all in their own little oases, making sacrifices, making friends with professional people.' Those who have survived in Ireland usually have a special reason. Perhaps an heir married a Yorkshire heiress; Lord Londonderry married a Durham coal heiress; Ascendancy widows married trade; their children, while appreciating the unaccustomed central heating in the old house, would apologize for the tycoon's vowels.

Kilbracken enjoys this game of inverted chic played by 'Chablis socialists': 'Mine were in textiles in Yorkshire.' Admittedly his is not an old title. His grandfather, a fervent admirer of Gladstone, was his private secretary and in 1909 was created a Baron by Edward VII. He chose Kilbracken as a title after an appealing hamlet of whitewashed cottages near the family home Killegar, close to the border with Northern Ireland.

Lord Longford beams; the banter could go on for hours but he ends it adroitly, quoting something about ' "the gap-toothed Ponsonby in Grattan's parliament", a favourite quotation of my brother's.'

Kilbracken orders another whiskey. 'The Ascendancy led a segregated life in Ireland, they were patronizing and felt superior to the people whose land they were visiting. Pompous people do not survive in Ireland.'

John Godley, born in 1930, was first taken to 'this strange wild place' called Killegar when he was six. Twenty years later it was his. He heard the news of his father's death as he travelled to New Zealand where he had been expected at the centenary celebrations in Canterbury, a province founded by his great-grandfather.

The new Lord Kilbracken was not at all sure he wanted his inheritance; life had been rather exciting. He was not a farmer by nature and certainly had not grown up at Killegar. He had gone to Eton, where he won poetry prizes, and then to Oxford where he enjoyed some success dreaming about winning racehorses the night before a meeting. His greatest coup was predicting a win for the Maharajah of Baroda, seeing in a dream the princely colours of terracotta and scarlet chevrons and even the name of the jockey, who was called Britt. The horse, Baroda Squadron, romped home at Lingfield in June 1947.

Although John Godley passed out top of more than a 100 candidates for the Foreign Service he was lured to a 'mouvementé' life. A pilot of distinction with the Fleet Air Arm during the Second World War, he felt impelled to send his medals and decorations back to the Queen as a protest against Ulster's Bloody Sunday.

His first instinct had been to sell the old house, but on his way home with time to think, he told himself firmly: 'God, Killegar is me and when three centuries have conspired to bring it to me . . .' He telephoned his brother from Sydney – 'He is the economist, brilliant, always being invited to shape up the finances of the Dominican Republic but not asked to advise in Ireland' – and cancelled the sale.

Getting back to Killegar he was overwhelmed by warm proprietorial feelings of 'this is my field – that is my grandfather clock.' He had been left less than a thousand pounds and decided to make money by offering accommodation, advertising in the New Statesman for 'guests' who would get full board and lodging for £180 a year; over half the applicants were unmarried women. Other well-paid assignments enabled him to buy another cow for the old stately byre. He once escorted Jayne Mansfield, the blonde busty film star, which meant more good publicity and several nice new additions to the herd. 'I got deeply into farming, rearing Herefords.'

His whole life oscillated between Killegar and London, though in 1971 the house was almost totally destroyed by fire. Anything left was thanks to the speedy action of the handyman, 'Little Johnny

Fyfe', aged seventy-nine. The next five years were spent rebuilding what was left of the decaying Georgian house, its weathered golden stone now overgrown with clematis and roses. Nobody ever used the hall door so the honeysuckle was free to clamber wildly round the white columns. Balmain models used to pick their thin high-instepped way round through the French windows, for the ascetic and persistent peer attracted any number of unlikely helpers.

John Kilbracken, they always said, had an elusive quality and liked to remain the roamer, the charmer, the Kipling cat who walked alone. Then quite suddenly eight years ago he experienced 'a little twist, a little madness' and married an Australian girl, disappointing a host of hopeful Lady Kilbrackens.

Homely waitresses in the House of Lords, who are chatted to constantly by the peerage, wheel and fuss round him, he is so thin. 'Have you enough honey?' and 'Would you like another toasted tea cake?'

Now divorced, his joy is a son called Sean, aged seven, for whom he has written a children's bird book.

'It is,' Kilbracken says wryly, 'of all my books the most successful.' Where better to write than Killegar, where in summer dragonflies hover over the lake which Kilbracken thinks of fondly as being 'the colour of Guinness'. At other times, depending on the beech trees and the seasons, it is deep green or gold.

In 1984 he faced bankruptcy. 'I had done a hell of a lot there. It had been costing a ridiculous amount of money. It was an albatross. So I decided eight years ago to get out of farming,' and with a dry triumphant smile he added: 'I shot the albatross.'

In his farmhouse kitchen, where you lift the latch and walk in, there may be someone playing the violin, a vet may be tending a sick lamb watched by a pale child from the north, an artist stretching her long Italian legs in front of the fire, while the Good Lord tramps up a hillside in wellingtons. Suddenly a shriek echoes through the house, another woman friend has just been frightened by a mouse in the lavatory.

Kilbracken says his most valued friends are a mixture of Catholics and Protestants living within eight miles of the border. Intellectual contacts, he says, are a little further away, but within ninety miles. Deprived children from sensitive villages, north and south, are invited to Killegar where they learn to be children again, are taught to fish by the owner, to sail and to vault over haystacks on this rather barren land.

Thomas Pakenham says: 'The big house in Ireland may be extinct in twenty years, they once used to be turned into lunatic asylums.'

'Ireland,' says Kilbracken, 'is a lovely place to be born and to die in but not for living.' Meanwhile he can while away afternoons in the Lords and wait for his visa for Afghanistan.

35

DROIT DE SEIGNEUR

Stories of curses, licentiousness and fairies are the magic of the celebrated Celtic twilight, where the good find faerie glens to live happily ever after in a land of honeybees and tumbling streams where they dance in 'uncontrollable gaiety', the 'Bright Ones', perpetually young.

Simple folkloric tales with a beginning, a middle and an end abound. Some had the sophisticated quirky enchantment of James Stephens' *Crock of Gold* written in 1912, the time of the Irish Literary Renaissance. It concerned 'the Philosophers, who were able to hear each other thinking all day long', smoked long clay pipes and were not too keen on their wives whom they called the Grey Woman and the Thin Woman. These ladies did not speak but had been taught to communicate by cracking their finger joints: '. . . they could make great explosive sounds which were nearly like thunder, and gentler sounds like the tapping of grey ashes on a hearthstone.'

It is the true stories in Ireland, not the make-believe, which have the strangest twist. 'Beware,' they say in Ireland 'a widow's warning or a curse;' they can destroy a family. An example was Lord Doneraile, the fourth Viscount, a dashing figure with bushy beard and roaming eye, a good-looking Rasputin with the same lusty appetites and a flamboyant figure in County Cork who believed merrily in the old principle of 'droit de seigneur'.

An elderly woman who had been a dairymaid at Doneraile from the age of thirteen remembered how the servants had to line up at the gates as he drove about in a coach and four, allegedly inspecting his estate each morning, but actually eyeing something sweet for after lunch. He was rather partial to a post-prandial walk and enjoying the company of pretty local village girls in the summer-house on the estate.

This 'taking one's pleasure on the county' was not limited to hunting and shooting but included other outdoor sports, and was fairly common practice even for rather bleak Evangelical land-owners. William Ponsonby Barker, who had an estate in the rich farmlands on the borders of Tipperary, would make his selection as he presided at family prayers, taking a maid up to bed, justifying it on the grounds that he needed a 'human hot water bottle' though what he said in the summer is not known. If the girl, eyes downcast, was not too fresh after a day hauling coal and wood, he would sprinkle her with eau-de-Cologne. Once, mistakenly picking up an inkwell in the dark, he claimed that he had been teaching 'the poor creature' to write.

An old lady told Miss Clodagh Anson in Lismore that one of her Waterford ancestors had mentioned a local girl in his will, stipulating that she should be given three bags of oats a year. 'It was,' Miss Anson says, 'quite good' – the equivalent of five shillings. Others were not so caring.

Henry Briscoe of Tinvane, an impecunious squire of a diminishing estate in Tipperary with gargantuan appetites, claimed he dare not throw a stone at any child in the town of Carrick on Suir 'for fear it might be his own'.

Not all the girls in the village were shy of Lord Doneraile; some were happy enough to catch his eye, glad to while away the afternoons with him dallying in the conservatory. It was one of the earliest in Ireland with its stained glass and ornate tiled floor although weeds now sprout from the roof. Or they might be taken for a stroll by the charming Awbeg River, wooed under a willow tree or by the lily pond. It was better than making sodabread in a thatched cottage, shouted at by a crabby grandmother to bring in the turf.

A concealed summerhouse in the garden and a secret path meant the girls need never be embarrassed or embarrassing, seen at the heavy imposing front door of Doneraile Court. An elegant house it was originally bought by the St Legers from the poet Edmund Spenser's son in 1627. Perpetuated in the fashionable St Leger race at Doncaster, which they founded, it is the Doneraile family name.

Doneraile burnt down but was rebuilt in the early eighteenth century, with handsome windows and views of the park where the deer would gather on ominous occasions. It was in this house that Elizabeth, the mischievous daughter of the first Viscount, once hid when the Freemasons were holding a meeting. They were furious when they found her hiding behind a grandfather clock in the library. She had overheard their secrets, seen them in their aprons, so they had to initiate her, forcing her to take vows and wear Masonic clothes.

Edward VII when he was Prince of Wales would come and shoot with Lord Doneraile. The Court produced almost as many home-reared pheasants as Sandringham. The Prince of Wales was a first-class shot but once it was too much for the Doneraile gamekeeper, who was Scottish and could not bear to see any more carnage. The birds were falling at such a rate, he spoke out. 'Your Royal Highness,' he said, 'I'd ask ye to shoot the burrids not to murder them.'

Lord Doneraile loved hunting, but hated to think of the fox meeting any other end. A tenant farmer on the estate shot a marauding fox which had been dining nightly on his chickens and then realized with horror that, if Lord Doneraile found out, he could be evicted from his house. Doneraile did hear about it, from his gamekeeper, and ordered him to dig up the fox while he looked on. The gamekeeper was mortified when a ginger puss was exhumed, craftily substituted by the wily tenant farmer. He kept his house but, it is said, Doneraile shot the gamekeeper.

He would be damned by an old woman, cursed not because 'he once beat a priest with a stick' but because her own granddaughter was pregnant by him. Pulling her black shawl close to her head she swore at him: Lord Doneraile would die barking like a dog, and rooks would never nest again at Doneraile or come back until the family had gone.

Her shame turned the village to a savage anger, but Doneraile still took no notice. If a girl had been seen on the estate, the men would hunt her down. Often news was brought to them by a strange misshapen figure with a stump like a tail, not unlike the hunchback of Notre Dame except he was tall and could run a hundred miles a day. This hairy messenger loped around the countryside; the children used to torment him but the young girls trembled because of the speed with which he could carry news. If there was a hint that a girl had been with Doneraile, the village men pursued her remorselessly and she would be taken again by the first to catch her in a strange primeval triumphant vindication.

Doneraile had a pet fox which he took with him everywhere. One day when he was in his coach on the way to Mallow, the little fox gave him a savage nip and also attacked the coachman.

Ignoring the Earl of Mountcashell's advice that an 'infallible cure' for a bite by a mad dog was 'two grains of Native Cinnabar', Doneraile, who always knew where to find the best, left this remote part of Cork and, taking his coachman with him, went to Paris to see the great Pasteur. The coachman followed Pasteur's instructions and would settle in America where he had a happy and fulfilled life. But Doneraile, who was easily bored and had never been forced to do anything he disliked, abandoned the treatment and developed rabies, dying a dreadful death, barking like a dog and fulfilling the old woman's prophecy.

The tiny bedroom where he died is empty now and no one talks about that night, not so very long ago, 26 August 1887, when the barking became uncontrollable and a groom and a gardener had to peg him down and smother him with a feather pillow. Now the rest of the curse would follow and the family, as predicted, would leave Doneraile.

After 1887 Doneraile never seemed to prosper again. Lord Doneraile's daughter had married Lord Castletown and they both enjoyed 'flitting around' in an extraordinarily free lifestyle. She died first and he built a canopy over her grave so that he could leave her peaches and chocolates. Children would creep into the graveyard at night and pinch these loving tokens, making him perfectly happy in the belief that Lady Castletown had popped in to enjoy his thoughtful gifts. He still haunts Doneraile quite regularly.

The seventh Viscount was in his eighties when he inherited: a sheep farmer who had to be resurrected from New Zealand to gamely take over Doneraile. His wife Mary, younger than he, was wealthy in her own right and they poured money into the estate. She lovingly grew flowers and vegetables and would watch the deer in the park from the bow window of the dining room or from her chintzy dressing room.

When her husband, Hugh, died at Doneraile Court in 1956, the doctor who had been attending him noticed how the deer were standing around at the front of the house in a still group. He mentioned this to Lady Doneraile, who said softly: 'Oh yes if the lord dies they know and form a semi-circle in the lawn field.'

After her husband's death, Lady Doneraile relied on a pet goat she called Gigi for company. He was keen on cigarettes and enjoyed being fed some 'Passing Clouds' from a cigarette box when he skipped in through the French window into the Pink Drawing Room on summer evenings. But Doneraile Court was too much for her on her own, so she moved to a smaller house, ironically near the famous summerhouse, where she lived until her death in 1958.

A possible heir for Doneraile was traced to California. He came back to Ireland, but somehow never established his claim, just threw money around the village, and vanished. The estate went to the Land Commission and the 25,000 acres were taken over by the Forestry Commission. A close Doneraile relative suggested: 'So many of us were born on the wrong side of the blanket.'

Today Doneraile Court retains a certain formality and daunting presence even though it is now virtually empty, lived in only by Arthur Montgomery, a young and optimistic curator. Gradually the tall rooms are being restored to eighteenth-century reds, blues and Chinese gold. There are few treasures left in a house which once held a contemporary copy of Charles I's death warrant – this was sent to the British Museum – a sword of Nelson's given to one of the Doneraides for safe-keeping and a chess set made from human bones found in one of the boudoirs. A St Leger had been in charge of French prisoners of war who carved the chessmen from the bones of their dead friends. In decline, the family were observed eating off priceless crested gold plate and, when asked why, declared that the maids tended to break china while gold merely bounces.

Montgomery is aware of the ghost of Lord Castletown. 'I hear him trying the handles of two or three of the ladies' bedroom doors . . . I am not afraid; he was very unhappy at the end of his life, and when his wife died, he was broken hearted and blamed the house for everything.'

The deer still behave strangely. When Arthur Montgomery arrived as curator he went amongst them, but was impaled by a tame buck called Rudolph and might have been killed had two foresters not rushed in and saved him.

There is a sunny light in the small room where the romping fourth Viscount died his strange and prophetic death. When volunteers came to help clear out Doneraile they threw out the cot which was chained to rings in the wall: 'alas' and Arthur Montgomery shakes his head.

The last Lady Doneraile would never allow anyone into this tiny room; she was ultra sensitive about this part of St Leger history. There are several branches of the family living quite simply in villages near by who are very curious to see where their ancestor died 'barking like a dog'.

Straggly high grass measures up to the tombstones in the Protestant churchyard in Doneraile. As you go through the Gothic gates, the aristocracy are on one side and the butlers, cooks and men who drove the ponies on the other. But the Doneraile seemed to have many close relatives. There is a stone to the seventh Viscount 'Hugh, a church warden' and to his wife Mary, 'a gracious lady'.

It all seems ancient history and yet because this is a tiny village with six pubs and a few small drab cottages, the stories told by the old people are still vivid and entertaining. The rooks are nesting once again in the park.

An old man with a cheery red face: 'Call me "Sir Mikey" ' Callaghan, a sunny carefree seventy-four year old in Doneraile, is haymaking for two genteel Ascendancy sisters. Both reed thin, as they sit on the steps of their white Georgian house, framed by pink roses, they leave you in no doubt that they belong to a most distinguished family which settled in Ireland in Norman times. 'We are the Harry Barrys,' they chorus, an unusual landowning family because it remained staunchly Catholic.

With sweet refinement they pour Mikey 'just one' sherry in a Waterford cut glass, which makes him even merrier and more roseate. As he recites a verse about the naughty fourth Lord Doneraile, they dimple and blush at the old man's irreverence. 'You never thought we were so gay.'

'I'm going to make a little 'cock' on the grave of Doneraile, he's our Lord,' he says, waving a pitchfork in the air and executing a twirl, and it is all curiously medieval.

36

MAKING THE VISITORS' FEET WET

The chastely grey Georgian mansion rises gauntly from raped woodlands; only the bushy rhododendrons are irrepressible.

Lissadell, home of the Gore-Booths with its legacy of heroism, mental fragility and decay, is probably one of the most romantic houses in Ireland and the saddest. It still has its classical grandeur, but the Ballysadare limestone now seems the colour of mourning.

In its heyday, Yeats made much of his visits to Lissadell, where he found 'all things in good taste' and was inspired to write a haunting poem celebrating the wistful beauty of two Gore-Booth daughters, Constance and Eva:

> The light of evening, Lissadell,
> Great windows open to the south,
> Two girls in silk kimonos, both
> Beautiful, one a gazelle.

The lovely artistic Constance, who scratched her name 'Con' on a window-pane with a diamond ring in May 1893, is a bit of an embarrassment to this Protestant Ascendancy family which arrived in Ireland in Elizabethan times and found itself, quite out of character, throwing up an Irish patriot, Countess Markievicz.

The strings have gone from a delicate green and gold wooden harp which once perhaps stirred the young Constance as she sat dreaming with her sister Eva on the sort of summer evenings which no longer seem to bring the same peace and happiness to Lissadell. Now the air, even in June, is tinged with regret.

There are no flowers outside except wild ones. You sweep in, past a mournful still lake where from April onwards the hardy chatelaine, Miss Aideen Gore-Booth, aged sixty-eight, likes to swim sheltered only by stunted bushes like Greek olive trees. On under archways of dripping green trees – it has always just been raining in Ireland, or is about to. A path of primroses to enchantment has been torn up and all the daffodils which carpeted the woodland and hill near the house have been uprooted, and spaces yawn where trees have been seized. The Ox Mountains and Ben Bulben across Sligo Bay seem silent witness to these indignities.

In the grim porte-cochère, Miss Gore-Booth, little pearls in her ears, with a jaunty shocking pink scarf and ivory stockings, is just about to lock up. The house in this magical corner of Sligo with more than a hint of aching gloom is open to the public. White haired in her sleeveless navy blue puffa jacket, she looks just like any landowner's wife, sister or aunt in Hampshire or Sussex who might be saying a cheerful goodbye to helpers and guides before going inside to the family home. But this is Ireland and Miss Gore-Booth is sole custodian, helper, cook, guide, mechanic and aesthete.

The hall is like a long abandoned Egyptian temple with old banana coloured walls where a sinister black bear leans forward on moth-eaten haunches, his yellow teeth bared and his outstretched paws worn away. Sir Henry Gore-Booth, the fifth Baronet, sailed to the Arctic in his yacht, the *Kara*, bringing back any number of stuffed animals and birds, whale bones and a moose's head.

The 'great sitting room as high as a church' with charming bow windows looking out over Sligo Bay and the Knocknarea mountains retains a frayed intimacy. Original red striped paper has faded to a raspberry water-ice except where a painting has been taken away, and then the regency colours are painfully vivid. Chintz covered chairs have been put invitingly together with a small table between, fashioned for talk and dreams. It was here that Yeats held his first seance; the Gore-Booths were always interested in Celtic folklore. Now nothing disturbs the dust, or the jaded withered plants. Some kitsch seaside souvenir china kittens with pink and blue ears look odd amongst the meltingly beautiful Sèvres porcelain.

Aideen Gore-Booth darts off to see to her brother Angus, a reclusive shadowy figure. 'Don't open all the doors,' she warns; 'I keep them shut because of the bats.'

Constance – the 'rebel countess' – was the eldest child of the fifth baronet, the seafaring adventurer Sir Henry Gore-Booth's five children; the others were Josslyn, Mordaunt, Eva and Mabel. She would also be the first woman elected to Westminster, the first woman minister of labour in Ireland and one of the few to abandon an Ascendancy background.

The Gore-Booths had a reputation for being genuinely caring landlords, yet as an impressionable child, Constance would remember being taken into the mud and stone cottages on the estate, and seeing how one room had to be shared with a cow or donkey, this deprivation giving rise to enduring jokes about pigs in Irish parlours.

Her early grace and bone structure brought many admirers to Lissadell. Already spirited as a teenager, when a guest had pestered her constantly during a formal dinner party and she found his hand on her dress once again, she held it up 'like a dropped pear', attracting everybody's attention, and said: 'Just look at what I have found in my lap.' If she thought an admirer who was also a local landowner was being unfair to his tenants she would disguise herself as a typical estate worker's wife and when she caught him being high-handed whip off the traditional black peasant shawl to confront him. Already this spoke of a character which would greet the news that she had been condemned to death with an extraordinary radiant insouciance. But she was later reprieved.

Constance and Eva were presented to Queen Victoria and did the London season. But Constance found society dull and would complain later to Eva: 'As you know, the English ideal of modern civilization always galled me. Endless relays of exquisite food and the eternal changing of costume bored me always to tears and I prefer my own to so many people's company. To make "conversation" to a bore through a long dinner party is the climax of dullness.' When she was twenty-five she enrolled at the Slade School. It seems late by today's standards, but with such a sheltered upbringing, it was quite racy to leave the protective gentleness of Lissadell and go to art college.

In Paris she met Casimir Markievicz, an artist who was a Polish count and a Russian subject, who had a wife who was dying slowly and a young son somewhere in the Ukraine. The Gore-Booths were not overjoyed when the couple married in 1900, their daughter insisting on the word 'obey' being omitted from the marriage service. Not only was 'Cassie' six years younger than his bride but he was a Roman Catholic. They honeymooned on his family's estate near Kiev and servants slept outside her door under blankets with the kind of devotion found amongst Indian staff.

An attractive Bohemian couple, Constance an actress, Casimir an artist, their house in Dublin attracted the literary, the musical and the theatrical. Their only child, a daughter Maeve born in 1901, was brought up by her grandmother Lady Georgina Gore-Booth, and had to be introduced to her busy mother when they met in a hotel in 1923.

Inflammatory rebel leaflets left lying around the cottage Constance and her husband rented in the Dublin mountains at Balally first attracted her to the Irish revolutionary cause. She was nearly forty at the time.

Her family took no particular notice when she organized a soup kitchen for strikers in 1913. It was something bountiful women of her class did constantly. However Ascendancy wives did not join the Irish Citizen Army, serve several jail sentences in Holloway, Ireland and Aylesbury, become Roman Catholics or announce as they lay dying: 'I am a pauper.'

The Count, not always faithful, decided to go back indefinitely to Russia. In the spirit of a true Edwardian feminist, his wife remarked airily that since the birth of her child, she no longer needed him as a husband. But at the huge farewell party for Casimir, an astute wardrobe mistress from the Abbey Theatre noticed 'how sad the Countess was that night'. But she had made her choice and would speak only of the 'joy of looking along a gun at the heart of an English soldier'.

She was soon known as the Red Countess for, though a dedicated rebel, Constance was accused of frivolity because she liked to wear a smart green tunic with silver buttons and a stunning hat with cocked feathers. When she visited America in 1922, she was intrigued by the vivid make-up worn by prostitutes and asked them for some tips.

Always a strikingly dramatic figure, she bounded through doors in a dazzling harlequin suit carrying her Mauser and an automatic, quite unlike her drab 'revolutionary sisters' in their deliberately sombre clothes. They did not care either for her high-pitched voice; of course it was the English accent they could not stomach even though she nearly died for Ireland. Casimir laden with flowers was at her bedside when eventually she died of peritonitis in 1927, aged fifty-nine. Three thousand people went to her funeral in Dublin and eight lorries were needed to carry her flowers.

Amongst the clutter of silver-framed photographs of elegant straight-backed Gore-Booth women with luxuriant dark hair, there is a souvenir of the Countess's centenary – she was born in 1868 – and a memento of a poem written for her when in prison on her birthday in 1917 by Eva, who always addressed her as 'dearest old darling'. The rebel in the family would sign her thank you letter 'Con[vict] 12'.

A soft voice remarks: 'The cook was terribly shy.' Aideen Gore-Booth reappears in happier mood and, more relaxed, is glad to explain the witty, vast full-length figures, solemn in tweed suits, painted on either side of the Egyptian-style black marble fireplace in the dining room. The forester, the gamekeeper and the butler all posed and were painted straight on to plaster by Casimir Markievicz. They are there for posterity, feet at an angle as if about to begin an Irish dance. They have a distinct Russian flavour. Markievicz gave them staring unemotional faces as if for icons. Between these Irish Gullivers, the sisters Eva and Constance appear fey and charming in rose-sprigged hats in a traditional portrait by Sarah Purser.

When people go round the house, Aideen Gore-Booth is immensely irritated by idle flattery: 'I hate it.' The visitors who come are often curious about the decline of this once grand

Protestant house with its elaborate Old Masters in Florentine frames, so many now 'gone to be restored'.

'A Dutchman said all the pictures here were rubbish; well, I like a good rattle, I don't like hypocrites. I like to see what is in people.' And maybe this is why she is so respected, in a sensitive area, not far from the border and only a few miles from Lord Mountbatten's summer house called Classiebawn. Gabriel Gore-Booth, another unmarried sister, worked as his land agent. Until his assassination by the IRA in 1979 Mountbatten had gone each summer to this part of Sligo which never lost its enchantment for him. The house belonged to his wife Edwina's family, a neo-Gothic confection built by Lord Palmerston. Here Lord Mountbatten could go lobster-potting, mackerel fishing and shrimping and enjoying carefree, happy times surrounded by energetic grandchildren.

On the morning he was killed, Aideen Gore-Booth had a curious premonition and went to the lake where she wept twice: 'I had this gloomy feeling and then I heard Mountbatten was dead.'

Her sister Gabriel tried to run Lissadell, until her death. 'She was wonderful on wood, just like our father, and she was good with men.' This was not in the Joan Collins film star sense, but meaning that she could manage the estate workers. There were days once when a hundred people worked at Lissadell and there were three thousand acres. 'And now nobody,' Miss Gore-Booth added philosophically. No acres either.

Strain and unhappiness show after years of battling, and of protecting her youngest brother Angus, who has not had the resilience to run Lissadell. She says, understandably: 'At times I feel so tired I could scream.'

For someone who had such a cherished childhood at Lissadell, the fact that Aideen Gore-Booth has survived the buffeting of a recent sad chapter in the family history is remarkable.

'Ours was the happiest household; nobody ever left. We had nurserymaids, butlers, cooks, valets who would only leave when they were getting married.' It was a house filled with books, including a travelling library of forty-eight miniature leather-bound books belonging to the cultivated Sir Robert Gore-Booth, fourth Baronet, who brought to Lissadell rare animals and

Egyptian artefacts from his foreign travels. A cultivated man who loved music he would mortgage the estate during the Famine so the hungry could be fed. It would take almost a century to pay off this debt which was about £50,000 and more than the value of the mortgage. But it would be cleared by his grandson Josslyn who had a strong social conscience. However it was not enough to appease his fiery sister Constance. During the 1920s, at the time of the Troubles, Sir Josslyn had to milk the cows himself until his hands bled as all the farm workers were on strike. One morning, seeing a letter from his rebel sister, he opened it with a smile of anticipation only to find it filled with rebuke, saying he should remember he came from a family of 'tyrants and usurpers'. About this time, she wrote to her sister from Mountjoy prison: 'I haven't given up the Bolshies yet: I believe that they will greatly improve conditions for the world.'

'Great-grandfather would actually spend all his money helping people during the Famine. At any one time there were thirty-six people begging at the door.' As a token Sir Robert was given a banner by the tenants which hangs in the billiard room.

When his grandson, Josslyn, Constance Markievicz's brother, inherited as sixth Baronet, he had a great sense of guilt about family wealth. A philanthropist, he set up co-operative creameries, but his great love was horticulture and he devoted years of his life to forestry, planting exotic shrubs and trees to tower above the demesne's grey stone walls.

As he grew up at Lissadell, the talk was of poetry and achievement. In a beaten wooden frame there is a copy of Yeats' poem, but the family were always ambivalent about him. 'My father did not care for Yeats.' Miss Gore-Booth is emphatic. In a prim voice she recited the first few lines: 'the light of evening . . . two "gels" in kimonas . . .' as if she did not think it very good poetry.

A local priest, Canon Colin Ward, an eighty-year-old firebrand, has been publicly outspoken about the Gore-Booths, describing the sisters as 'millstones round the neck of the people' and is quick to tell you: 'Yeats was never half as much at Lissadell as he liked to pretend. He was there only once. Why? Because they were county and he was merchant.' He chuckles and goes in to exhort his flock in the tiny Catholic parish church to move up to the front row which is always empty; the women obey. 'Are ye frightened somebody will be looking in your ear or what?' their pastor inquires. But the men prefer to stay down on one knee in the porch where they can have a quick drag at a cigarette during the collection.

Michael Gore-Booth, he says proudly, was buried in the Catholic graveyard instead of at the Church of Ireland at Drumcliffe where Yeats was married and is buried.

It has a stern Methodist feel, is overgrown, and in the church doorway there are leaflets with advice for rape victims, and for suicide and despair 'contact the Sligo Samaritans'. W. B. Yeats asked to be buried in the shadow of Ben Bulben simply and without fuss. His words 'Cast a cold eye on death . . . horseman, ride by,' luminously transform the drab grey granite.

The poet himself, who grew up in Sligo, young Yeats country, would be both 'terrible and gay'. He wrote about the apartness of the Ascendancy: 'No matter how rich we grew, no matter how many thousands a year our mills or our ships brought in, we could never be "County" nor had we any desire to be so. We would meet on Grand Juries those people in the grand houses, we would speak no malicious gossip and know ourselves respected in turn, but the long settled habit of Irish life set up a wall.'

For one thing Ascendancy families of the Gore-Booth calibre always did the London season. Aideen and her sisters were presented at Buckingham Palace. 'I remember we were given iced coffee as debs.' Even then there had been an acerbic awareness. 'We thought Edward VIII rather silly, not serious,' she remarked.

When Sir Josslyn died in 1944 – he had towards the end tended to winter in bed – his unfit heir Sir Michael Gore-Booth had a nervous breakdown and was eventually made a ward of court. Two other brothers, Hugh and Brian, who might have taken over the estate had been killed in World War II and a fourth brother, Angus, had returned from the war suffering from shell-shock.

At the beginning of the century, the Gore-Booths owned more than 30,000 acres and also had an income from property in Manchester. But much of the estate was sold up under the

Wyndham Land Act, leaving about two and a half thousand acres. The bulk of that was taken over by the Land Commission in the 1960s so that the estate was further reduced to 400 acres and the house. From now on Lissadell would be controlled by a court official but the day to day running of the estate was left to Miss Gabriel Gore-Booth the youngest of the four daughters. There were accusations of mismanagement and the sisters faced the indignity of a High Court order ruling that twenty-one head of cattle should be seized.

They fought desperately to save their cattle, and scenes were described in court, in a dry legal voice, that had they not been so tragic, would be rather comic. How on a bright morning Miss Gabriel Gore-Booth, aged fifty-four, was seen jumping a hedge and chasing her cattle through a meadow away from the drovers who were waiting with lorries; later she was joined by her sister Aideen, who entered more conventionally through a gate. The Supreme Court judge ordered the sisters to pay costs, but refrained from sending them to prison. They lost their cattle, though.

They would be helpless and further humiliated when most of the wonderful woods created by Sir Josslyn Gore-Booth as an enduring legacy for Lissadell were destroyed by court order, the timber sold to make ends meet. To see a tree cut down after a hurricane or with Dutch elm disease hurts; for the Gore-Booths this destruction was seeing the end of their Lissadell. Now all the sisters could hear was the insistent whine of a chain saw as great trees were carted away from woods with charming names like Shepherd Flat, Cat's Corner and Clancy's Gate.

This stripping of the woods was a scandal which shook Ireland's old families. The executioners were enthusiastic; there was unlicensed felling. 'Thousands of stumps' were clumsily camouflaged with oil and then moss, but the sisters knew every tree.

'All those woods, all those flowers.' Aideen Gore-Booth is suddenly sad and can hardly go on; she grieves especially over the vanished banks of primroses. When she remonstrated with the Forestry Commission doing the ploughing she was told the primroses were making the visitors' feet wet.

Josslyn Gore-Booth, aged thirty-eight and the son of Miss Aideen's youngest brother, is the heir to Lissadell. He worked as a head hunter in London but now owns a large house and land in the north of England: 'Call me a Yorkshire squire.' He administers the estate and goes to Ireland three or four times a year.

Lissadell was a place for school holidays. Josslyn Gore-Booth grew up in England but was catapulted early on into the traumatic litigation over the estate. At the time when it was being adminis-tered by the State solicitor on behalf of his late uncle, Sir Michael Gore-Booth 'but not very well,' he and his aunt went to court to protest, declaring that livestock had been removed, acres of woodland destroyed. 'We resisted the continuation of this state of affairs; the court agreed with us, but on condition that I took over; so the ownership passed to me.' It was something of a millstone for this father of two daughters who already owns a large house in Yorkshire, and feels that Lissadell was built in the days of huge families when armies of servants were available.

Defensive, battered by this Chekhovian drama, Miss Gore-Booth is not very comfortable in the new Ireland; it is not one she likes. She uses words like 'cheap' and regrets the eroding of what she thinks of as 'decent' values. She paints 'because it gets me away to a spiritual world.' It is an ascetic life, fairly frugal, but she has a peace about her.

It is a tribute to her that she is so welcome in the village. At the 'Yeats' pub – the poet would probably jump off the top of King's Mountain if he saw this 'modrun' building – the landlord had just died; the dogs were dry nosed and lethargic but she was welcomed by one of the strapping sons of the house as if an honoured guest. He watched approvingly as she enjoyed a huge portion of fresh salmon eaten with a sensual pleasure, little bits peaking out at the corner of her mouth. 'Normally I live on roughage and fresh fish like pollock from the lake cooked with herbs,' she says perkily, while customers sit in dark corners aware of her clipped accent and talking behind large hands.

It may be a rather unlikely place for this slim precise little person who never drinks but she is full of surprises: 'I rode a horse side-saddle for Channel 4. The first time I went on television I was very nervous but the floor manager said "I'll blow you a kiss" and I thought that was very funny so I relaxed. It was a programme about the Descendancy.'

'I suppose I was invited on television so people could see if I was as queer as they thought.' The word 'queer' in Ireland tends to retain its Oxford dictionary definition, meaning odd, or a bit off colour rather than homosexual.

Faintly autocratic, she is droll about the theory that the Anglo-Irish are all meant to 'have long noses and vivid love lives'. This virginal figure sniffs: 'The long nose is true in my case' and, with innocence, 'I love a bit of fun,' then asks, 'Did you know that women from large families have the least wrinkly skins?'

After a quick glimpse of a heron on the lake, Aideen Gore-Booth, who is a keen bird watcher, turns a giant key in the door of the shuttered house, her heels echoing in the hall. On the way to her bedroom past dismal strings of dried flowers she stops to answer the question whether she thinks of herself as Irish or Anglo-Irish. Without a moment's hesitation, she replies: 'I think of myself as a mongrel.'

37

A GREAT COMPLIMENT

'Blarney,' hissed Elizabeth I, spitting out the word in a fury. The Earl of Leicester had just written another long boring letter explaining why he had failed to capture Blarney Castle for his Queen.

Today Blarney means charm, 'a way with words'. People have been drawn to this castle in County Cork from all over the world. Kissing the Blarney Stone is not at all easy, and involves hanging upside down and hoping someone is holding on to you. Yet Russian ambassadors have arrived unannounced for a quick kiss and even Sir Winston Churchill succumbed, leaning backwards at a perilous angle from the parapet as if he needed the gift of eloquence.

Sir George Colthurst, sixty-one and an old Harrovian, owns Blarney Castle. He is the epitome of a jolly Ascendancy squire, shakes with laughter; there could be no better custodian of the famous Stone than this County Cork baronet. A rotund figure he finds it difficult to be taken seriously whether in the City, where he is with Lloyds, at Blarney, or at home in Edenbridge, Kent.

His son Charles Colthurst is exactly the same, and chuckles over the apt date chosen by his father to hand over the running of Blarney Castle, April Fool's Day 1986. Father and son have a chubby aura. With their resounding 'Ha, ha ha,' they exude an image of generous tables laden with barons of beef, good talk and firkins of foaming ale. To be in their company is to be immediately and inexplicably in good spirits and to see life through a hugely entertaining lens, not a foolish view, but a ticklish one.

The Castle was inherited by the Colthursts on the female side through marriage with a Jefferye ancestor in 1848. One Jefferye was a Minister Plenipotentiary at the Swedish Court so a portrait of Charles XII of Sweden hangs on the stairs. Unlike many Irish stately homes it could almost be called cosy. It is warm and comfortable, and has recently been thoroughly Laura Ashleyed: spriggy prints and bolder large flowery chintzes sit comfortably against pitch pine, Irish Sheraton painted cabinets, applewood and walnut furniture.

A little antiquity is to be found in the library where there is a vast eighteenth-century tapestry, a document from Elizabeth I, a deed by Godolphin who bought Blarney originally for £248 and leather-bound works of Voltaire in French. 'Oeuvres,' Charles Colthurst says with a smile; he read law at Cambridge; his friends love coming to Blarney to shoot and fish.

Life however is not all 'Ha, ha, ha' for young Charles, who in spite of roly-poly amiability, is dedicated and hardworking. He finds Blarney demanding and shrewdly appreciates his legal training in the running of this good-sized estate. His wife Norah, whom he recently married, is a solicitor also.

He drives a battered Land-Rover with a bleeper. 'How far can you go with delegation?' he asks, and in the end feels only he can be responsible for the 1,100 acres, the Castle farm, the forestry division and glorious gardens where four men were at work on the flowerbeds and lawns alone. It is in good order; there are swans on the lake, beautiful lawns and avenues full of azaleas. He got a bee man in from Kilkenny to get rid of several swarms. Bees also like Blarney.

Charles is much loved and the happy Castle atmosphere is refreshing, no hunched servants here but cheery girls, where five generations of Toomeys have worked. Pleasantly feudal when the hunt meets, the cry as stirrup cups are filled is: 'God bless the man who made the wine' and, when drained, a doleful 'God blast the man who made the glass.'

Sir George has a habit of suddenly bursting into Irish folk songs. Sitting bolt upright on a sofa, looking like a robin, he will warble unexpectedly: 'Have ye ever been to Drumcollogher?' This is a tin-pot village in Ireland but it captured the composer Percy French's imagination when he cycled through as a Land Commission agent. Sir George continues, rolling his rrs to give Drumcollogher a broguey burr '. . . I was over in London, of course I called on the Queen, the butler said she's out, she isn't about, in fact sir, she's not been seen . . .'

He has the Cork brogue to perfection. 'Says I, have you been to Drumcollogher, and the fine house we have there?' And he conjures up a vision of a puzzled royal footman in velvet breeches being questioned intently by this simple Irish country fellow who finds it hard to believe the Queen has never been to his village. '. . . and the fine house we have there . . . If your mistress would come . . .' Sir George then sings another about President Reagan's village Ballyporeen.

There is something about Ireland, and God knows the houses are not warm enough to invite nudity, but many much loved apocryphal stories are told of maids coming in with nothing on at parties, and butlers too. One of the best is about a Blarney butler appearing in the drawing room carrying a silver tray without a stitch on, not even a bow tie, on the day Sir George's grandmother was buried. A genteel soul who had been Lady Colthurst's companion went quietly up to the distracted butler and whispered, 'I think we need more sugar,' and he left the room.

But Sir George is not too keen on this story; he is a kind man, never patronizing and none of his stories are malicious. He prefers to recall the artful reply of another butler. 'We always had tea on a big copper tray on a bamboo stand. Well, one day we had finished and rang for the manservant, who came in and took the tray out; then we heard this terrible crash. My grandmother said, "Oh James, oh dear," all her fine bone china, but the butler answered quickly "Oi'm all right, Your Ladyship, Oi'm all right." '

Still benevolently feudal, Sir George feels that laughter is always the saving grace in Ireland: 'Nobody loses face and problems are solved.' An engaging raconteur, he enjoys the 'native wit' and the humorous relationship between the Irish and the Ascendancy and tells a story about Lady Cadogan, the Viceroy's wife, who loved Blarney. She was out for a run in a carriage with Sir George Colthurst one afternoon when she was shocked to see a man by the side of the road beating a donkey which could not pull the cart it was so heavily laden with turf, sticks and faggots. The Vicereine, as President of the RSPCA, was inflamed. 'George,' she said to her host, 'can you stop? I'll have to have a word with him. He knows who I am.'

Sir George Colthurst shook his head: 'You're wasting your time;' but he pulled up and watched Lady Cadogan, elegant in her Edwardian long skirt, go up to the man. 'This is a sorry sight,' she said, and upbraided him for beating the donkey and castigated him for committing one of the seven deadly sins. 'Didn't our Lord ride a donkey into Jerusalem and that is why he has a cross on his back, so you are committing a double sin, sacrilege and cruelty . . . You are,' she sniffed, 'a very bad man.'

The man listened patiently with that inherent County Cork courtesy, and then shook his head and quietly put his point of view, 'What your Ladyship says may well be true but if Our Lord rode this donkey into Jerusalem and didn't beat him, he wouldn't be there yet.'

The tale is almost as precious to Sir George as being called 'Me Auld Slob' by Dan Toomey, one of the oldest retainers; 'that's terribly good,' the ninth baronet explains, 'a great compliment.'

Conclusion

IN CLOVER

Nothing can change the colour of the sea in Ireland, its shimmering changes of mood, light to silvery grey to slate blue; the dark shiny green ivy over old Georgian windows with ancient curtains; genuine old lace; inside shaky Regency beds under carved eagles in the ceiling, frayed embroidered pillowcases; the charm of newly baked scones at tea in dusty chintzy first-floor drawing rooms; lilac, creamy white and purple, still flourishes in Ascendancy gardens; the wonderful hunting over springy grass, with the heady smell of honeyed gorse in the nostrils, cherry brandy in the hip flask, galloping on the best horses, on they go, the last of the Ascendancy, alongside the Irish squire, a bunch of violets in his hunting pink buttonhole, still a unique people titupping into oblivion.

The appeal of Ireland is described as a series of hugely enjoyable small shocks. The Anglo-Irish remain addicted; back from London, as soon as the train gets near the country station, they put out their heads to sniff the turfy air, that 'great old feeling'; they could never settle anywhere else. The Irish novelist George Moore once suggested that Ireland was 'a fatal disease', a country where a hangover is thought of as 'a damp soul', where Radio Telefis apologizes at ten o'clock, saying, 'We can't find the newsreader anywhere' as if he were a handkerchief; a bit of Irish music is played, five minutes go by, ten: 'Still we can't find him,' more diddley diddlededee. An evening without news, everyone agrees later, is 'grand'.

Those of the Anglo-Irish left, though a small band, remain confidently incontrovertibly grand, untouched by an Ireland irrevocably changed, one they could never understand; Mrs Richard Grove Annesley, appalled by new arrivals in Cork: 'I hear Killowen has been bought by people called Worcester. Worcester Sauce, I suppose.'

They need no pity. They have a distinction. Another of this formidable breed, Lady Cochrane, sitting in a Lebanese garden as Beirut reverberated with gunfire and the sky was grey with fighting, went on with her tapestry, far away from Woodbrook her home in County Wicklow with its concert hall big enough for the London Symphony Orchestra, splendid cricket ground and pretty golf course where champions play and balls go into the sea.

Educated to do nothing, work still has a stigma. Lord Inchiquin admits sadly, 'We are the first generation to work.' The brighter ones represent Sotheby's and Christie's in Ireland and do very well, but these fine art experts may still be referred to scathingly by the Anglo-Irish as 'obsequious auctioneers'.

The Irish nation is one of inconsistency and double standards. It has an ambivalence which says 'Brits out in Northern Ireland' but proudly advertises a hotel by saying 'The Prince of Wales Slept Here.' They love royalty. But if you ask southerners what in their hearts they feel about a united North and South, there will be a sad shake of the head. Not all are enthusiastic, but must keep *sotto voce*. In the North they still ask whether someone is a Protestant or Catholic Jew.

Frederick the Great, urging his troops to surge forward once more during the Seven Years War, bellowed: 'Rascals, would you live forever?' Today the Anglo-Irish are a little like those exhausted soldiers or the guests who have enjoyed such good hospitality, they have overstayed; they are sensitive about their place in Ireland but saved by a sense of irony, good manners. They are suitably low key, fully understanding what they symbolize in modern Ireland today; some even fake Oirish accents.

Those who can afford it send their sons from Ireland to public schools: Eton, Charterhouse, Harrow and Wellington, where they are inevitably nicknamed 'Boggy', sons who come home after a spell in the City or Hong Kong bringing new wives, some French, some Belgian, but soon the pretty dower house begins to pall and the women are complaining, 'C'est le dregs.'

Yet in Dublin you are still deafened by a chorus of screeching seagulls sitting on bridges over the River Liffey, a city with wonderful bookshops and wide streets. In the gold Italianate formality of Cardinal Newman's University Church in St Stephen's Green, twinkling with pink and white gladioli, a priest speaks about a job being a privilege, the cure for Aids: 'fidelity to one partner', and about Dublin's underprivileged areas; and a voice from the back answers, 'I know them well' as if it is a private conversation, and the air has a subtle sweet scent of alcohol.

A November evening, crunchy autumn cornflake leaves on impressive streets, Georgian buildings in the traditional pinks and Lincoln green, but now with desk lamps while architects and advertisers work in these graciously proportioned rooms, creating slogans like Éireann Rich Gravy, and outside a blue plaque to George Bernard Shaw.

Spicy-flavoured Irish dinner-table talk, fast, sharp, full of allusion, about books; usually at least a few of the people in the dining room will have written novels or histories.

Ascendancy women, lively, with high-boned thin faces, wondering if enough can be salvaged for another meal tomorrow. With their pale intensity, some lack a softness; survival is demanding; their men are not famous for knuckling down to tackle either the dry rot or the bank balance, equally mouldering. They are looked after by servants brought out of old people's homes; they write to friends on sawn-off greeting cards. Even if the house is being sold over their head, still the old courtesy: 'Sherry, Daff?'

But the twentieth century has not been kind to the aristocracy in general, the peerage of Ireland in particular, where striped black and white cows called Moillies graze on the lawn of an Armagh estate; Old Masters are found behind hedges and under hay; hens peck from Meissen bowls.

But it is enough that the Palladian stone is still silver in the rain.

The Ascendancy love this haunted land, and sitting in their libraries, reading just the spines of their precious first editions, often pristine, gives reassurance. They are saved too by an unworldly innocence, a touching trust yet a sheer determination about where they belong and are going to end their days.

The Irish say they would hate it if the Anglo-Irish died out, bearing out Harold Macmillan's experience as Prime Minister, when he found: 'It is the second-rate people who despise each other.'

There are no RMs anymore. 'It is rare to meet a rural Protestant who matters.' Nuala O'Faolain, one of Ireland's brightest young commentators whose words tumble out in bright Joycean phrases, works for the old Ascendancy newspaper *The Irish Times*, where Catholics these days 'dress like Protestants in tweeds; normally Catholics are in nylon shirts.'

Maybe the Anglo-Irish 'just are,' she says. They do not play a part but 'tend to be stewards of provincial racecourses'. There will be no conservatives left in Ireland when the last of them have gone.

Nothing can stop them loving Ireland, its vulnerability and the dignity which breaks the heart, the geniality, the terrible land in the west, even with its poor economy; they love the country as the Russian loves even the icy wastes. Irish farmers are so lazy there are still butterflies and wild flowers, safe from spraying chemicals in fields where coats of arms lie chipped in sweet grass speckled with clover.

The fear in Ireland is that there will be only one more generation of Anglo-Irish, that this picturesque breed is about to disappear. The Irish pay them the highest compliment. They are, they say, the last of the 'old originals', belonging to a very magic vanishing world.

PICTURE CREDITS

COLOUR PICTURES

Lady Mollie Cusack Smith *Ann Morrow*
Lady Mollie Cusack Smith as a child
  *Reproduced by courtesy of Mollie
  O'Rourke*
Mrs 'Melon' Daly *Ann Morrow*
Lord and Lady Dunsany *Ann Morrow*
Olivia Robertson and Lord Strathloch
  © *Daily Express Magazine*
Door in Clonegal Castle *Ann Morrow*
Cratloe *Reproduced by courtesy of Gordon
  and Sylvia Brickenden*
Dunguaire *Ann Morrow*
Lord O'Neill *Reproduced by courtesy of
  Lord O'Neill*
Molly Keane *Ann Morrow*
Lord Altamont reading to his daughter
  © *Liam Lyons*
Lord Erne and his Swedish wife *Ann
  Morrow*
Lord Dunleath *Ann Morrow*
Lady Jennifer Bernard *Ann Morrow*
'The Gay Mice' *Ann Morrow*
Norah and Leila Storr with the Hon.
  Mrs Lycester Storr *Reproduced by
  courtesy of the Blake sisters*

BLACK AND WHITE PICTURES

The gallery at Strokestown *The Irish
  Architectural Archive, Dublin (I.A.A.)*
View of Strokestown *I.A.A.*
Family Group © *Strokestown Park House*
Portrait of Olive Pakenham Mahon ©
  Strokestown Park House
Olive Pakenham Mahon as a child ©
  Strokestown Park House
Jim Callery *Ann Morrow*
14-year-old Miss Cary Barnard
  *Reproduced by courtesy of Mrs Melosine
  Daly*
Miss Melosine Cary Barnard at her
  presentation *Reproduced by courtesy of
  Mrs Melosine Daly*
The Rosse family *Ann Morrow*
Lady Altamont with her daughters ©
  Town and Country Magazine
The first sign of Famine *I.A.A.*
Lord Mountcharles *Ann Morrow*
Bunratty Castle *Shannon Development*
Lord and Lady Castlemaine *Reproduced
  by courtesy of Miss Joyce Walpole*
Richard Grove Annesley at Annes Grove
  Reproduced by courtesy of Patrick Annesley

The O'Conor-Nash family *Ann Morrow*
Desmond Guinness *Ann Morrow*
Adare Manor up for auction *I.A.A.*
Aerial view of Adare Manor © *Hunting Aerofilms*
Horace Holroyd Smyth on a deer cull *Reproduced by courtesy of Catherine Fleming*
Tessa and Jeffry Lefroy *Ann Morrow*
The West Waterford Hunt *Reproduced by courtesy of Catherine Fleming*
Catherine Fleming with the Duchess of Devonshire et al *Reproduced by courtesy of Catherine Fleming*
Drawing room in Castle Bernard *Reproduced by courtesy of Lady Bernard*
Somerville and Ross sailing near Castletownshend *Reproduced by courtesy of Captain and Mrs Chavasse*
Captain Dodson in fancy dress *Reproduced by courtesy of the Blake sisters*
Staff at Stanhope Lodge *Reproduced by courtesy of the Blake Sisters*
Curraghmore *I.A.A*
Wall paintings at Lissadell *I.A.A.*
Doneraile *I.A.A.*

INDEX